P9-DNZ-784

JEFFERSON DAVIS

Other Works by

ROBERT McELROY

•

KENTUCKY IN THE NATION'S HISTORY

THE WINNING OF THE FAR WEST

GROVER CLEVELAND, THE MAN AND THE STATESMAN

LEVI PARSONS MORTON, BANKER, DIPLOMAT AND STATESMAN

THE PATHWAY OF PEACE
(The Sir George Watson Lectures for 1926)

IN THE NAME OF LIBERTY
(An Edition of the Speeches of William Bourke Cockran)

THE REPRESENTATIVE IDEA IN HISTORY
(Tsing Hua Lectures for 1916-1917, in China)

THE UNITED STATES OF AMERICA
(In Benn's Six Penny Series, London)

•

JEFFERSON DAVIS AT THE BEGINNING OF HIS POLITICAL CAREER
From an engraving made from a daguerreotype. New York Public Library

Jefferson Davis

The Unreal and the Real

BY

ROBERT McELROY

Ph.D., LL.D., M.A. and D.Litt. (Oxon), F.R.Hist.S.

*Harold Vyvyan Harmsworth Professor of American History
in Oxford University; Fellow of the Queen's College;
Sometime Edwards Professor of American History
in Princeton University*

VOLUME I

HARPER & BROTHERS PUBLISHERS

New York and London

1937

JEFFERSON DAVIS

Copyright, 1937, by Robert McElroy
Printed in the United States of America

All rights in this book are reserved.
No part of the book may be reproduced in any
manner whatsoever without written permission.
For information address
Harper & Brothers

10/7

FIRST EDITION

I-M

E
467.1
. D26M24
vol. 1

TO

DUNBAR ROWLAND

AND TO THE MEMORY OF

WALTER LYNWOOD FLEMING

82362

EMORY AND HENRY LIBRARY

CONTENTS

—

ILLUSTRATIONS

———

VOLUME I

INTRODUCTION

A biographer, writing as he does for a generation later than that in which his character lived, must have regard to the interests and ethical standards of that generation, and, as these alter with changing generations, the life of every leader must be written again and again; with each new writing there must be new points of emphasis, a new use of evidence. Jefferson Davis was conscious of this when he wrote: "If history as now written is accepted, it will consign the South to infamy." He was confident, however, that later generations would do justice to his moral rectitude, and that of the millions who followed him. "We do not fear the verdict of posterity on the purity of our motives, or the sincerity of our belief," he assured Bishop Galloway; and to another friend he said, "In asserting the right of Secession . . . I recognize the fact that the war showed it to be impracticable, but this did not prove it to be wrong." He was even confident that the basic issue of the Civil War, which he interpreted, not as slavery, but as the right of each State to determine the conditions upon which it would remain in the union, was "bound to reassert itself, though it may be at another time and in another form"; and no one can doubt that this principle has so reasserted itself. Woodrow Wilson restated it in the brilliant phrase, "the right of men everywhere to choose their own ways of peace and of obedience." The British Commonwealth of Nations, and the League of Nations both definitely assert that any member State may "depart in peace," if the union fails to maintain conditions which satisfy it; and peaceful secessions have already tested this right, and confirmed it.

This inevitable change of standard was evident during Davis' life, in the appearance of new viewpoints regarding both slavery and secession. Thomas Jefferson had defended the Louisiana purchase upon the ground that it would make the condition of the slave more tolerable, by enabling slavery to occupy new territory and thus to increase the means of subsistence to be shared by slave and master. In Davis' youth this argument was considered merely as a contribution to a then dominant economic problem; but as he grew to manhood, the slavery question entered a new stage, an ethical stage, and he was pilloried as the champion of an impious cause when, in 1848, he re-stated Jefferson's argument in these words: "If the opponents of slavery wish to emancipate the slaves they are taking the wrong course. Slavery cannot be abolished without a long series of preliminary preparations. . . . The most judicious course is to let the institution alone and permit it to spread itself through the adjacent States, so that it may assume a new and more liberal character. The practical and useful emancipation of the slaves will not be the labour of one generation. The slave must be made fit for his freedom, by education and discipline, and thus made unfit for slavery. As soon as he becomes unfit for slavery, the master will no longer desire to hold him as a slave."

To the *Impatient Abolitionist* of Davis' generation, such a statement stamped the speaker as a man eager to forge for ever the fetters of the bondsman. In vain did he explain, as Jefferson had not had to explain, that he cherished no such sinister design. He considered himself, then as ever, the sanest type of Abolitionist, and his interpretation of the inevitable result of restricting slavery to the States where it already existed was summed up in the words: "There is no policy which would perpetuate and rivet that institution for ever on this country, so surely as that which confines the slaves to the present limits in which they are held. There must— to render emancipation practicable—be a door opened, by which they may go out; and that door towards the equator. All who understand their habits and constitutional peculiarities must admit this. . . . Increasing in number year by year, the impossibility of emancipation will augment also, until he only can deny that the system must be perpetual who is prepared to see the slave become the master, to convert a portion of the States of this Union into negro possessions, or, to witness the more probable result, of their extermination by a servile war." Clearly, his view was then what it remained throughout his life, that patient emancipation was desirable, and that by it alone could the problem be solved without serious injury to the people of either race.

Lincoln too was a *Patient Abolitionist*, and feared the effects which would follow hasty emancipation. In his debates with Douglas he declared that he would be willing to wait a hundred years for the complete destruction of slavery, if only he could be certain that it was "in the process of ultimate extinction." He believed, however, in opposition to both Jefferson and Davis, that it would be in process of ultimate extinction only when rigorously restricted to the States where it already existed. "Keep it out of our new territory," he said, ". . . restrict it for ever to the old States . . . and give it time. It will not be accomplished in a day, a year, or two years, but a hundred years at least, but it will come at last." In his Message of March 6, 1862, he declared, "Gradual and not sudden emancipation is better for all."

Moreover, Davis and Lincoln agreed that, pending this long process of extinction, it was the duty of the Federal Government to see that slavery in the States was protected as property: and Lincoln, in his first Inaugural Address, reaffirmed his allegiance to the Fugitive Slave law. Their disagreement, therefore, lay not in the field of abolition, but in their views concerning the effect which the extension of slavery into new territory would have upon that institution and its future abolition. They agreed also that slavery was an incident in the war, and an incident for the existence of which the South was not more to blame than the North.

It is difficult, if not impossible, for a twentieth-century mind to understand Davis' conviction, not shared by Lincoln, that, for the long period of transition at least, slavery was slavery "by decree of Almighty God"; the best possible relationship between a superior and an inferior race; the most humane system yet found of coöperation between capital and labour; and there are many men today who believe that the position of labour, under *laissez-faire*, is little superior to the form of slavery which Davis defended.

It would be unfair to judge Davis as political opponents of his generation judged him, though all normal minds, South and North, now agree as to the horror of human slavery; and few competent students will deny that it might have been destroyed with less disastrous results, moral as well as political, had the *Patient Abolitionists* been allowed to control.

A similar shifting of standards is apparent when we study the problem of secession as it appeared in Thomas Jefferson's time, and as it appeared in the days of Davis. Jefferson, President of the United States, could write, without serious suspicion of treasonable intent, "These Federalists see in this acquisition [of Louisiana] the formation of a new Confederacy, embracing all the waters of the Mississippi on both sides of it, and a separation . . . from us. . . . If it should become the great interest of those nations to separate from this, if their happiness should depend on it so strongly as to induce them to go through that convulsion, why should the Atlantic States dread it? But especially why should we, their present inhabitants, take sides in such a question? . . . The future inhabitants of the Atlantic and Mississippi States will be our sons. We leave them in distinct but bordering establishments. We think we see their happiness in their union, and we wish it. Events may prove it otherwise; and if they see their interest in separation, why should we take sides with our Atlantic rather than our Mississippi descendants? . . . God bless them both and keep them in union, if it be for their good, but separate them, if it be better." But, when Jefferson Davis, in 1861, reluctantly joined his State in a secession which he had long opposed, he was denounced as a traitor.

Davis was not a traitor, but a devotee of the union, as he believed the Fathers had planned it, based upon the sovereignty of the member states; and let him who today is not insisting upon the absolute sovereignty of his nation as the condition of "a more perfect union" among nations cast the first stone.

Sound patriotism is a progressive passion, attaching itself to ever larger units, as man's interests expand with advancing civilization. From cave to clan, from state to nation and to empire: this much we have seen. Is there another step which will extend man's patriotic allegiance to the present area of his economic activity, namely, the world? Is it possible to put behind some League of Nations a sentiment of devotion such as has been honestly given to each successive unit of an ever-widening political organization?

In the ancient city of Peking stands a cottage over the door of which is written:

> "I live in a very small house, but my windows look out upon a very large world." The necessity of this broader vision which Davis realized at times, though dimly, must, if the world's progress is to continue, be one day inscribed upon the parliaments of all nations.

ROBERT McELROY

Rhodes House,
Oxford,
June, 1937

JEFFERSON DAVIS

CHAPTER I

"CLEANLY BRED, MACHINELY CRAMMED"

THE Welsh have been called "Militant Nightingales": but what has that to do with Jefferson Davis? Perhaps much. In ancient Wales, the bards or national poets were a gifted nobility, enjoying hereditary privileges and honoured by prince and people alike. When the Scriptures first appeared among them, they loved most the story of David, Bard of Israel: and, when baptized, frequently adopted his name, calling it Dyfedd, in the earlier periods, Dayfedd, in the thirteenth century; and in course of time Davy, Davie, and Davis. As a result the name Davis is said to be thirty-second in frequency among family names in England and Wales; and Jefferson Davis was the descendent of a Welsh John Davis, Davie, or David, according to the orthography which one selects. Recent theories of chromosomes and genes, associated with the name of Thomas Hunt Morgan, seem to give a new meaning to the word, heredity; and if there is a Welsh chromosome which transmits militancy, Jefferson Davis certainly received it: though the gene of music may have passed him by.

John Davis migrated to Philadelphia in the first year of the eighteenth century. Here his son Evan was born and, having married a Mrs. Williams, became the father of Samuel Davis. In the latter's early childhood, the family moved to Augusta, Georgia, where the father died, leaving his widow with little save two sets of children. Her two sons by her earlier marriage enlisted in the patriot army when the Revolution began, and Samuel Davis, was sent, like David of old, to carry supplies to his

1

half-brothers. Like David, also, he chose war rather than obedience to the parental order to return home, and remained with the army, winning his spurs as a mounted gunman. Later, he formed his own company of infantry, and did his part in banishing the invading Britons from Georgia and the Carolinas.

At the end of the Revolution, which Macaulay characterizes as the war that "threw away thirteen colonies," he returned home to find his mother dead and her property wrecked. He sold his share of what remained of his inheritance, 200 acres of land, and removed to Augusta, where he was met by the good fortune which sometimes comes to the soldier who survives the ordeal by battle. He was granted twelve hundred acres of land, four miles south of Washington, Georgia, was elected Clerk of the Courts; and thus provided with a decent living, won a handsome Scotch-Irish lassie, Jane Cook, who, according to family tradition, was a niece of the famous Revolutionary general, Nathanael Greene.

We have from Jefferson Davis' own pen a description of the pair. His mother was noted for her beauty and sprightliness of mind, much of which she retained to extreme old age. His father, he writes, was "unusually handsome, and the accomplished horseman of his early life among the 'mounted men' of Georgia, . . . a man of wonderful physical activity, . . . usually grave and stoical . . . and of such sound judgement that his opinions were law to his children, and quoted by them long after he had gone to his final rest."

For the first few years of his married life, Samuel Davis was content to cultivate his Georgia farm: but it was not long before the new West called him as it called so many of his generation, and after a preliminary study of possible locations, he selected Kentucky, and secured six hundred acres of land in what later became Christian County. At a point, since known as "Fair View," he cleared land, built a house, purchased a small stock of blooded horses, and settled down to the work of breeding racers.

The Davis family increased, however, more rapidly than their income, and in time they added to the occupation of farming and horse-breeding, that of the maintenance of a Wayfarers Rest. Here, on June 3, 1808, was born the last of a truly frontier family of ten children and was named Jefferson in honour of the great leader then approaching the end of his second term as President of the United States. The cradle in which Jane rocked him is preserved in the Confederate Museum in New Orleans: but the house no longer stands. Its later history, however, is interesting. During the Nashville Centennial of 1897, it, and the cabin in which Abraham Lincoln was born, were taken down and re-erected at the Centennial grounds as objects of popular interest. After the exhibition, the Davis cabin was sold and exhibited by its purchaser in various cities and towns of the South. When it ceased to attract sufficient interest to justify further exhibition, it was stored in Richmond according to the *New Orleans Daily Picayune*, but no one knows its present location, if indeed it still exists.

Psychologists tell us that the first decade of childhood establishes the ethics of manhood. Davis' first decade was spent in an atmosphere where devoutly religious ideals blended with the institution of human slavery in a way which no twentieth-century mind can understand. It was a monstrous union; but one blessed by the Church, and accepted as God's plan for man at the family altar. Already the evils attending large plantations and the overseer system, with absentee owners, were apparent in the plantation states; but Kentucky, never a plantation state, exhibited few of those evils. There master and slave were in constant, personal contact and, as a result, Jefferson Davis' childhood experiences with slavery showed few of the more hateful aspects which marked it farther South.

In Davis' third year, his father, in his turn, heard the call of "farther South," and Kentucky could not hold him longer. He disposed of his farm, assembled his caravan of wagons, bundled

in his ten children and an orphan whom Providence had brought
to his hospitable door, and whom he had adopted, and with his
wife beside him, and his household slaves in attendance, faced
southward, bound for St. Mary's Parish, Louisiana, which lay
beyond six hundred miles of wilderness, with scarcely an intervening village. Bayou Têche, near the present town of Franklin,
was the first site selected for his new home; but mosquitos, followed, in a sequence then not understood, by malaria, caused
another migration which landed them, in 1812, in Wilkinson
County, Mississippi. Samuel here secured a small farm, and
while his family camped in the open, constructed, with such
help as he could secure, a comfortable brown frame dwelling. As
early as practicable, Mrs. Davis had the ground around the house
laid out as a flower garden, with rose-hedges separating it from
the orchard, and soon it blossomed in the wilderness. A niece
wrote of it in later years: "The memory of the old home is to me
'like dew on a parched and withered garden.' "

Jefferson Davis' earliest memory of "Poplar Grove" was not
of the garden, however, but of whisperings of the massacre of
Fort Mimms, where, he later wrote, "many of our neighbours
died in fulfilment of the noblest motives of human action, to give
their lives that others may live." As he was but five years of age,
when the Creek chief, Weatherford, and 1,000 braves stormed
that little fortress, killing 400 men, women, and children, he
could have been but dimly aware of the war waging against
England and her savage allies, though he doubtless heard much
conversation about the massacre, and about Andrew Jackson,
who rushed to the rescue of the remaining inhabitants of the
region, leading an army of 2,500, and there displayed for the first
time his wonderful qualities as a military leader. In breaking the
power of the Creeks, he won advancement, receiving, on May 31,
1814, a commission as major-general in the regular army.

When Davis reached school age his parents faced the question
of how to educate him. At five, he had been sent to "Old Field,"

a log cabin school, a mile from his home: but there remains no record of his progress, save that it had been so unsatisfactory that his father, despite the mother's wishes, decided to send him back to Kentucky, where he would have more effective teaching. Having made the long journey himself, Samuel Davis knew its difficulties, and began the search for a friend who would add the boy to his own caravan bound thither. Soon an ideal conductor was discovered in Major Hinds, the officer who had announced to Jackson the advance of the British at the battle of New Orleans, and who had since been appointed general of the Mississippi militia. Hinds' party included his wife, a sister-in-law, a niece, and a son, Howell Hinds, a lad of about Davis' age. There were, of course, servants, mule-drivers, and the ordinary equipment for such a journey, before steamboats had begun to run upon the Western waters, or stage-coaches to make journeys through its forests.

The trip was an adventure such as came to few boys, even in frontier days, and its details remained for ever clear in Davis' memory. His writings contain frequent reference to it, even to the very last year of his long life. Mounted upon stout little ponies, and followed by a file of pack-horses, the two boys absorbed every detail, heedless of fatigue, and thrilled by the knowledge that they had to pass through the Choctaw and Cherokee country, where the youthful imagination could picture a Chief Weatherford behind every tree, a new Tecumseh hiding in the recesses of every canebrake. They had no fear, however, for had not Major Hinds fought with Jackson? That there was no longer cause for fear from the now subdued savages of the region, boys engaged in such a journey could scarcely be expected to credit. "The only good Indian is the dead Indian," ran the familiar frontier maxim, and there remained many live Indians in the great wilderness where the caravan passed the long weeks of the journey. At times, while fording rivers, they met parties of white men bound southward, carried by the current upon rough rafts, and many persons, who had gone down the river in flatboats, Davis later recorded, "walked back through the wilderness to Kentucky, Ohio, and elsewhere. We passed many of these, daily." At night, they camped, using their own equipment, or stopped at what he calls "Stands . . . log cabins . . . occupied by white men who had intermarried with Indians," the Inns of the Wilderness.

"When we reached Nashville," continues Davis' narrative, "we went to the 'Hermitage.' Major Hinds wished to visit his friend and former companion-in-arms, General Jackson. The whole party was so kindly received that we remained there for several weeks. During that period I had the opportunity a boy has to observe a great man—a standpoint of no small advantage—and I have always remembered with warm affection the kind and tender wife who then presided over his house.

"General Jackson's home, at that time, was a roomy log house. In front was a grove of fine forest trees, and behind were cotton and grain fields. I have never forgotten the unaffected and well-bred courtesy which caused him to be remarked by court-trained diplomats, when President of the United States, by reason of his very impressive bearing and manner." General Jackson "inspired reverence and affection which has remained with me through my whole life. . . . My confidence and respect for him increased in after years. My affection and admiration followed him to the grave, and cling to his memory. . . . My first vote was cast in favour of him for President."

The visit at the Hermitage over, the caravan resumed its march, landing Jefferson Davis at last in Washington County, Kentucky, where he entered a school bearing the name of St. Thomas Aquinas, and conducted by Dominican fathers. The fees were one hundred dollars a year, reduced to ten dollars, if necessary, and were payable in coin, English pounds, or other currency, as suited the resources of the parents.

As the youngest boy, and one who paid his full dues, Davis was given quarters in the room of one of the fathers and there spent three of the most susceptible years of his life, years which permanently coloured his attitude toward Roman Catholicism, although, as he testified in later life, no attempt was made to proselyte him. Indeed, the fathers discouraged the idea of his adopting the Roman faith, when at the age of seven, and deeply impressed with the spirit of the place, he suggested to one of his ghostly advisers that he be allowed to become a Roman Catholic. Father Wilson listened patiently and sympathetically, and then, as Davis later recorded, "handed me a biscuit and a bit of cheese, and told me that, for the present, I had better take some Catholic food."

At St. Thomas, furthermore, Davis saw the institution of slavery serving holy orders; and heard the revamped arguments in its defence which churchmen had piously repeated since Las Casas used them to justify the first man-stealing expedition along the African coast in the days of Prince Henry, the Navigator. The school was run in connection with an agricultural estate, stocked with blooded cattle and worked by slaves, and slavery as the child saw it here in no wise destroyed the belief, in which he had been reared, that it was an institution ordained of God.

During the first year of Davis' life at St. Thomas' another lad, seven months his junior, was playing on the banks of Nolin Creek, thirty miles away, but in 1816 this lad's father, Thomas Lincoln, blood brother to the "wind that tramps the world," sold his forlorn home at Knob creek for ten barrels of whisky and twenty dollars in cash, rounded up his family, including little Abraham and crossed the Ohio river to spend his remaining days, in regions "for ever free" by virtue of the ordinance of 1787.

Today, the world knows the grim details of how Lincoln was trained for the leadership of the anti-slavery movement in those early days of Indiana and Illinois. But the story of how Davis was educated for leadership of the pro-Slavery South has still to be traced in such scattered references and odd documents as chance has preserved. The "ifs" of history are alluring. What changes would have occurred had John Hampden and Oliver Cromwell carried into effect plans, apparently once formed by them, to migrate to America? What changes would have occurred had George Washington been allowed to carry out his design of becoming a midshipman in the British navy? And it is not less interesting to speculate upon the result which would have followed had Samuel Davis migrated with his family into the free territory north of the Ohio; and Thomas Lincoln taken Abraham south into the "black-belt." In all likelihood, American history would have been altered by such an interchange of personalities, but altered, probably only in incidentals; for the great currents which later placed these two Kentuckians face to face, as leaders of opposing causes, were too powerful to have been changed in essentials by the lives of any two individuals.

In the meantime, Mrs. Davis had been pleading for her son's return to his home. Before the arrival of his tenth birthday she had won, and Samuel Davis reluctantly made plans for the return journey, which was now comparatively easy, as steamboats were making regular trips on the Mississippi. A passage was taken for the child on the *Ætna*, and Charles Green, a young Mississippian, who had been studying law in Kentucky, then the home of many eminent lawyers, took charge of him during the journey, which was uneventful. He has, himself, left the story of his arrival at home. "I found my dear mother sitting at the door, and, walking up with an assumed air to hide a throbbing heart, I asked here if there had been any stray horses round there. She said she had seen a stray boy, and clasped me in her arms." He then sought his father, to see whether he too would know him. The father's instant recognition disappointed him somewhat, and his eager kisses embarrassed him. "I wondered," he said, "why my father should have kissed so big a boy."

At once it was found that in that section of Mississippi it was not then possible to have one's son and educate him, too. The schools close at hand were poor, the teachers for the most part untrained, and the majority of the students ill-disposed toward learning. When these facts became clear, Jefferson, now ten years of age, was sent to Adams County, to what was called "Jefferson College," whose principal, James McAllister, was a man of learning. Shortly afterward, however, Wilkinson Academy was organized by a Bostonian, John A. Shaw, and Jefferson was brought home. Here he soon proved that he too was "ill-disposed toward learning," and, resentful also of the stern discipline which the principal maintained, he confidently went to his father for sympathy. He found it of a very wise kind. "It is for you to elect whether you will work with head or hands," his father answered. "My son could not be an idler." "Hands" won and a cotton-picking task was assigned instead of a school desk. After one day's work in the burning Mississippi sunshine, however, Davis decided that his intellectual interests had revived and was allowed to return to school, where he showed by good work that he had assimilated the lesson. "You may lead a horse to water, but you can't make him drink," or as Woodrow Wilson once revamped it, "You may lead a fool to knowledge, but you can't make him think." By this test, Davis demonstrated that he was no "fool."

In 1821, Shaw reported him ready for college, and Transylvania, in Lexington, seemed the natural choice. It had been organized in 1785, and now had 383 students. It had lived through many controversies, and had come to be looked upon as one of America's leading institutions of learning. Its president, Horace Halley, a Yale graduate and a Unitarian clergyman, who had had a brilliant career in Boston, was distinctly liberal and modern, as standards then stood, and in consequence had been accused of many sins, including socinianism, pelagianism, and want of faith in a personal devil. One critic had said of him that he was an infidel, and planned "to expel Christianity from Transylvania as it had been expelled from Harvard"; another, that, "though answering to a sacred title, he hesitated not to visit the theatre, to permit cards and dancing in his family, to divest the Sabbath of all idea of sacredness, and even to visit the racecourse, and become one of the judges of the races." Unmoved by such attacks, however, Dr. Halley had gone his way, confident in the sanity of his views, and conscious of the potentiality of his position.

How much of this characteristically bitter religious controversy had come to the ears of Davis' parents cannot now be determined. As they had lived in Kentucky, it is likely that some news of it had reached them, but it did not deter them from their plan, and in September, 1821, Jefferson Davis presented himself to Dr. Halley for entrance to the Freshman class. Having met the tests, he was duly matriculated, and his parents became liable for a fee of thirty dollars a year, for tuition, and an admission fee of five dollars. The Catalogue of 1826 thus estimates the additional annual expenses of a Transylvania undergraduate: "Board, or diet, can be obtained by those who have rooms in the college for one dollar and fifty cents a week. Board, washing, lodging, fuel, and lights can be obtained in private families for two dollars and fifty cents per week. The annual expense of all these items, including tuition, is about $112, to those having rooms in college, and about $130 to those lodging in private families."

All details having been settled, Davis found himself associated with a body of undergraduates, many of whom were destined to high positions in the life of the nation. When, in later years, he was serving his first term as United States Senator, he was one of six students of Transylvania who held seats in that Chamber. He remained in college until the end of his Junior year, enjoying the life and the beauty of surroundings, which has made the Blue Grass region famous. He enjoyed also the friendship of Henry Clay, a trustee of the university, already a commanding figure in national politics, and whose son was Davis' fellow student, and congenial comrade.

J. W. Jones, a classmate, later a Congressman and later still Davis' biographer, recalled Davis, the undergraduate: as "always gay and brimful of buoyant spirits, but without the smallest

tendency toward vice or immorality. He had that innate refine-
ment and gentleness that distinguished him through life. . . .
He never was perceptibly under the influence of liquor, and he
never gambled." His career shows also that his father's cotton-
field experiment had worked a real conversion: for he no longer
desired to escape the machinery of education. He studied with
special diligence the Greek and Latin classics and developed a
love of political philosophy which he never lost, and of history,
which was his favourite diversion throughout life. At the end of
his Junior year he passed his examinations with a rank sufficiently high to make him eligible for the coveted honour of
Junior orator at the commencement exercises, and this with his
personality caused him to be selected. He chose as his subject,
"Friendship," and delivered his oration in a manner which won
applause from audience and student body alike.

It had been Davis' intention to finish his course at Transylvania
and enter the University of Virginia, but at this point his brother
Joseph, a prominent member of the Mississippi bar, secured for
him an appointment to a cadetship at West Point, where, protested his mother, boys are "trained for vice and the army," and
his academic life came to a sudden end.

In the second decade of the nineteenth century, under the
superintendency of Major Sylvanus Thayer, the National Military
Academy of West Point held a high reputation as a place of
scientific education. Cadetships, then under the direct control of
the President, were the object of keen competition, although the
selection depended upon presidential favour rather than competi-
tive examination, and there were, it was said, at least thirty appli-
cants for every available appointment. There are no records to
show what influences Joseph Davis had been able to command
in his brother's interest. We know only that, on March 11, 1824,
John C. Calhoun, Secretary of War, made out a cadet's commission for him, and President Monroe signed it. It was forwarded
to Natchez and on to Transylvania. In consequence, Davis did

not receive it until July. His reply, dated Lexington, July 7, 1824, Transylvania University, is of military brevity:

"The commission of cadet granted the undersigned March 11th, and remitted to Natchez, on account of my absence was forwarded here. I accept it.

"Am not able to go on before Sept. for reasons I will explain to the Superintendent on my arrival.

"Yours & C.

"JEFFERSON DAVIS."

Three days before the date of this letter, Samuel Davis died at his farm in Mississippi; but the fact was not known to Davis when he accepted the appointment. Indeed, almost a month later he acknowledged the letter, which had conveyed to him the tidings. "I cannot describe the shock my feelings sustained at the sad intelligence," he wrote. . . . This is the second time I have been doomed to receive the heart-rending intelligence of the death of a friend. God only knows whether or not it will be the last. If all the dear friends of my childhood are to be torn from me, I care not how soon I may follow."

Professor Fleming has called attention to the many and varied influences of these the most formative years of Davis' life. "His teachers . . . at St. Thomas were Englishmen, at Jefferson College, Scotsmen, at the County Academy a Bostonian, at Transylvania . . . Scotsmen, New Englanders, French and Irish." His religious contacts had been equally broad, Baptist at home, Catholic, Presbyterian, and Unitarian at school and college; an education calculated, though certainly not intended, to make him a cosmopolitan with a predisposition toward international-mindedness.

Colonel Henderson, the famous English biographer of "Stonewall" Jackson, speaks of West Point as a "university," for reasons hard to discover, as candidates were examined for entrance only in reading, writing, and arithmetic; and when the examiners discovered that Davis had studied Greek, all further questioning was waived. His qualifications having been declared sufficient, he subscribed to the oath which bound him "to serve in the army of the United States for a period of five years, unless sooner discharged"; read the rules almost puritanical in their prohibition of cards, tobacco, and passing the limits without permit, and having spent this period of probation at Gridley's Hotel, where prospectives slept "three in a bed," he was assigned quarters in South Barracks, which, like the other West Point buildings of his day, has since been removed to give place to the Gothic of the present Academy. His room was eleven feet square, and was shared by two other cadets. No furniture was provided by the government, each cadet being required to contribute his share, and in consequence the quarters were far from luxurious. For the hours of study by day, three chairs, a small table, and scant bookshelves sufficed: and for night three mattresses were spread on the floor, where the cadets slept soundly until reveille summoned them to parade and another day. Water, each man fetched for himself from a neighbouring spring. The Hudson served as a bath during mild weather; but, in winter, the cadet must make shift with a small tub placed before his log fire, which took its start each day from a tinder-box, in lieu of matches.

At the end of his second year, Davis moved into larger quarters in North Barracks, where the extra seven feet of space was more than compensated for by two more room-mates, five, in an eighteen-foot-room, with living arrangements as before, well outside the present-day sanitary code. Such simple, indeed Spartan, surroundings made intimate friendships easy: and such friendships lasted through life. Albert Sidney Johnston and Leonidas Polk, later the "fighting Bishop" of the Confederacy, were two years ahead of Davis as cadets, but were his closest friends; Robert E. Lee and Joseph E. Johnston, though slightly older, were his juniors by one year at West Point, and there seems to have been little intimacy with either.

The intellectual side of the Academy was as Spartan as its physical conditions. Every waking hour had its duties. The schedule we have from the contemporary testimony of Theodore Sedgwick, Jr., who wrote in July, 1824: "The exercises of each day, at this time of the year are as follows: at 4.30 A.M. the reveille drum beats, when we all attend roll-call, soon after which, the officer of the day inspects the rooms, sees that beds are made, rooms swept, and none in bed, and reports all those whose beds are not made, whose rooms are not swept, or who are in bed. At six o'clock, we go to breakfast at our boarding-houses, at seven o'clock we attend prayers . . . after which studies and recitations commence, and continue till one o'clock when we go to dinner; at two o'clock we have another roll-call, when the studies commence again. . . . At six we have a drill, and at seven we sup; at half past eight we have a roll-call in the lecture-room; at nine the inspector sees that all are in their rooms, and reports all who are out and at ten he inspects again, when all are required to be in bed." Sedgwick adds this bit of criticism: "The Academy is under the sole direction of Captain Partridge, who has under him three professors and one French master. . . . The branches which are taught are Mathematics, Philosophy, Military Science, Ethicks, Belles Lettres, Practical Geometry, Topography, Greek, Latin, French, and Music. Fencing is likewise taught."

Leonidas Polk, wrote: "I think in point of mathematics and philosophy and the other sciences dependent on these two, this institution is inferior to none in the United States," and not satisfied with the breadth of this generalization, he added, "and I may say . . . the world. . . . Most of the authors we study are selected from the French, some of them translated into English, others not." This sounds more learned than the facts warrant, for the cadets were not more proficient French scholars than the students of other educational institutions of America, and Colonel de Vernon's *Science of War*, in a poor translation, was sold as a "pony" at twenty cents a copy, and freely used.

Of all the subjects taught at West Point at the time, however, the one which history has most emphasized, was "Constitutional Law." Before Davis' arrival, it had been taught by the Chaplain, the magnetic C. P. McIlvaine, later Episcopal Bishop of Ohio, a man whose influence upon the cadets seems to have been very great; and the text-book which he had used was *A View of the Constitution of the United States of America*, by William Rawle. This fact gave rise to the contention that Davis, Lee, and the other Confederate leaders who were trained at West Point had been taught at government expense the views which they later defended in the Civil War. But this conclusion is wholly upset by a statement from Davis himself. On July 1, 1886, he wrote to the Hon. R. T. Bennett: "Rawle on the Constitution was the text-book at West Point, but when the class of which I was a member entered *the graduating year*, Kent's *Commentaries* were introduced as the text-book on the Constitution and international law." As this subject was taught only in *the graduating year*, it is evident from Davis' own words, so often used to prove the contrary, that he did not use Rawle's text-book at West Point.

Nor did he derive his views upon the right of secession from McIlvaine, who, as Douglas Freeman tells us, was no longer at West Point when Lee studied there. As Lee entered in 1825, it is evident that McIlvaine could not have been Davis' teacher in his Senior year, 1827-28. As a matter of fact, Lee never subscribed to Rawle's views, and the research of over a century has produced no evidence that Davis derived his opinions from Rawle, either while at West Point or in later life. As he had studied at Transylvania only two decades after the publication of the Kentucky Resolutions of 1798, the chief author of which was his political ideal, Thomas Jefferson, it is far more likely that he got his theory of the right of secession there.

The lasting importance of this question is shown by the fact that when Davis was under impeachment for treason, his chief counsel, the illustrious Charles O'Conor, declared that with so admirably prepared and so overwhelmingly conclusive a brief as Rawle's *View*, it would be easy to defend him against the charge. And William B. Reed, another of his counsel labouring under the same misapprehension, wrote later, "If the case had come to trial, the defence would have offered in evidence the text-book on constitutional law [Rawle's *"View"*] from which Davis had been instructed at West Point by the authority of the United States Government, and in which the right of secession is maintained as one of the constitutional rights of a state."

One of the rules of West Point prohibited the receiving of extra money from outside, the desire being to oblige the Cadets to live upon their pay and rations, and it required talent, therefore, to find much outside recreation. Necessary expenses accounted for, out of an allowance of twenty-eight dollars a month, the cash balance must have been low indeed. But even under such discouraging conditions, Jefferson Davis managed to leave behind him the memory of something accomplished, something done, in the way of amusing himself. It is a matter of record that he was one of a group court-martialled a certain night for drinking at Benny Havens', a public house some two miles from the Academy, and, when caught in the act, as Captain Hitchcock reported, "he exhibited extreme embarrassment . . . [which] might have proceeded from being found in the circumstances I stated, but a part of it I attributed to the use of spirituous liquors."

Penalties for such offences were not light, and four of the offenders were dismissed from the Army. Davis, with Hays, was "pardoned and returned to duty," partly, no doubt, owing to the high average of his conduct chart, partly perhaps because of the skill with which he presented his case in the written report which each offender was allowed to make. Davis argued that the order not to frequent Benny Havens' had not been officially promulgated, and was therefore something less than law; and that the cider and porter which they enjoyed there were not, in the opinion of the chemist, "spirituous liquors," and closed his brief with the touching eloquence, "It is better a hundred guilty should escape than one righteous person be condemned." The obvious inference, that he was, in this case, that one righteous person strangely resembles a non-sequitur; but he received the pardon which restored him to the rights of the righteous. The military report of the case was as follows:

Engineer Department,
Washington, Aug. 29, 1825.

M. A. Orders No. 19.

At the General Court Martial of which Major W. J. Worth of the 1st Regiment of Artillery is President, first convened at West Point, in the State of New York, by virtue of Orders No. 41 issued by the Adjutant-General of the Army on the 19th. of May 1825 was reconvened by virtue of orders No. 62 issued by the same officer on the 22nd. day of July last which Court commenced its sessions under the second convention on the 30th of July and continued it by adjournment to the 8th of August last was tried

· · · · · · ·

Cadet Jefferson Davis on the following Charges and Specifications, viz.

Charge 1st. In this that the said Jefferson Davis did on Sunday the 31st. July 1825 go beyond the limits prescribed to Cadets at West Point without permission.

Charge 2nd. Violating the 1408th. Paragraph of the General Army Regulations.

Specifications 1st. In this that the said Cadet Davis on Sunday the 31st. July 1825 at some place in the vicinity of West Point did drink spirituous and intoxicating liquor.

Specifications 2nd. In this that the said Cadet Davis on

Sunday the 31st. July 1825 did go to a public house or place where spirituous liquors are sold kept by one Benjamin Havens at or near Buttermilk Falls and distant about two miles from West Point.

The Prisoner pleaded to the 1st. Charge and its Specifications, Guilty; to the 1st. Specification 2nd. Charge, Not Guilty; to the 2nd. Specification 2nd. Charge, Guilty; to the 2nd. Charge, guilty of violating so much of the 1408th. Paragraph of the General Army Regulations as prohibits going to a public house or place where liquors are sold and not guilty of the remainder.

The Court after mature deliberation on the testimony adduced find the Prisoner Cadet Jefferson Davis guilty of both the 1st. and 2nd. Charges preferred against him and their Specifications. The Court sentence him to be dismissed from the service of the United States; but in consideration of his former good conduct respectfully recommend the remission of said sentence. . . .

The foregoing proceedings are approved.

Cadets . . . and Davis in consideration of the recommendation of the General Court Martial are pardoned and will return to their duty. . . .

> By order of the Secretary of War:
> (sg) Alex. Macomb,
> Major-General,
> Inspr. of the Mil. Academy.

This was the only occasion when Davis figured in a court-martial: but it was not the only time that he risked such an experience. For again he allowed Benny's to endanger his military career, and this time his escape was due to his heels rather than to his head. Alarmed while drinking, Davis and his companion, Emil La Serre, sought escape by a cliff route, where Davis stumbled and fell some forty feet, narrowly escaping with his life. When his anxious comrade called him from above, he answered with a laugh; but months were required to restore the laughter to the drillgrounds, so severe had been his injuries.

A third wandering from the straight and narrow path took the form of a projected but illegal Christmas party, at which Davis and other informed Cadets proposed to show the uninformed how to make eggnog, that drink of enticing flavour and high potential. Benny furnished the explosives; Davis delivered the invitations, and Robert E. Lee and Joseph E. Johnston were among those who accepted the summons. But before the glorious moment of tasting arrived, the authorities made their appearance and Davis was sent to his quarters, under arrest. "Fortunately for him," says Fleming, ". . . after some hilarious noise, he went to sleep and did not get into the riot which followed." That riot soon developed into a free-fight between some of the remaining Cadets and officials, and its aftermath was nineteen Cadets court-martialled and dismissed. But Jefferson Davis, who had not been among the rioters, remained. There is, too, a story, in a letter to W. L. Fleming, June 12, 1908, from James Augustus Bethune, to the effect that "Davis and [Joseph E.] Johnston had each a 'gallantry' with the tavern-keeper's daughter (at West Point) and that, upon their repairing to Old Fort Putnam to settle the dispute by a fisticuff, Johnston, being heavier but not so tall, gave Davis the worst of the fight."

On the whole, Davis won at West Point only a fair rating in scholarship. He graduated twenty-third in a class of thirty-three. His conduct rating was 120 demerits the first year, 70 for the second, and 137 for the third. Two hundred a year would have meant dismissal from the Academy. The training had not confirmed the ambitions formed at Transylvania, but had developed his natural bent toward military studies, and his equally natural interest in mathematics, philosophy, and history. Nothing in his career predicted a brilliant future; but he carried with him from West Point the high sense of honour and devotion to duty which is of the essence of the profession.

CHAPTER II

ARMY DAYS

I N HIS autobiography Jefferson Davis thus treats the subject of his short career as an officer in the Army of the United States: "I graduated in 1828, and then, in accordance with the custom of cadets, entered active service with the rank of lieutenant, serving as an officer of Infantry on the Northern Frontier until 1833, when, a regiment of dragoons having been created, I was transferred to it. After a successful campaign against the Indians, I resigned from the army in 1835."

While in no sense epoch-making, this period of his life illustrates his character. His first station was Jefferson Barracks, St. Louis, where he made his appearance in September, 1828, as brevet Second-Lieutenant of the First Regular Infantry. Soon, however, he was assigned to duty at Fort Crawford, in the Indian Country, far to the north, and better known to later generations as Prairie du Chien. It stood near the junction of the Wisconsin and the Mississippi, commanding a wilderness occupied by savages, and was thus the frontier guardian of civilization, upon the northern border of the Illinois tribes, and the starting-point of their raids against the Iroquois. From Davis himself we have an account of his arrival: "Being . . . something of a martinet, I arrayed myself in full uniform and made my way to the regimental headquarters. The Colonel and Lieutenant-Colonel being absent—or perhaps one or both of these positions being vacant— the command of the regiment had devolved upon Major (afterward Colonel and brevet Major-General) Bennet Riley. The Major was not in, and I was directed to the Commissary to find him. Repairing to the place indicated, I found Major Riley, alone, seated at a table with a pack of cards before him, intently occupied in a game of solitaire. In response to my formal salute, he nodded, invited me to take a seat, and continued his game. Looking up after a few minutes, he inquired: "Young man, do you play solitaire? Finest game in the world! You may cheat as much as you please and have nobody to detect it."

This was a drab beginning for a young and ardent West Pointer, with a proper idea of the dignity of his profession; though highly characteristic of the life of a frontier camp of the early nineteenth century.

Davis' later frontier record, as it appears in Cullum's *Officers and Graduates of West Point*, is equally drab. The following details alone appear:

"Served: on frontier duty at Fort Crawford, Wis., 1829, Fort Winnebago, Wis., 1829-1831; Yellow river, Superintendent Saw-Mill, 1831, Fort Crawford, Wis., 1831, Dubuque mines, Ia., 1832. Jefferson Barracks, Mo., 1832, and Fort Crawford, Wis., 1832-33."

To examine critically the many thrilling adventures which time has added to Davis' modest statements of these days would require a separate volume. No man can become, as he later became, a great political figure, without having his career, at every stage, decorated with evidences of super-manhood. But the historian, interested in facts alone, and such drama as those facts justify, will find little of moment in his earlier frontier life. There is the story of the daring young Lieutenant Lumberjack, caught in a deadly current, reminiscent of Scylla and Charybdis; the story of the same heroic young Lieutenant, sick unto death with pneumonia, lying on his hard bed for months, far up the Yellow river, directing as best he could the operations of his men, and attended by his faithful slave, Jim Pemberton, who scorned to take advantage of the ordinance of 1787, which made a slave in the Northwest territory forever free. But these and many similar tales find no confirmation in the documents.

When Davis returned to Fort Crawford, he found Colonel Zachary Taylor in command, and soon developed an interest in the Colonel's daughter, Sarah Knox Taylor, which interest, the Colonel, later known as "the General who never surrenders," was far from encouraging. Many explanations of this fact have been given, some plausible, many fantastic. In musty records, we find one incident, however, which may well help to explain it. A fragment from a memoir of a Pottawottomi Chief, one Shaubena, describes an Indian wedding attended by Taylor, Davis and other officers. "Among the wedding party," it runs, "was a young squaw of great personal attraction, who danced in her Indian style with much grace. Lieutenant Davis became fascinated with her charms, and danced with her in almost every set. He would do many remarkable things, sometimes changing the order of the dance to suit his fancy. When quadrilles were danced, he would change into a waltz, so he could have his arms around the waist of the young squaw; then again, freeing himself from her, he would dance with all his might, causing his tall form to jerk and wiggle as it swayed to and fro; sometimes jumping up and down in quick succession, and yelling at the top of his voice, in imitation of the Indians at the door. Colonel Taylor and Captain Smith took no part in the dance, but sat in one corner of the room, looking on, and almost splitting their sides with laughter. . . . The young squaw, feeling herself insulted in the presence of the company, became indignant, and informed her brother of it. Her brother, a tall, athletic Indian, was very angry . . . and felt determined to punish the offender. Being quite drunk, his brain frenzied by anger and whiskey, he went up to Lieutenant Davis, and in bad English accused him of insulting his sister, at the same time pulling his nose. Davis, who never lacked courage, pushed the Indian from him, and drew forth a pistol. The Indian, with a fiendish smile, drew from its scabbard a long scalping-knife, and was prepared to meet his antagonist in a deadly combat. The dance stopped, the women screamed, and all was confusion and alarm; everyone expected to see the death of one or both. . . . But in an instant Colonel Taylor sprang between the combatants, and thereby prevented the effusion of blood."

This incident reminds one of Herodotus' sprightly story of the young man who danced himself out of a bride; for when Davis settled down to the task of winning Zachary Taylor's daughter, he found the father less willing than the maid. To protesting friends of Davis', Colonel Taylor declared curtly that he had no desire to acquire Davis as a son-in-law. This feeling was increased before long by a difference of opinion in a court martial in which Lieutenant Davis ventured to vote against the Colonel's wishes in a matter of military punctilio. It was not an important point, but both Davis and Taylor were determined, and there was already friction between them. Almost half a century later, Davis was still arguing his position. "I was right," he wrote on April 25, 1879, "as to the principle . . . but impolitic in the manner of asserting it. . . . The colonel assailed me harshly, imputing to me motives the reverse of those by which I was actuated. Then I became wrong, as angry men are apt to be." In the end, Taylor forbade Davis the house and swore, "by the Eternal," that he should never become a member of his family.

What history calls "the Code" was not yet dead on the frontier, and Davis' irritation now drove him to the determination to challenge the colonel. He accordingly approached Captain McRee with the request that he act as his "second," only to be told how absurd it was to plan the death of the man whom he wished as a father-in-law. Mrs. McRee was called into council, seconded her husband's refusal, and declared that if Davis would master his temper, she could manage to bring him, at times, into Miss Taylor's company, and facilitate his suit. And so matters stood when trouble with the Indians called Davis into active service in the field.

The Black Hawk war was the result of an attempt to alienate uncivilized lands by the not too civilized method of purchase from Indians who lacked the white man's views upon real estate. In 1804 the United States government had acquired by what white men call a treaty of purchase from the Sacs and Foxes some 50 million acres of land located in what is now Missouri, Illinois and Wisconsin. The hereditary chief of the Sacs, Mucatah Muhicatah, better known by the name, Black Hawk, who had signed the agreement, understood little of the idea of individual ownership of land. "I touched the goose quill to the treaty," he later complained, "not knowing . . . that by that act I gave away my village." "Gave away" was very near the truth, as the value received amounted to not more than $1,000.

After the sale and contrary to the agreement, Black Hawk had remained at the mouth of Rock River, upon the alienated lands, where white settlers had stolen his crops and mistreated his people. To avoid an Indian war, the government had from time to time sanctioned gifts to sweeten the bargain which Black Hawk showed an increasing tendency to disregard, although in 1830, the Sacs and the Foxes assembled at Prairie du Chien had for the second time ceded the territory to the United States. Still Black Hawk was sullen and threatening, and in 1831, Governor Reynolds, with a volunteer army, had forced him to cross to the west bank of the Mississippi, where, angry and defiant, he had prepared for war.

General Henry Atkinson had next given 60,000 bushels of corn, valued at $3,000, as the price of peace, and for a few months it seemed that Indian affairs had again been quieted by bribery. But the corn was soon only a sweet and rapidly passing memory, while the alienation of the lands remained a very bitter one. "My reason teaches me," Black Hawk declared, "that land cannot be sold. The Great Spirit gave it to his children to live upon. . . . Nothing can be sold but such things as can be carried away." He accordingly issued a warning that "his heart was bad," raised a

British flag, and having sent emissaries to the "Dirty Water People," the Winnebagoes, to ask for help, mustered his braves, consulted his wise men, and all signs being propitious, recrossed the Mississippi, on April 6, 1832, and the Black Hawk war was on.

By May 10th, Taylor's First Infantry was in motion, and Lieutenant Davis with it. At the battle of Wisconsin Heights (July 21) he had his first glimpse of his profession in action, and it was grim enough, for it was soon evident that the handful of regulars who garrisoned the frontier could not check the invasion. Governor Reynolds again called upon the citizens of Illinois to volunteer for the defence of their homes, and almost every man of fighting age responded. It was not the response of "embattled farmers," but of state militia, as the law of Illinois required each of her sons to "provide himself with a good musket, fusee or rifle, with proper accoutrements"; the officers to be armed "with a sword and pair of pistols. . . ." It declared, moreover, that any one who, when called for, refused to serve, either personally or through a substitute, should be treated as a deserter. From the conscientious objector, the law demanded one dollar and fifty cents a year, in lieu of service. Thus, in theory, every able-bodied citizen of Illinois was a soldier, even before Black Hawk's swoop, though from Lieutenant Davis' standpoint he left much to be desired by way of equipment, drill, precision, and more especially discipline. The law further stipulated that officers were to be elected by the soldiers after five days' notice, a provision which launched the careers of not a few whose chief interest was political rather than military—the type most detested by the West Pointer.

Among those chosen for leadership was the captain of the Sagamon County militia, Abraham Lincoln. "Out of work, penniless, a candidate for office," says his biographer, Beveridge, he had "promptly volunteered for thirty days' service against 'the British Band,' as Black Hawk and his warriors were called," the

Chief having fought for England in the War of 1812. The word "volunteer," as Beveridge explains, is misleading. "Lincoln's service," he says, "was service according to law, but his political friends later defined it as 'volunteer service' for the defence of frontier settlers . . . from the savage 'tomahawk and skelping-knife.' "

Elected captain, certainly for qualifications not remotely connected with what Davis considered military, Lincoln waited with his company to be mustered in. Mrs. Davis, in her memoir of her husband, presents an interesting picture of the scene of his enlistment: "Two lieutenants were sent by Scott to Dixon, Illinois, to muster the new soldiers. One of these lieutenants was a very fascinating young man, of easy manners and affable disposition; the other was equally pleasant and extremely modest. On the morning when the muster was to take place, a tall, gawky, slab-sided, homely young man, dressed in a suit of blue jeans, presented himself to the lieutenants as the captain of the recruits, and was duly sworn in. The homely young man was Abraham Lincoln. The bashful lieutenant was he who afterward fired the first gun at Fort Sumter, Major Anderson. The other lieutenant, who administered the oath, was, in after years, the President of the Confederate States, Jefferson Davis." Mrs. Davis gives, as her authority, the Rev. Dr. Harsha, of Omaha, who claimed that his story had been corroborated by the then Chaplain at Fort Snelling, and by another (left nameless) who declared that "he had often heard Mr. Lincoln say that the first time he had taken the oath of allegiance to the United States, it was administered by Jefferson Davis."

It is a pleasing picture, lacking only the incident of complete proof to make it history: the rough young Lincoln, "unkempt, disreputable, vast," to adopt Kipling's not too flattering characterization of "the American," facing, upon the Western plains the trim, military figures of Anderson and Davis, "cleanly bred, machinely crammed," sent to commission him as captain. Whether

Davis and Anderson actually rendered this service has been often questioned. Mrs. Davis says that her husband "remembered swearing in some volunteers, but could not substantiate what seems a probable story." Whoever commissioned Lincoln, however, he made a pleasing impression upon the historian and poet, William Cullen Bryant, who was present and described the Sagamon company as "hard-looking . . . unkempt, and unshaved, wearing shirts of dark calico, and sometimes calico capotes," and Captain Lincoln as "a raw youth, in whose quaint and pleasant talk," he found himself deeply interested. He was dressed in a suit of blue jeans, and, when the recruiting officer approached, waved a long arm towards a motley crowd on his right, saying: "I am the captain of this company."

To Lincoln, if we may judge by certain expressions in his later speeches, the Black Hawk war was a not very serious affair. When on the march, his men frequently lolled in the shade of the trees, or at night lay round the campfire, listening to their captain's stories until the lights were ordered out. In defiance of the dignity of the service, which meant so much to Davis, Lincoln raced, boxed, and wrestled with all comers. By the end of his thirty days' enlistment, he was "the most popular man in the army," to quote a member of his company, but his popularity was due to no deeds of military prowess, no hairbreadth escapes. He himself later summed up the experiences of that month in the words: "In the days of the Black Hawk War I fought, bled, and came away. . . . I had a good many bloody struggles with the mosquitoes, and although I never fainted from loss of blood, I can truly say I was often very hungry." He declared that he did not break his sword, because he had none, despite the Illinois militia law; but bent a musket "by accident." He also spoke of gallant charges on the wild-onion beds.

In striking contrast to Lincoln's outwardly flippant view of this service in the Army of his country, is the seriousness with

which Jefferson Davis viewed it. Without Lincoln's keen sense of
humour, and with perhaps a keener sense of the issues involved,
he helped in the chase of the bloody invaders, pressing them so
persistently that they found it difficult to gather supplies. By the
middle of July they were near starvation, and the pursuing regulars were themselves so short of food that they had to be content
with little more than raw pork and dough. And as Davis pursued,
he admired; for the gallantry and resourcefulness of Black Hawk
and his fellow savages were magnificent. "We were one day pursuing the Indians," he said later, "when we came close to the
Wisconsin River. Reaching the river bank, the Indians made so
determined a stand, and fought with such desperation, that they
held us in check. During this time the squaws tore bark from
the trees and made little shallops, in which they floated their
papooses . . . across to an island, also swimming over the ponies.
As soon as this was accomplished, half of the warriors plunged
in and swam across, each holding his gun in one hand over his
head, and swimming with the other. As soon as they reached the
opposite bank, they opened fire upon us, under cover of which
the other half slipped down the bank and swam in like manner.
This was the most brilliant exhibition of military tactics that I
ever witnessed, a feat of most consummate management and
bravery, in the face of an enemy of greatly superior numbers. . . .
Had it been performed by white men it would have been immor-
talized as one of the most splendid achievements in military
history."

It would be a profitless task to follow the details of such military operations as are involved in a fight between civilized and
savage warriors. The inevitable catastrophe for Black Hawk came
on August 2, 1832, when, in the battle of Bad Axe, he met an
overwhelming defeat, losing 190 warriors, by death or capture.
Leaving twenty-four white victims dead upon the field, the Chief
and the Prophet with a few savage survivors escaped to an island

above Prairie du Chien, still closely pursued by a detachment under Lieutenant Davis, whose account is as follows:

"It was reported that the Indians were on an island in the river above the prairie, and Colonel Taylor sent a lieutenant (Lieutenant Davis) with an appropriate command to explore the island. He found Black Hawk . . . with a few Winnebagoes who said Black Hawk had surrendered to them, and that they wanted to take him to the fort and to see the Indian agent. The lieutenant went with the Indians to the fort, and reported to Colonel Taylor, among other things, his disbelief of the Winnebagoes' story. The . . . old soldier merely replied, 'They want the credit of being friendly and to get a reward. Let them have it.' "

General Scott then ordered Robert Anderson with the steamer *Warrior* to proceed to Fort Crawford, get General Street, who as agent of the Winnebagoes was now in charge of Black Hawk, and bring him with his prisoners to Fort Armstrong. While on his way, Anderson fell ill with cholera, and Colonel Taylor sent Lieutenant Davis to relieve him of the detail.

When he made his first inspection of the boat, Davis was accompanied by General Street, who shook hands with each prisoner in turn, until they came to Black Hawk. Seeing the old chief with irons on his wrists, he turned to Davis, and suggested that they be removed, and upon Davis' replying that it might not be safe, "Sir," answered Street, "I hold myself personally responsible for this man's safety and good conduct." "If you direct it, General," Davis replied, and turning to his orderly, sent for the boat's blacksmith to file the irons away.

When Davis and Street reached Fort Armstrong with their prisoners, General Scott came out in a small boat to meet them and ordered Davis to convey the prisoners to Jefferson Barracks, St. Louis, as cholera was raging at Fort Armstrong. To Black Hawk's disappointment, he himself refused to board the boat, for fear of spreading the dread disease. Black Hawk's comment upon the precaution was:

"The war chief looked well, and I have since heard was constantly among his soldiers, who were sick and dying, administering to their wants, and had not caught the disease from them, and I thought it absurd to think that any of the people on the steamboat could be afraid of catching the disease from a well man. But these people are not brave like war chiefs, who never fear anything."

In his further account of the journey, dictated to his interpreter, Antoine Leclair, Black Hawk says that he "started to Jefferson Barracks in a steamboat, under the charge of a young war chief [Lieutenant Jefferson Davis] who treated us all with much kindness. He is a good and brave young chief, with whose conduct I was much pleased.

"On our way down, we called at Galena, and remained a short time. The people crowded to the boat to see us; but the war chief would not permit them to enter the apartment where we were— knowing, from what his own feelings would have been, if he had been placed in a similar situation, that we did not wish to have a gaping crowd around us." And further, as watching his ancestral lands fade from his view: "I reflected upon the ingratitude of the whites when I saw their houses, rich harvests and everything desirable round them, and recalled that all this land had been ours."

At St. Louis, Davis delivered his charges to Brigadier-General H. Atkinson, known to the Indians as "The White Beaver." "We were now," continues Black Hawk, "confined to the barracks, and forced to wear the *ball* and *chain*! This was extremely mortifying, and altogether useless. Was the White Beaver afraid that I would break out of his barracks and run away? Or was he ordered to inflict this punishment upon me? If I had taken him prisoner on the field of battle, I would not have wounded his feelings so much, by such treatment, knowing that a brave war chief would prefer *death* to *dishonour*! But I do not blame the

White Beaver for the course he pursued—it is the custom among
white soldiers, and, I suppose, was a part of his duty."

From St. Louis, Black Hawk was sent to Fortress Monroe,
where later Davis was himself to know the humiliation of wearing the ball and chain, though denied the consideration with
which he had treated his savage prisoner. In recognition of his
services to his country, he was advanced on March 4, 1833, to the
rank of first lieutenant of the First Regiment of Dragoons, then
stationed at St. Louis, and, shortly after, when the regiment was
ordered to Fort Gibson, was made its adjutant. He frankly declared, however, that the real heroes of the war were Black Hawk
and his savage followers.

Fort Gibson commanded a region so lovely that the poet Long-
fellow sent thither, in later years, that immortal creation of his
fancy, Evangeline, in her search for her lost lover, Gabriel. She
found, not Gabriel, but a charming Shawnee woman also seeking
a lost lover:

> "And there they wept together,
>   For their helpless fate,
>   The white and the Indian maiden."

Here too lingered the memory of Washington Irving's visit of
October, 1832; and his French guide, Antonie Tonish, remains
a delightful character in American literature.

That strange empire-builder, Sam Houston, had also lived
near Fort Gibson, in the Cherokee Country, from 1829 to 1832,
after his sudden and unexplained separation from his young wife
soon after the wedding, and his abandonment of his post as Governor of Tennessee. He had come alone, to ask the hospitality of
the aged Indian chief, "Johnniecake," and had been received as an
honoured son of the tribe. Here he had consoled himself with an
Indian wife, had led the wild life of a savage, and had won
among his fellow tribesmen the not too flattering nickname of

"Big Drunk." We have a record of a later meeting between Davis and Houston, in 1834, when the latter confided his intention of going to Texas, breaking it off from Mexico, and annexing it to the United States; he went even farther in his confidences, declaring his intention of becoming governor of Texas, United States senator, and President. When the last-named ambition should have been realized, he added that he wanted "Davis for his Secretary of War," a suggestion which Davis may well have ascribed to the habit of drink which had made Houston so notorious.

Two years had passed since Davis left Fort Crawford, and, against his desire, the daughter of its commanding officer; but that he had written to her and perhaps seen her more than once is evidenced by a letter from Fort Gibson, in which he speaks as an accepted suitor. He therefore informed the still irreconcilable father that his marriage with Knox would take place in the near future. Knox added the statement that as she had waited two years for his consent, which was still withheld, and, as nothing derogatory to Davis' character had been offered as excuse for the refusal, she would marry without consent. When Colonel Taylor waxed eloquent, and more than eloquent, at these announcements, Captain Kearney, a fellow officer of Davis', ventured to plead his friend's case; to which Taylor replied: "I will de damned if another daughter of mine shall marry into the Army. I know enough of the family life of officers. I scarcely know my own children, or they me," and though adding, "I have no personal objections to Lieutenant Davis," he remained obdurate.

During one of Knox's pleadings for her lover, she said to her father: "The time will come when you will see, as I do, all his rare qualities." This proved to be true, but that time was not yet.

One of the least appealing incidents in the life of Edward Gibbon, the historian, is that in which his father commanded him to give up the woman he loved. He tells us that: "I sighed as a lover, but obeyed as a son." Davis and Miss Taylor were of a different type. They continued to urge their case through friends, and at the same time planned for a married future outside the Army. Davis had studied his chances of promotion, even to the rank of captain, and had found them far from encouraging. Few vacancies were likely to occur, and the probability of new posts being created was slight. Ganoe's *History of the United States Army* tells us that for the West Point graduates of 1836 there were no vacant posts, and that they had to be attached as brevet second lieutenants to the companies to which they were assigned. He adds that 117 of Davis' fellow officers resigned in that year chiefly because of the discouraging outlook for promotion. It was therefore wisdom, not pique, which caused Davis' decision.

The story of Davis' "runaway match" has taken many forms: The two "eloped in a sleigh to Galena and were married there"; "Davis lifted his bride from an upper window of her father's house, crossed into Iowa and they were married on the boat by a Roman Catholic priest"; "they were married in St. Louis in a house standing on the corner of Monroe and Hall Streets"; "they took four horses from her father's stable and made a joint getaway with George Wilson and Miss Mary Street"; "they compelled an Indian to row them down to Turkey River, on the Iowa side, and there they were married"; "they went to St. Louis and . . . the colonel heard of them there, and had them brought back."

Imagination is the life of fiction, but the death of history. All of these stories, and many more, have masqueraded as history, but are pure fiction, "baseless scandal," as Davis called them. What really happened is that Mrs. Gibson Taylor, aunt of the bride-to-be, continued to plead with Colonel Taylor to withdraw his objections; and that finally he reluctantly agreed, provided the wedding should take place at Mrs. Gibson Taylor's home in Kentucky. Captain McRee thereupon engaged Miss Taylor's passage from Fort Crawford to Louisville on a St. Louis steamboat, and she sailed to join Davis; a licence was procured, and, just before the ceremony, Knox wrote to her mother:

Louisville, *June 17, 1835.*

You will be surprised, no doubt, my dear mother, to hear of my being married so soon. When I wrote to you last I had no idea of leaving here before fall; but hearing the part of the country to which I am going is quite healthy, I have concluded to go down this summer and will leave here this afternoon at 4 o'clock; will be married as you advised in my bonnet and travelling-dress. I am very much gratified that Sister Ann is here. At this time having one member of my family present, I shall not feel so entirely destitute of friends. But you, my dearest mother, I know will retain some feelings of affection for a child who has been so unfortunate as to form a connexion without the sanction of her parents, but who will always feel the deepest affection for them whatever may be their feelings toward her. Say to my dear father that I have received his kind and affectionate letter, and thank him for the liberal supply of money sent me.

KNOX.

The records show that Davis married June 17, 1835, and resigned less than two weeks later.

CHAPTER III

PLANTATION DAYS

THE part of the country referred to by Knox Taylor in the letter to her mother, written on her wedding day, was Warren County, Mississippi. In lieu of the interest which Jefferson Davis had in his father's negroes, which had passed into the service of Joseph Davis, the latter had transferred to his brother 890 acres of his own plantation, "Hurricane." Unfortunately, however, as later events proved, Joseph Davis neglected to make over a clear title to Jefferson Davis, who therefore led his bride to a home not legally their own. "Brierfield," as the new plantation was called, was, however, hardly a home, as it consisted of a mass of tangled undergrowth, trees and briers, potential but certainly forbidding from the point of view of a bride, and by no means so healthy as it had been reported. It and Joseph's own plantation lay in a bend of the Mississippi River, known as Palmyra Bend, twenty miles below Vicksburg. Originally a peninsula, as appears upon some of the early maps, it had been made into an island by a change in the course of the river. It was, therefore, to Palmyra Island that Jefferson Davis brought his bride, across seventy feet of water with a six-mile current. For one less inured to isolation than Colonel Taylor's daughter, the sense of loneliness would doubtless have been overpowering. But young Mrs. Davis had been reared on the frontier; and the silence of her island home may have seemed to her friendly rather than appalling.

Up to this time, Davis had had no long or close relationship to any one section of the country. Kentucky and Mississippi alike had been hardly more than incidents in his roaming life. But from this moment Mississippi became his sovereign state, the object of the veneration which one gives to one's sovereign. Moreover, this new home had a unique appeal. Virginia and Kentucky had, and still have, such distinctive features as to make their inhabitants Virginians or Kentuckians, rather than mere Americans or Southerners. South Carolina has similar characteristics, and her sons proudly declare themselves South Carolinians. The Mississippi of Davis' plantation days, on the contrary, was a cross section of the Nation, with a population recently come from every part of the country, and had not had time to become distinctly Mississippian. In 1800 the state had only 5,000 inhabitants; by 1840 it boasted 375,000. Of its leading politicians of the period, Jacob Thompson had migrated from North Carolina, Henry S. Foote was a native of Virginia, John A. Quitman was a New Yorker, Robert J. Walker had come from Pennsylvania, Sergeant S. Prentiss was a Maine "Yankee," a term said to have been the Indian rendering of the French, "Anglais"; and Davis himself had been born in Kentucky. Thus it is evident that Davis, fresh from the army, was little less a stranger to Mississippi than were the leaders among his contemporaries.

The new state had not yet adopted the theory of the right of secession, lately strongly held in the North, but now discarded there and dominant in South Carolina; for, in 1834, a Mississippi State Democratic Convention had unanimously resolved, "that a Constitutional right of secession from the Union on the part of a single state, as asserted by the nullifying leaders of South Carolina, is utterly unsanctioned by the Constitution, which was framed to establish, not destroy, the Union." It would seem, therefore, that there was little in the atmosphere of his new home calculated to make of a man who had always served the nation, an ardent worshipper of local sovereignty. But already slavery was beginning the creation of a different attitude, a fact which the legislature suspected as little as they suspected that the new

JEFFERSON DAVIS IN PLANTER DAYS

planter at "Brierfield" was one day to lead the disciples of the right of secession.

The prime requisite of a plantation was a body of slaves, and these Jefferson Davis proceeded to secure. By certain depositions, in manuscript form in the State House at Jackson, we are reminded of the revolting process of purchase. "I belonged to Jefferson Davis before the war," says one deposition. "He buy me from Mr. Wyley. . . . When they had us up in a row, at Natchez, Moss Joe [Davis] said, 'I didn't buy you, he,' pointing to Moss Jeff, 'bought you, and he is your master.' . . . He bring me at 'Hurricane' and put me to work there. . . . He bought me, Old Uncle Robert, Aunt Rhina, Rhina No. 2, William and Jack, Frances, and Charley, Old Charley, Solomon, Betsy, Fanny, Moses, Jeffrey, Young Hagar, Kizziarch and Old Hagar." With the help of these and other slaves, especially that of the superior, one might almost say the super-slave, James Pemberton, Davis took up the task of converting "Brierfield" into a home. But fever prevented.

Olmsted, in his famous *Journey*, records a conversation with the owner of one of the great plantations in the fever-ridden districts, in which the latter said: "I would as soon stand fifty feet from the best Kentucky rifleman and be shot at by the hour, as to spend a night on my plantation in summer." And in commenting upon rice culture, Olmstead wrote: "During the summer, from four to six months at least, not one rice planter in a hundred resides on his plantation, but leaves it with all his slaves, in charge of an overseer. . . . Rarely," he adds, "is there more than one white man upon a plantation at a time during the summer." Davis' mother-in-law, Mrs. Zachary Taylor, even better acquainted with such plantations than was Olmstead, apparently felt apprehensive, and warned her daughter not to remain at "Brierfield," to which Mrs. Davis answered, "Do not make yourself uneasy about me; the country is quite healthy." Her husband, however, was less confident, and started with his bride to his sister's home, "Locust Grove" plantation, in Louisiana. But the dreaded fever was already in their systems, and developed as they journeyed southward. Soon after their arrival, both were at death's door. On September 15th Davis, from whom the desperate state of his wife had been concealed, was roused by the sound of her voice singing, as it proved in her last delirium, a song associated with the days of their courtship. In disregard of orders and of caution, he rose from his bed and rushed to her room, only to find that she had suddenly passed into unconsciousness, from which she never returned. She died on September 15, 1835, less than three months after her marriage.

For years after his wife's death, Davis lived the life almost of a hermit. On his return from a visit to Cuba, where he had been sent to shorten his convalescence, he joined his brother at "Hurricane," unwilling to live alone in the home which he had begun. Here he passed eight years supervising his own plantation as an absentee landlord, and doing it so effectively as to win praise from his brother, who had doubted the ability of an army-trained man to succeed in such an enterprise. He rarely left the island, and his days were filled with the care of his crops and his slaves. The nights and slack periods were given to study, and to long discussions upon political and economic questions with his brother, who was so much his senior as to be more like a father.

Joseph, says N. W. Stephenson, was "a commanding figure. . . . Though a Democrat, he had gone over, in the bud of his fortunes, to that new phase of democracy which retained Jeffersonian theories while practicing aristocracy. A risen man, he was born a 'founder,' the type England invariably seizes to 'reinforce' the House of Lords." Jefferson Davis later described him, in terms perhaps exaggerated by affection, as "a profound lawyer, a wise man, a bold thinker, a zealous advocate of the principles of the Constitution, as understood by its founders, with a widespreading humanity, which manifested itself especially in a patriarchal care of the many negroes dependent upon him, not merely for the supply of their physical wants, but also for their moral and mental elevation, with regard to which he had more hope than most men of his large experience. To him, materially as well as intellectually, I am more indebted than to all other men."

The Davis theory as regards the managing of slaves was that force should be used very sparingly, and that self-government should be encouraged, organized and carefully supervised. In consequence, says Fleming, "no negro was ever punished except after conviction by a jury of blacks. This jury was composed of 'settled' men; an old negro presided as judge; there were black sheriffs or constables; witnesses were examined as in white courts, and the punishments were inflicted by the negroes." The masters retained the right to modify the sentences, or to grant full pardons; and not infrequently intervened to prevent, not too much leniency, but a too rigorous punishment for minor offences.

Moreover, the slaves were entrusted with many duties which ordinarily fell to white overseers, or white helpers. At "Brierfield," the overseer was Jim Pemberton, the slave who had accompanied him to his frontier service in the Northwest. Until Pemberton's death, in 1850, slave and master worked for the common good, being friend and master as well as slave and owner. Together they studied the slaves, seeking the occupation best suited to each. One "Brierfield" negro was encouraged to keep a store, which the Davises patronized. Others looked after the plantation nursery for black children. Some made themselves useful in connexion with the storerooms which carried the plantation's stock of implements, medicines, saddles and harness, household goods, and even sweetmeats. Moreover, they were allowed the privilege, common on the best southern plantations, of cultivating patches of land, the products of which, vegetables, fruits, pigs, chickens, etc., they were free to sell to the master or to any other market that offered. And there were also recognized rights for the negroes, and duties for the owners, not unlike the mediaeval customs of Europe. "At the birth of a negro child," writes Fleming, "an outfit was given, and at death the burial clothes, and food for those who 'set up.' When a negro was ill, the master furnished or paid for delicacies; and for a wedding he provided the dinner and the finery." A dentist came regularly to both plantations, and every care was taken to keep the slaves not only fit for work, but happy.

Under such conditions, the plantation ran smoothly and brought in an ample income. And Davis reared a body of slaves who proved that self-discipline is not incompatible with slavery. Even after emancipation, the Davis slave was pointed to as an example of what the system had produced. "If all slave-owners," writes Eckenrode, "had employed the methods of Jefferson Davis, slavery would have had just claim to be considered a beneficent institution."

The Davis theory, however, had not the remotest resemblance to the theory of the Virginia "Bill of Rights" that: "All men are by nature equally free," or to the "Declaration of Independence," which had assured the world that "all men are created equal." He believed, and never ceased to believe, that God had created the black man unequal to the white man, in all cases. On April 12, 1860, he assured the United States Senate that he believed in the equality of the white race, differences existing among them being attached, he declared, to individuals, not to the race. A man might lose his equality by committing a crime, or by lack of education. These, he said, are personal. But the negro had been deliberately created by God unequal to the white man, a different creature, and no amount of education, or of wisdom, could make him an equal. "When Balaam's ass talked as a rational being," he added, "the miraculous event became a matter of record; but rational beings have brayed like asses many a time since Balaam's ass spoke, and no man took note of it." His meaning clearly was that no amount of wisdom could alter the fact that the ass was an ass, and that a negro, even though grown as wise as Socrates, would still be a negro, and therefore an inferior.

Among the negroes themselves, furthermore, he recognized no equality. The plantation labourer was of lower social status than the household servant, whose higher function it was to minister to the more personal needs of his owners. Such distinctions within the race he considered alterable by a change of occupation; but the chasm placed by the hand of God between the white man and the black could never be bridged. The man who makes the assertion that black can be equal to white, he once scornfully declared, "proves to me *his* equality with the negro. He proves to me no more." Eckrenrode properly interprets him when he says that to Davis "Democracy does well enough where distinctions are artificial; it fails where differences are real. The *Social Contract*, the *Declaration of Independence*, the *Rights of Man*, did not alter the fact that a gulf yawned in the lower South between Nordic civilization and Ethiopian barbarism." Such a theory made every white Southerner feel himself an aristocrat; and this the North, long freed from the presence of negroes in large numbers, could never understand. But the sense of having inherited that aristocracy, strange, fictitious, fantastic, as we now know it to have been, meant more in pre-Civil War America than is sometimes realized. It held loyal to the "Lost Cause," even in its darkest hours, millions of men who owned no slaves, and reaped no other benefit from the institution.

His years at "Brierfield" implanted in Davis' mind two convictions which never left him; first, that emancipation could not solve the negro problem; and second, that the only hope for improvement in the condition of the negro lay in the slow process of fitting him for economic competition with his white superiors. In his opinion, sudden emancipation would destroy a race, unfitted to compete. He believed in the measurable perfectibility of the negro, and honestly sought to advance him; but always with the conviction that he could never become the white man's equal. "In all past history," he once said in the Senate, "the race is doomed by the Creator to occupy the attitude of servility."

With "Brierfield" plantation in mind, and "Brierfield" days were the only days in which he ever came into responsible personal relationship with slavery as a system of labour, it is less difficult to understand such a speech as that of 1860 in which he said: "There is a relation belonging to this species of property . . . which awakens whatever there is of kindness or of nobility of soul of him who owns it; and this can only be alienated, obscured, or destroyed by collecting this species of property into such masses that the owner himself becomes ignorant of the individuals who compose it. In the relation, however, which can exist in the Northern territories, the mere domestic association of one, two, or at most half a dozen servants in a family, associating with the children as they grow up, attending upon age as it declines, there can be nothing against which either philanthropy or humanity can make an appeal." And in one of his many talks with Dr. Craven, during his prison days, he said that "the papers bore evidence . . . of increasing hostility between the races, and this was but part of the penalty the poor negro had to pay for freedom. The more political equality was given or approached, the greater must be the social antagonism of the races. In the South, under slavery, there was no such feeling, because there could be no such rivalry. Children of the white master were often suckled by negroes. . . . It was under black huntsmen the young whites took their first lessons in field sports. They fished, shot, and hunted together, eating the same bread . . . sleeping under the same tree with their negro guides. In public conveyances there was no exclusion of the blacks, nor any dislike engendered by competition between white and negro labour. . . . And while there might be, as in all countries and amongst all races, individual instances of cruel treatment, he was well satisfied that between no master and labouring class on earth had so kindly and regardful a feeling subsisted. To suppose otherwise required a violation of the known laws of human nature. Early associations of service, affection, and support were powerful. To these self-interest joined. . . . The attainment of political equality by the negro," he added, "will revolutionize all this. . . . Emancipation throws the whole black race into direct and aggressive competition with the labouring classes of the whites, and the ignorance of the blacks, presuming on their freedom, will embitter every difference. . . . The negro will have to pay, in harsh social restrictions and treatment, for the attempt to invest him with political equality."

Much the same idea was expressed later by A. J. B. Beresford Hope when he assured the people of England: "There is a law which you may think hard, prohibiting the liberation of slaves above and below certain ages; but this is in reality a provision for their benefit, seeing that the master is bound to maintain all infants, and all aged people who have worked out their strength in his service. . . . By President Lincoln's blessed proclamation the masters, hundreds of thousands in number, are all simultaneously declared to be relieved from this obligation, while the babe and the veteran, the sick and the feeble, are left to hobble out on the highway and die in the ditch, free for ever from their antecedent claim upon their no longer masters." One is disposed to look with less suspicion upon that purely economic theory when he recalls the fact that it made its appeal to Lincoln himself, who, when contemplating emancipation, was asked how the freed negroes would live. In reply, he told of a man who claimed that he had discovered a new and cheaper method of raising pigs. Fence a field, he said, and sow it with potatoes. When these mature, turn in the pigs. When someone suggested that the pigs might one day find the ground frozen, and what would they then do for food, Lincoln's reply showed that he understood the difficulty. "Root," he answered, "or die."

Just as Davis saw slavery in an almost ideal light, Olmstead and Mrs. Stowe saw the other side of the shield. The minds of these great and honest critics were focussed upon its evils, while Davis always tended to think of its benefits. In the end he had to admit, and did admit, that "the whites are better off for the abolition of slavery," though even then his earlier memories caused him to add, "It is an equally patent fact that the coloured people are not."

To the twentieth-century mind, it is almost inconceivable that men could have retained a deeply religious faith and at the same time have claimed a sanctity for their human possessions: but at the time of Jefferson Davis' youth and young manhood, the combination seemed natural and defensible upon religious grounds. Olmstead recorded this fact with astonishment: "Men talk in public places, in churches and in barrooms, in the stage-coach, and at the fireside, of their personal and peculiar relationship with the Deity, and of the mutations of their harmony with the Holy Spirit, just as they do about their families and business matters," including of course the important question of the cost of slaves.

Davis inherited his attitude towards slavery, as he inherited his attitude towards the absurd set of regulations known as "the Code," according to which gambling debts are more sacred than other debts, and a man may give satisfaction for insulting another, by arranging a deadly combat. If a gentleman "Commit an offence against the feelings of a gentleman," he once said in the Senate, "he then redeems, as far as may be, that offence by giving him redress," to which Senator Collamer replied, "If a gentleman intentionally insults me, I am to invite him out that he may shoot me, and that is called satisfaction?"

"It may be," answered Davis.

It is the exceptional man who questions the ethical soundness of the principles governing the society in which he has been born and bred, and few recognize the crimes inherited from their ancestors, their very loyalty acting as a screen, to hide from them the nature of the sins made sacred by inheritance. But the world moves onward and upward, otherwise vain would be our striving, and today the grandchildren of conscientious defenders of slavery find it hard to understand that they could be just, and yet justify the institution, as a hundred years hence our grandchildren will be equally perplexed over many attitudes and practices of today.

Since coming to "Brierfield," in 1835, Davis had paid little attention to the practice of politics, although he had devoted much time to the study of its theories. On February 9, 1839, he wrote to a friend: "You perceive that when I write of politics I am out of my element and naturally slip back to seeding and ploughing." But, although he little suspected it, his seeding and ploughing were almost over, and his political activities, for which his days of isolation had done much to prepare him, were close at hand. Locally, he was known as a reader of books, an encyclopaedia of information: he read Latin and Greek and was a student of English history and literature as well as that of his own country. Up to this period, he had seen only America, but he had seen far more of it than most Americans of his day, and had seen it as the servant of the nation, not of any one section or state.

The educated Southern planter, and not all of them were educated, had inherited a tradition of political leadership, and a deep sense of political responsibility. It was natural, therefore, that when in 1843 the dominant Whig party of Warren County, Mississippi, found themselves facing an inter-party strife between two Whig candidates for the state legislature, the Democrats should have seen their opportunity to introduce Jefferson Davis, a move said to have been initiated by the Mississippi leader, Robert J. Walker. How happy the suggestion was, is indicated by the following letter, sent to the Vicksburg *Sentinel*, on November 1, 1843, by a prominent aspirant for the same post:

Dear Sir—Have the kindness to state that I have informed Major Davis, if he would become a candidate I would support him, and urge his election; this I will gladly do. But if he should decline, or fail to receive the nomination, then my name may be offered, *and on that event only*. I have for years past lent some aid in rolling back a tide which overwhelmed this country, and should much regret, if, at this late day, after the many sacrifices of the party, and when for the first time victory is within our grasp, any untoward circumstance should eventuate in defeat— I am determined such result shall be traced to no action of mine. I am for principles and not men, and will support any good and true man, who may receive the nomination. I shall only ask, in the language of Mr. Jefferson, "is he honest, is he capable, and a friend to the Constitution?"

> I have the honor to be
> Your Friend,
> J. B. WILLIAMSON

November 1, 1843.

The same issue of the *Sentinel* announced Davis' nomination and commented as follows:

CANDIDATE FOR THE CITY AND COUNTY

Elsewhere in our paper of this morning, will be found the proceedings of the Democratic Convention, which met yesterday for the purpose of selecting a candidate to represent the city and county. It will be seen that JEFFERSON DAVIS, Esq. received the unanimous nomination of the party, a gentleman, who, should he be elected, will do honour to himself and his constituents. Mr. Davis is a sterling Democrat, a man of unsullied private character, talents of a superior order, extensive political information, and judging from the structure of his remarks before the convention, a fine public speaker. There may be some in the county to whom Mr. Davis, from the secluded privacy in which he has lived, is unknown, to these we repeat, Mr. Davis is what we have stated, *a man, every inch a man,* of whom the Democracy of Old Warren should be proud.

Let us rally now around the man of our choice and the victory is ours!! To secure it, *action* and *union,* on the part of our friends are alone necessary. Let every democrat, every anti-bonder walk up to the polls on Monday, and cast his vote for the regularly nominated candidates, and we shall be certain to come out triumphantly victorious!!

Davis' own account of the incident, which marks the beginning of his political career, is as follows:

"The canvass had advanced to a period within one week of the election, when the Democrats became dissatisfied with their candidate and resolved to withdraw him, and I was requested to take his place. The Whigs had a decided majority in the county, and there were two Whig candidates against the one Democrat. When I was announced, one of the Whig candidates withdrew, which seemed to render my defeat certain; so at least I regarded it. Our opponents must have thought otherwise, for they put into the field for the canvass—though himself not a candidate—the greatest popular orator of the state—it is not too much to say the greatest of his day—Sergeant S. Prentiss; and my first speech was made in opposition to him. This led to an incident perhaps worthy of mention.

"An arrangement was made by our respective parties for a debate between Mr. Prentiss and myself on the day of election, each party to be allowed fifteen minutes alternately. Before the day appointed I met Mr. Prentiss to agree upon the questions to be discussed, eliminating all those with regard to which there was no difference between us, although they might be involved in the canvass. Among these was one which had been decided by the legislature of Mississippi, and had become in some measure an historical question, but which was still the subject of political discussion, viz., that of 'Repudiation.' On this question there was a slight difference between us. He held that the Union Bank bonds constituted a debt of the state. I believed that they were issued unconstitutionally, but that as the fundamental law of the state authorized it to be sued, the question of debt or no debt was one to be determined by the courts; and if the bonds should be adjudged to be a debt of the state, I was in favour of paying them. As, therefore, we were agreed with regard to the principle that the state might create a debt, and that in such case the people are bound to pay it, there was no such difference between us as to require a discussion of the so-called question of 'Repudiation,' which turned upon the assumption that a state could not create a debt, or, in the phraseology of the period, that one generation could not impose such obligations upon another. There was another set of obligations, known as the 'Planters' Bank bonds, the legality of which I never doubted and for which I thought the legislature was bound to make timely provision."

In spite of this and many other clear statements showing how utterly groundless was the charge later made as Civil War propaganda, that Davis was responsible for Mississippi's repudiation of her bonds, he was compelled, to the end of his life, to face this unjust accusation. Robert J. Walker, who had called him from his retreat at "Brierfield" to lead a forlorn hope for his Democratic machine, officially carried the propaganda to Europe, where he laboured to convince friends of the South, that its leader was a notorious American repudiationist. "That lying emissary to England," Davis later commented, ". . . represented me as the author of repudiation in Mississippi, though he, being actively engaged in state politics at the time, knew that I . . . had no connexion with the transaction." This unequivocal denial was confirmed by one of Davis' most violent critics, Edward A. Pollard, who wrote that Davis' "previous connexion with the local politics of Mississippi could only have been of the slightest kind." Yet, as late as November 5, 1861, an American admirer of Davis wrote from London to the Honourable C. J. McRae: "It is generally supposed here that President Davis was a prominent actor in the repudiation of Mississippi bonds, and he has been styled the 'Father of Repudiation.' You will readily see how important it is to the fiscal credit of our Confederation to disprove this rumour and I wish you would send me some official denial that will set the matter at rest on this side, and which can be published. I have understood that President Davis was never a member of the legislature of Mississippi, so that he could not have been the Mr. Davis who is reported to have sneered at the 'crocodile tears' of the bondholders, and it will be very impor- tant to show this. The official attestation of the facts by the Gov- ernor or Secretary of State of Mississippi will be all that is necessary." The requisite denial was easily obtained; but the story fitted so well with the needs of the hour that denial produced little effect, and, even after the war was over, the story was ruth- lessly employed, and even extended, to cover other repudiation activities with which Davis again had no connexion, as proved by the following letter which he wrote in 1870:

Private   Memphis Tenn. 9th April 1870
R. S. Guernsey Esqr.

Sir, In reply to your inquiry I give you such information as my memory affords, and writing for your use, and in the midst of many engagements, will not attempt to prepare such a paper as would answer for publication, but only to make a statement which you can cull and reduce to the form suited to your purpose.

I took no action "in the U. S. Senate in regard to the payment of the Missi. State bonds," that subject not having been before the Senate. But while a Senator I twice acted thereon in the follow- ing manner. In the year 1848—*I think*—my connexion Thos. E. Robins of Missi. visited me in Washington City and we devised a plan for the payment of the Missi. Union Bank Bonds by the voluntary subscription of those citizens of the State who were willing thus to adjust the claims of the holders of those bonds, which had some ten years before been declared by the people of the State to have been issued in violation of the State constitu- tion and therefore devoid of legal validity. Mr. Buchanan was then Secty. of State for the U. S. and gave to the project such favourable consideration, that contrary to the practice of his Dept. he gave to Mr. Robins, letters to officials in England which put him in a quasi public character.

Mr. R. J. Walker, late a Senator of Missi., was then Secty. of the Treasury: from him we derived no assistance. Mr. Robins failed in the attempted negotiation with the Bondholders, who probably overestimated the legality of their claim, or underestimated the morality and pride of the people in whom they were invited to confide.

Again in the year 1859, I believe, an article was published and copied by various newspapers which arraigned the integrity of Missi. in regard to her public debt and appealed to the sympathy of the world in behalf of the Widows and Orphans who were represented to have been brought to want by the repudiation of Missi. Bonds, in which their means had been invested. As a Mississippian I chose to expose the hypocrisy and the falsehood of the accusation, by the publication of an article of which I have no copy left in my possession. The substance of it was to show to the public that Missi. had issued two sets of Bonds, one for the Planters Bank and another for the Union Bank—that the first had been on the open market, and had not been repudiated, but admitted to be a debt legally binding on the State; that the last named Bonds which had been pronounced void as having been issued in violation of the Constitution had never been on the open market, and could not have been an investment for the means of Widows and Orphans: that those Bonds had been purchased for the U. S. Bank of Pa. and sent by that institution to England to be deposited as collateral security with the creditors of that Bank.

As your inquiry is of personal history it may be well to add, that all the statements which represent me as the leader of "Repudiation" in Missi. or as a follower of the doctrine, are without the least foundation in fact. My course in the two instances was prompted by sensibility for the good name and affection for the people of the State in which I was reared & of which I was then a Senator. After twelve years of absence from Missi., at school and in the U. S. Army, I returned to the home of my childhood in 1835. My residence was in a very secluded place and I had no connexion with the politics of the country until 1843, before which date the Union Bank bonds had been issued, sold, the money squandered, and the obligation of the state denied, or, in the common parlance, "the debt repudiated."

I never held any office whatever in the State Government, or served in either branch of its Legislature, or ever had any connexion with either of its Banks, not even that of a debtor.

If this seems needlessly full, it has been made so because of the persistent and widespread misrepresentation to which I have been subjected, in connexion with the Missi. Bond question. The "Defence of Missi.," referred to, was published in a newspaper at Washington, D. C., probably the *Constitution*, and I have been told was cited by R. J. Walker in a pamphlet issued by him in England during the War. I have not seen that pamphlet, but if it gave the date of my article it may enable you to find it, or at least to fix its date about which I am very doubtful. . . .

With all this evidence easily obtainable, Winfield Scott repeated the story in his *Autobiography*, and Theodore Roosevelt put it into his *Life of Thomas H. Benton*, phrasing it, in true Rooseveltian definiteness, as follows: "Before Jefferson Davis took his place among the arch-traitors in our annals, he had already long been known as one of the chief repudiators. It was not unnatural that to dishonesty towards the creditors of the public he should afterwards add treachery towards the public itself." When Davis wrote in protest, and offered to prove the falsity of the charge, he received in reply a letter from the Colonel's secretary curtly declaring, "Mr. Theodore Roosevelt declines to have any correspondence with Mr. Jefferson Davis."

The brief legislative campaign of 1843, source of this senseless abuse, resulted, as Davis had expected when accepting the last-hour nomination, in his defeat—a defeat which marked the end of Jefferson Davis, the planter. From that moment to the day of his capture, as President of the Confederate States of America, he belonged to the public; for like Lincoln's later defeat for the United States Senate, at the hands of Stephen A. Douglas, his unsuccessful candidacy for the state legislature marked him as a leader, and insured him another opportunity. This came the following year, 1844, when, as a delegate from Warren County which had instructed for Martin Van Buren, who sought a second term as President of the United States, he ventured to plead before the Mississippi Convention the superior qualifications of John C. Calhoun for the presidential nomination. "I wish nothing which I may say to be referred to a willingness to depreciate the high, just, and often-acknowledged claims of Mr. Van Buren," he said: ". . . The points of my preference for Mr. Calhoun will be merely indicated to you; because, resting as they do upon bases so well understood, any elucidation of them is uncalled for." He urged the convention to note that for free trade, the annexation of Texas, the honest and efficient administration of the Executive Department at Washington, and the proper establishments for the defence of Southern harbours, Calhoun was the best available candidate; and moved, "that our delegates to the national convention, in the event of any contingency which shall defeat the purpose for which they are appointed, viz., the termination of Martin Van Buren for President, and James K. Polk for Vice-President, shall consider as our second choice, John C. Calhoun for President, and Levi Woodbury for Vice-President."

The convention recognized the impression which Davis had already made, by placing him at the head of their candidates as elector-at-large, and he at once began preparations for a campaign which he felt would be important, whatever the choice of the Democratic National Convention. According to his scholarly habit, he sought campaign material from the most reliable sources. On March 25, 1844, he wrote to Van Buren:

"The Democratic Convention of this state which decided in your favour as the candidate of the Democracy for the next Presidency, placed me on the electoral ticket for the state—and in view of the approaching presidential canvass, and with no doubt of the ratification of the National Convention of so much of our action as refers to yourself, I have determined to call upon you for answers to three points which I expect to be opened and think could not be otherwise well closed." The points, written in the form of a separate letter of the same date, were:

"Your opinion on the following questions:

First, The annexation of Texas to the Territory of the United States.

Second, The Constitutional power of Congress over slavery in the District of Columbia.

Third, The Tariff of 1828 and whether your vote on that bill was entirely the result of the instructions you received."

These questions had been subjects of special study by Davis, during his eight years of seclusion at "Hurricane." The first, he felt, should be answered in the words of Andrew Jackson, "We must regain Texas, peaceably if we can, forcibly if we must." The second was meant to elicit a clearly pro-slavery answer, and the third, which concerned the tariff of 1828, represented a contest which had almost caused Davis to resign his commission during the Black Hawk war, so great had been his indignation at the possibility of the Federal Government's attempting to coerce the sovereign state of South Carolina. Had he known that Van Buren's mind was already occupied with the elusive thoughts, to be embodied within a month in his fatal "globe letter," which cost him the nomination, he would have hoped for little in the way of definite answers to any of these questions, and it is safe to say, in the absence of documents to prove the contrary, that Van Buren gave him little new material for the campaign, in

which that too astute Presidential aspirant was diligently trim-
ming his sails to catch either east or west winds.

On the day that Davis sent his questions to Van Buren, he
wrote also to Senator Allen of Ohio:

Hurricane Mi., *25th March, 1884.*

HON. SEN. ALLEN of Ohio,

Dr. Sir,

The sick man knows the Physician's step, but I assure you that
if breaking a long silence to ask a favour of you should expose
me to the suspicion of remembering you only because of my
trouble, the fact is nevertheless quite otherwise. I am one of the
Presidential "electors" for the state of Mississippi, and though I do
not doubt the democratic character of our people, I fear false
statements and false issues in the approaching canvass and expect the Whigs to make great exertions. I wish you to aid me
with any statements which can be made available against the
charge of *defalcation,* and extravagance under Mr. Van Buren's
administration, against the present Tariff as productive of revenue,
against the U. S. Bank, against the charge of improper removals
from offices, and if there be such statement the removals in the
first year of Harrison and Tyler's administration. Further, I
should be glad to have the evidence of Mr. Clay's refusal to
divide the resolution of censure upon President Jackson for the
removal of the deposits and the rule of the Senate in relation to
the division of questions, Secretary Taney's report on the removal
of the deposits from the U. S. Bank, Secretary Poinset's annual
report recommending reorganization of the militia and answer to
call of the House on the same subject. Was not President Van
Buren one of the first to point out the unconstitutionality of the
military districts as projected in that answer? . . . I have mingled
but little in politics and, as you perceive by this letter, have an
arsenal poorly supplied for a campaign. Labour is expected of
me and I am willing to render it. I believe much depends on this

Presidential election, and that every man who loves the Union and the Constitution *as it is* should be active. . . .

He himself was exceedingly active, and his gifts as a speaker made him an effective Democratic campaign orator, first for the nomination of Van Buren, and later for James K. Polk when Van Buren's "globe letter" had made his nomination impossible.

After the election of November, 1844, which made Polk President, and war with Mexico certain, Davis had only to mark time until January, 1845, when his electoral vote was to be cast. He spent much of this period in planning a new future at "Brierfield"; for, the distress caused by the loss of his first wife having yielded at last to the healing influences of time, he had become attached to Miss Howell, of Natchez, and hoped for an early marriage. The couple had met in earlier years, and again shortly before the opening of the pre-nomination campaign, after which Miss Howell had remarked: "I do not think I shall ever like him as I do his brother, Joe. Would you believe it, he is refined and cultivated, and yet he is a Democrat." Before February, 1845, however, the refined Democrat had won.

Upon the Mississippi steamboat which carried Davis to Natchez for the wedding, he found himself face to face with his former father-in-law, Zachary Taylor, now a general and on his way to his post as guardian of the Mexican border. Time had softened Taylor's resentment for the defiance of old days, and they met as friends, and travelled as comrades.

On February 26th, while Taylor was still moving southward towards the scenes which were to make him President, Jefferson Davis and Miss Howell were married. After the ceremony, the bride and groom paid a visit to the groom's sister, at Locust Grove, where together they stood beside the grave of the first Mrs. Davis. Thence they travelled to Woodville, Mississippi, for a visit to his mother and sisters, and, the honeymoon over, repaired to the seclusion of "Brierfield," now a prosperous estate.

As the result of eight years of hard work and careful management, Davis' bank balance and income justified a higher scale of living. He therefore planned a new residence and, during the planning, there emerged an unfortunate "incompatibility of temper," not between bride and groom, but between the bride and Joseph, whom Mrs. Davis had so lately preferred to Jefferson. Joseph, she later declared in a deposition, was "bitter at times against all his family, except his wife, and at times engaged in controversies of very irritating character." For a time, therefore, controversy advanced more rapidly than the new house; for Mrs. Davis had her own ideas concerning the plans, while Joseph, as the donor of the estate, ventured to have his, and to express them in not too conciliatory language. From the abundant evidence, of depositions of residents of the plantation, both white and coloured, it is clear that "Brierfield" was at such times by no means an Utopia. But, as it chanced, these unhappy circumstances affected Davis very little. His planter-days were over though "Brierfield" continued to be considered his home until it was occupied as a concentration camp for freedmen in 1863—"a negro paradise," as he called it.

Before the end of his first year of marriage he was invited by the Mississippi Democratic leaders to run for the office of representative-at-large in the national congress. "It was a singular coincidence," writes Eckenrode, "that the leader of the secession cause appeared in politics at the very moment of the issue that made secession inevitable," namely the annexation of Texas.

Davis was quite ready to accept the nomination: but before it was actually made, an anonymous writer, signing himself "Cato," sent a communication to the Vicksburg *Sentinel*, doubtless designed to involve him in a local controversy of extreme bitterness. After several fulsome paragraphs, praising "his urbanity of manner, his gentlemanly deportment, his kind feelings," and the "brilliancy, beauty and force of the recent speeches of this leader" who had "stepped forth like the fabled goddess, fully armed to do battle," "Cato" proceeded to business: "Should he receive the nomination of the coming convention, he will no doubt permit an humble individual who wishes him well . . . to request his views on a subject about to be agitated in our next legislative councils, and at present dear to the democracy of the Union. I mean what is commonly known as the 'Briscoe bill,' in its original form as introduced by the Senator from Claiborne. This inquiry will not be considered impertinent when I explain myself. . . . At the convention of Monday last, a resolution was introduced, supposed at the time, and still thought to be adverse to the bill. This resolution, if I am not mistaken, was advocated by Mr. Davis or claimed to have been so by the enemies of the bill. Some of his friends, however, insist that from the confusion that prevailed at the time and the ambiguity of some of the proceedings, his views and feelings have been misinterpreted. Be this as it may, it is right and proper that he should be fully and fairly located, that the people who now see him, *as through a glass, darkly,* may have a clear and distinct view of all his political features. The friends of the measure desire this exposition; its enemies cannot object to it. The fate of Rome, and perhaps of Caesar, may depend upon it."

The Briscoe bill, which had been passed in January, 1843, prescribed "the mode of proceeding against incorporated banks for a violation of their corporate franchises, and against persons pretending to exercise corporate privileges." "It gave the ancient writ of *quo warranto* special sanction against banks which were not able to redeem their bills. Under it, proceedings by *quo warranto* were instituted against nearly every bank in the state," in order "to get rid of the debts due to them," by dissolving the banks themselves.

The question was meant to compel the candidate to take a decided position in a local conflict which had developed great bitterness; and Davis was on the unpopular side. He at once prepared, however, a definite and comprehensive answer, and requested the editor of the *Sentinel* to hasten the publication of his next edition, in order to allow the convention to consider his views before its adjournment, although it was his belief that it would make his election impossible.

His reply opened with the statement, "I have no opinions which I wish to conceal, . . . and no other request than that this answer shall not be construed into an admission of my being a candidate for any office. . . . The question has been changed from its true nature, the rights of creditors against the obligations of debtors, into an issue of banks against the country, and its laws. Were the latter the true question, I certainly have no favour for the banks which could draw me from my duty to the country. . . . I have never owned a share of bank stock nor borrowed a dollar from a bank."

Continuing, he divided public opinion into three classes. "1st— those who hold that when forfeiture is adjudged against a bank all debts to and from it shall be expunged, the personal effects ('escheat to') become the property of the state and the real estate revert to the original grantor.

"2nd—that after forfeiture the state shall appoint a receiver to collect the assets of the bank for the benefit of the state.

"3rd—that after forfeiture of franchise, trustees shall be appointed under penal restraints, and with sufficient security, to collect the assets and dispose of the property of the corporation for the benefit of the creditors and stockholders. Among the third class, Sir, I arraign myself."

In defiance of repudiationists, he expressed his scorn for a law which "will permit an agent to lend out the money of his employer to personal or business friends, and then by an act contravening his duties as an agent, debar the employer from pursuing his money in the hands of the borrower . . . or will permit a banking corporation to throw its notes into circulation and by refusing to redeem them, deprive the noteholder of his remedy against the effects of the bank, or . . . release the debtor from the obligation of his bill given for the notes of the bank and throw the loss upon the noteholder." In one crisp sentence he summarized his view: "The few borrow, the many hold the notes of the bank; it surely must be elsewhere than in the ranks of the democracy, that advocates are to be found contending for the exemption of the few, by sacrificing the rights of the many." Not content with this answer, and alarmed lest his position should again be misunderstood, Davis prepared, printed, and circulated at his own expense a pamphlet declaring his unalterable opposition to repudiation.

He was, of course, promptly attacked by the "repudiationists" as a Democrat who stood for the payment of the repudiated bonds; but he was the most available candidate, and, despite bitter opposition, his nomination and election followed.

As a duly elected representative of his congressional district, it became Davis' duty to present to his neighbours "Mr. [John C.] Calhoun, . . . to me the guiding star in the political firmament," whose political fortunes had brought him to Vicksburg, on his way to a convention at Cincinnati. Fully conscious of the importance of this, his first speech as congressman-elect, he wrote his address of introduction, embodying in it, with painstaking care, his views upon the political issues of the day. Calhoun's fame brought together a great assembly, a survey of which made Davis so apprehensive, that he requested his young wife not to look at him during the speech. His nervousness, however, was forgotten as he faced his audience, and in Calhoun's presence, presented his own confession of faith: low tariff, sound currency, the annexation of Texas, and a strict construction of the Constitution. A wise instinct had warned him to steer clear of the doctrine of nullification, which was his visitor's favourite theory, but, to Davis, unsound and unprofitable. His speech was a success. In delivering it he had found words not written in his manuscript, and ideas which the hyperaesthesia of the occasion brought to his mind, and "from that day forth," says Mrs. Davis' *Memoir*, "no speech was ever written for delivery. Dates and names were jotted down on two or three inches of paper, and these sufficed."

The impression made by this speech is attested by Calhoun himself, who, five years later, recalling the incident, predicted that his own successor as leader of the South would be the young scholar-planter, Jefferson Davis.

CHAPTER IV

SIX MONTHS IN CONGRESS

NINE months after the inauguration of James K. Polk as President, Jefferson Davis took his seat in the House of Representatives, an unusual achievement for a man who had held no civil office, legislative, executive, or judicial, in the state which he was to represent: and who had, but two years before, emerged from an almost hermit-like seclusion. He was thirty-seven and, if we may quote the later opinion of the *New York World*, a paper not predisposed to give him excessive praise, he was "the best equipped man, intellectually, of his age, perhaps, in the country." He was, as one of his biographers has said, a man whose "faults were those of a bookish, solitary nature." Bookish he remained throughout life; but a bookish man of action; and it is fair to say that more errors in American politics have been due to unbookishness than may be charged to bookishness.

At Washington, Davis at once began training for a federal career, and almost at the beginning, was known as "a scholar and a thinker," to quote the words of Gamaliel Bradford. Such men were much needed at this time when America was facing a rising tide of controversy, and Davis' rapid progress in politics was due, not only to personality and a gift for leadership, but also to the fact that he had studied deeply and had definite knowledge, as well as conviction, upon the two great issues of the day: the rights of slavery and the rights of sovereign states. His chief danger lay in the fact that he had acquired a legalistic point of view, a predisposition to argue from what has been to what ought to be. Law alone is never sufficient; for law is static. It is content to

61

defend the *status quo*. There must always be kept open an easy appeal from unjust law to justice; otherwise the appeal from law to force will keep itself open.

Davis' studies had given him control of a wealth of historic data to justify the two positions, that slavery has a right to exist because the law and the Constitution had allowed it to exist; and that the states, once sovereign, had not lost their sovereignty. From these he argued, skilfully and with sound legal logic, that property in slaves must be given as adequate protection as any other property; and that a state may leave the Union at its pleasure, not by revolution, but by the peaceful exercise of established legal right. This he maintained at his coming into politics, and this he continued to maintain to the close of his life. His mistake was not that he loved the Constitution too little, but that he loved it, not as it had become, but as it had been, refusing to make allowance for the fact that custom makes more law than statute, and that custom had already gone far in interpreting the Constitution in such a way as to endanger, if not destroy, the theory of the absolute sovereignty of the individual states.

Thus, at the very threshold of his political career, he deserved the title, later given him by Dunbar Rowland, of "Jefferson Davis, Constitutionalist." The tragedy of his life was due to his inability to recognize that the future already belonged to those who, with Daniel Webster, loved the Constitution for what it might become by virtue of its flexibility, its capacity to grow and alter as need should arise. Already Webster's capacious brain, to quote Woodrow Wilson, had so interpreted the Constitution that "its sanctions could be made to cover every change that added to the unity or the greatness of the nation." Blaine later wrote of Webster's reply to Hayne: "It corrected traditions, changed convictions, revolutionized conclusions. It gave the friends of the Union the abundant logic which established the right and power of the government to preserve itself." Wilson adds the opinion, that Webster had "found little difficulty in overwhelming the argu-

JEFFERSON DAVIS

From a portrait at Westmoreland Club

ment for 'nullification.' It was the argument for state sovereignty . . . which he was unable to dislodge from its historic position."

Davis had welcomed the defeat of the Calhoun idea of nullification: but he scornfully rejected the theory that state sovereignty must followed it into the category of what had been. He believed that the Constitution should be preserved, administered and accepted in the form and with the meaning which it had when it left the hands of its authors. To him those who, by any method other than the formal amendment which its clauses provided, altered its original intent and meaning were its despoilers; and he eagerly dedicated his powers to the task of resisting the changes which custom had already made. Thus he unconsciously arrayed himself as the champion against change, which is evolution, a fact which explains much, otherwise inexplicable, in this conscientious defender of an institution, justly doomed, and of a constitutional ideal already passed into history.

On December 8, 1845, Davis took the oath which made him a member of the Twenty-ninth Congress of the United States. Almost from the first, he was made to appreciate the fact that, under the American system, every Representative and every Senator must ultimately face situations in which he is compelled to choose between serving the interests of his immediate constituents or becoming again a private citizen; to think too far beyond the immediate demands of these constituents, being to make room for an ever-present rival. Burke's conception, that every British member of Parliament represents the nation as a whole, is a noble conception; but it was not then, and is not now, that of America. If today an English representative rejects commands from his constituency, which he regards as unwise, immoral, or impracticable, he can be given another, and so retain both his seat and his judgment. The American system banishes her daring and adventurous thinkers; England retains hers in the nation's service, and harvests the fruits of their independence.

There can be little doubt that Davis, like Calhoun, entered national politics with the conviction that a public man should think in large terms, and that a national representative should think in national, if not international, terms. But there is also little doubt that each, yielding by degrees to a pressure as constant as the atmosphere, became subject to local thinking.

N. W. Stephenson wrote with justice: "Only an extreme partisan of Davis would claim for him a commanding position in the Twenty-ninth Congress." But the same may as properly be said, without disparagement, of most "cub" congressmen. A Henry Clay could, and did, seize leadership as soon as he took his seat; but most of the nation's congressmen respect the established convention, that new members should be seen and not heard, and Davis restrained, at times with difficulty, his eloquence, and was in general content to watch and hear the men about him. Of these he most admired Calhoun, though he admitted that both Clay and Webster were his superiors in oratory, an accomplishment, he said, for which Calhoun had "perfect contempt."

Already Calhoun, once regarded as the most nationalistic of statesmen, was clearly the leader of the sectionalists; and Davis, still maintaining a broader point of view, regretted the change. When urged, early in the session, to support a rivers and harbour bill, on the ground that it would help the state of Mississippi, he replied: "I feel, Sir, that I am incapable of sectional distinctions upon such a subject. I abhor and reject all interested combinations." Like many a delegate at the world assembly at Geneva, today, he spoke, and spoke honestly, in terms which neither his predisposition nor his position as custodian of the interests of his constituency allowed him to put into action.

Fortunately, however, his constituency at the moment cared little about his views upon nullification, which was now a dead issue. Fortunately, also, secession was not at the time of vital interest to them; as under the leadership of Walker, the Mississippi Democracy had declared that doctrine "utterly unsanctioned by the Constitution." And it was perhaps most fortunate of all that Davis' studies had landed him squarely in the Calhoun camp upon the ever-present tariff issue. To him, as to them, all protective tariffs were tariffs of abomination, believing, as Hadley later believed, that they represent "an attempt to prevent local powers from developing their own industries as they please." A revenue tariff he recognized as necessary under existing conditions, but felt that it should be kept down to the lowest possible rates. "Everything that will bear a duty," he said, ". . . should have the duty imposed on it which it can pay, and then we should scale down to the lowest duty that will furnish a sufficient revenue to the government. I wish . . . that no Secretary of the Treasury ever again should have to send in an estimate of the cost of collecting the duties from imports, that the custom-houses were abandoned, and the army of retainers of the Federal Government employed to collect the taxes through *impost* duties, dispersed among the people. I should like to see free trade existing throughout the Union, with all its fraternizing effect on the nations, with all its beneficial results to the labouring masses, each receiving that which can be made elsewhere cheaper than he could produce it himself, and each exchanging that which nature and the industrial habits of his country enable him to produce more cheaply than others."

Davis' first definite impression upon the House of Representatives was made on December 19, 1845, by a speech on the then pending question of "Native Americanism and the Nationalization Laws." Among savage nations, he said, "a stranger was counted an enemy, and the same word designated both; but, as civilization . . . advanced and prevailed, the gates of admission were gradually thrown open. Like another celebrated system which prevails in this country, namely a protective tariff, this barbarian doctrine of exclusion has been called 'the American system.' Such a doctrine was never heard among the patriots of the Revolution. . . . Did gentlemen forget, that among the signers of the Declaration of Independence were eight 'actual foreigners, and nine who were the immediate descendents of foreign parents?'" Emerson once said of Plato, "his broad humanity transcends all sectional lines." The same might fairly be said of Davis at this stage of his development. "To live for one's country, in its broadest, truest sense," he said, " is . . . to live for mankind."

After this outburst, too brief to stand as a maiden speech, but sufficient to mark him as a man of definite opinions, he lapsed again, for a time, into the traditional silence of a new member, but one intent upon the great issues under discussion. His silence, however, extended only to debates in Congress. As the representative of a constituency, he regarded it as his duty to watch over the legitimate interests of his state, and to defend his party associates before the public. On January 30, 1846, in reply to certain vague insinuations concerning Robert J. Walker, now Secretary of the Treasury, he published in the Vicksburg *Sentinel* a brief article, defending his fellow Mississippian whose energies were needed for "the accomplishment of those great objects, the divorce of bank and state and the repeal of the protective tariff of 1842." "Mississippi has now, for the first time in her history," he said, "a representative in the Executive Cabinet. We have believed that our interests were unjustly neglected by the Federal Government; we find the Secretary of the Treasury, with his acknowledged ability, labouring for us. . . . Shall vague rumours shaped by private spleen—shall dark suspicions anonymously thrown into circulation—be permitted to rob your public servants of the only reward the honest politician seeks, the approbation of those to whom his time and toil have been given?"

This speech points to a suspicion of unfair treatment of the South, and to the belief that the interests of the Free States were opposed to those of the Slave States. Already he had begun to feel that government based upon the theory that the majority have the right to rule invites majority tyranny, and to seek means of defending the minority from majority exploitation. Already local thinking was beginning to take the place of the nationalistic or internationalistic thinking which had characterized his speech on "Native Americanism," and he was rapidly being brought into closer sympathy with Calhoun than with either Clay or Webster.

The great issues before Congress, in the early days of 1846, were of a character calculated to increase suspicion regarding the aims of the majority, already dominantly "Northern" and "Free Soil." Walker was pressing free-trade views, soon to find legal lodgment in the Walker Tariff of 1846; and the "interests" were opposing, and demanding protection. Davis believed that the Walker Tariff would furnish adequate revenue, and at the same time preserve what he later called "the great Democratic feature of spreading its application over a large number of articles and imposing duties *ad valorem* upon all." The Oregon question, too, involving British-American interests, and the dangerous subject of slave property, was at a critical stage; and the memory of the Revolution, and of the War of 1812, gave efficacy to the arguments of heated orators who assured the country that one of the advantages to result from war would be emancipation from the control of the manufacturers of Manchester and Birmingham, although the campaign cry of 1844, "54° 40' or fight," was already being slowly overwhelmed, through wise leadership, by the later "49° and be thankful."

With a full appreciation of the potential value of Oregon, Davis combined a soldier's understanding of the horrors of war: and on February 6th broke his silence to declare in Congress that war should be "a dread alternative . . . the last resort," and that upon the basis of the rival claims in Oregon, it would be as unwise as it was unnecessary. There is, he said, one portion of Oregon, "where we have possession above the treaty, and over which we can exercise all the rights not inconsistent with the trade permitted to England: another portion in which, admitting the Nootka Convention to be still in force, we have, with England, a joint right to trade and settlement," and between these "the condition of a joint right in England and the United States to occupy for fur trade." This joint right should not be disturbed. In the end, Polk's administration dropped the "whole of Oregon" contention and compromised on the line of the 49th parallel. The President's suggestion had been defeated, as had Davis' demand for the continuance of slavery during the territorial stage of the area; for slavery was definitely prohibited.

Long before the Oregon question became dominant in American politics, circumstances, led by Sam Houston, had separated Texas from Mexico, as Houston had earlier declared to Davis his intention to separate them, and in 1845 Houston and Jackson with other determined imperialists had procured its annexation to the United States. The resulting boundary controversy, which precipitated war with Mexico, had reached a critical stage before Davis' election to Congress, before at Natchez he had cried, "God speed" to Zachary Taylor, sent to guard the American claim.

After leaving Davis at Natchez, Taylor had led his army of occupation into Texas and had set himself to guard what he considered her western boundaries. A collision with Mexican soldiers, guardians of the boundary, as they interpreted it, had resulted on April 23rd, and President Polk, on May 11th, had declared in a message to Congress: that "Mexico has passed the boundary of the United States . . . and shed American blood upon American soil. War exists, and exists by the act of Mexico." At once the soldier awoke in the congressman, and Davis, next day, informed his constituents that the treaty of peace should "be made at the City of Mexico, and by an ambassador who cannot be refused a hearing, but will speak with that which levels walls and opens gates—American cannon." And he showed his readiness to do his part, by a letter to the Vicksburg *Sentinel*. "I should like to command a Warren [County] regiment," he wrote. ". . . I look to the movement of our forces . . . with a strong desire to be a part of them. My education and former practice would, I think, enable me to be of service to Mississippians who take the field. If they wish it, I will join them as soon as possible, wherever they may be." The judicial poise of the statesman had given way to the impetuous loyalty of the soldier, and like a soldier, he offered himself, accepting without too much examination, the decision of "war guilt" which Polk's proclamation had placed squarely upon Mexico.

A few days later, Davis rose in Congress to support a resolution of thanks to General Taylor for his conduct as guardian of the American frontier. His brief speech shows little of his usual tendency to trace cause and effect; or even to weigh the question of justice. His country was at war, and he would support her. "As an American whose heart responds to all which illustrates our national character, and adds new glory to our name," he said, "I rejoice with exceeding joy at the recent triumph of our arms." Even so had Spanish patriots rejoiced over Cortez's victories, which the world was at that moment reading in Prescott's brilliant volumes. Davis' generation had not outlived the belief that a man owes allegiance to the crimes of his country. Grant too rejoiced at the victories of Americans in Mexico, although he later declared that "Polk's war" was "one of the most unjust ever waged by a stronger against a weaker nation," and even Lincoln voted for supplies while denouncing the ethics of the war. "Let him that is without the same fault" among us "cast the first stone"—at them and at Davis, eager to plant the American eagle upon the heights of Mexico's capital. Of Taylor himself, Davis spoke in terms of praise which held no memory of an ancient controversy.

"The world held not a soldier better qualified for the service he was engaged in," he declared; and subsequent history proved that in this opinion he was not far in excess of the facts. "Seldom in the annals of military history has there been [a victory] in which desperate daring and military skill were more happily combined. The enemy selected his own ground, and united to the advantage of a strong position a numerical majority of three to one. Driven from his first position by an attack in which it is hard to say whether professional skill or manly courage is to be more admired, he retired, posted his artillery on a narrow defile, to sweep the ground over which our troops were compelled to pass. There, posted in strength three times greater than our own, they waited the approach of our gallant little army.

"General Taylor knew the danger and distribution of the band he left to hold his camp opposite Matamoras, and he paused for no regular approaches, but opened his field artillery, and dashed with sword and bayonet on the foe. A single charge left him master of their battery, and the number of slain attests the skill and discipline of his army."

At this point, he paused to answer a criticism recently made against the graduates of West Point, in general: and in answering it used an expression which seemed to Congressman Andrew Johnson designed to ridicule him, because of the humble conditions out of which he had emerged. Johnson had been a tailor, and Davis' words rhetorically challenged any critic to say whether "a blacksmith or a tailor could have secured the same results" as Taylor had secured. Johnson's temper was notorious, and his response to what he believed to be an insult was in his most bitter vein. He poured scorn and contempt upon the "illegitimate, swaggering, bastard, scrub aristocracy" of which he declared Davis a member.

At first Davis was mystified by Johnson's rage, but soon realized that what he had intended as a general statement Johnson had interpreted as a personal taunt. He therefore at once disavowed any intention of personal reference in his remark, and in a speech on the army pay bill, two days later, made a second apology in the words: "Among those to whom I have been long known no explanation could be necessary; but here, having been misunderstood, it seems to be called for. Once for all, then, I would say, that if I know myself, I am incapable of wantonly wounding the feelings, or of making invidious reflections upon, the origin or occupation of any man." Meticulously, he explained, that his sole aim had been to point out "the results of skill and military science," and to call attention to the fact that these could not be expected from men without military education. He had "named two of the trades of civil life, not that either one or the other could disqualify a man" from acquiring military skill: but that neither was calculated to give it. He pointed to the record as evidence that "on a former occasion, and for a similar purpose, he had made an extended allusion to many trades and professions," with no thought of being suspected of personal insinuations, and finished his apology with the words "war, like other knowledge, must be acquired. A military education does not qualify for civil pursuits, nor does preparation for any of the civil pursuits, in itself, qualify for the duties of a soldier."

To the average man this apology would have removed all sense of injury, all suspicion of ungenerous intent; but in capacity for cherishing hatreds, Andrew Johnson was far from average, and he hated Jefferson from that time forth and for evermore, elevating him to the position of the very incarnation of the superiority complex which he always saw in the leaders of the slaveocracy.

In the thrilling hours that followed this Mexican War debate in which Davis had won from John Quincy Adams the prophecy, "he will make his mark," Davis stood squarely behind the Democratic administration, despite the fact that Calhoun passionately opposed it upon many points. From the first gun, his heart was with his old commander, Taylor, and his comrades in arms; and even the fact that the South was beginning to look upon him as Calhoun's logical successor in the leadership of its cause could not tempt him to remain in Washington. Nor could his desire to support the administration in its preparations for war lead him to forget his states'-rights views which now caused him to resist a movement in Congress to confer upon Polk the power to appoint the general officers of the army. Such appointment, Davis indignantly declared, belongs exclusively to the sovereign states.

To take it from them by legislative action was unjustified; although it was the duty of the sovereign states to grant new powers whenever such were needed by the federal government. "If the states deny the means necessary to the existence of the government, nothing is more sure than that it will usurp them. If, on the other hand, the federal government, by indirection, seeks more than is proper to its functions," calamity will follow. "The harmony, the efficiency, the perpetuity of our Union require the states, whenever the grants of the Constitution are inadequate to the purpose for which it was ordained, to add from their sovereignty whatever may be needed, and the same motives urge us [Congress] to seek no power by other means than application to the states." These words are worthy of careful consideration by a generation witnessing the steady encroachment of the federal government upon powers which the Constitution clearly assigns to the states.

At about this time, another new member, Abraham Lincoln, of Illinois, made his maiden speech, being then in his first and only term in Congress. He took the occasion to uphold the right of revolution, a right which leads "to the liberty of the world." Of the two in later years it has been well said: "Lincoln sought to save the Union; Davis did not wish to destroy the Union; he sought to preserve states rights, under his interpretation of the Constitution."

Before the arrival of the eagerly awaited summons to lead a regiment of volunteers from Mississippi, Davis was called upon, as member of a committee of Congress, to write a report upon the question of whether Daniel Webster, notoriously careless in money matters, had been dishonourable in his use of secret funds as Tyler's Secretary of State, his enemies professing to believe that he had defaulted to the extent of some $5,000. In later times Davis thus recalled his part in the affair: "Mr. Webster was arraigned for an offence which affected him most deeply. He was no accountant; all knew that there was but little mercantile exactness in his habits. He was arraigned on a pecuniary charge—the mis-application of what is known as the secret service fund; and I was one of the committee that had to investigate the charge. I endeavoured to do justice, to examine the evidence with a view to ascertain the truth. As an American I hoped he would come out without stain or smoke upon his garments. But the duty was rigidly to inquire, and rigorously to do justice. The result was that he was acquitted of every charge that was made against him, and it was equally my pride and my pleasure to vindicate him in every form which lay within my power. No man who knew Daniel Webster would have expected less of him, had our positions been reversed. None could have believed that he would, with a view to judgment, ask whether a charge was made against a Massachusetts man or a Mississippian. No! it belonged to a lower, a later, and I trust a shorter-lived race of statesmen to measure all facts by considerations of latitude and longitude."

CHAPTER V

THE MEXICAN WAR

IN THE latter part of June, 1846, the voice of his sovereign, the people of Mississippi, called Davis from the duties of Congress to the stirring scenes of Mexico. "The Mississippi Rifles," composed of volunteers, had been formed for active service, and by common consent they demanded that Jefferson Davis should become their colonel. In consequence, they sent James Roach to Washington, to summon him to lead to Mexico a regiment of hard-riding, hard-fighting, Mississippi gentlemen, the "Rough Riders" of that day. Roach found him deep in tariff legislation, but eager to accept the call and start at once. President Polk, however, urged him to remain in Congress until the Walker tariff bill should be enacted into law, promising that in the meantime the necessary requisitions for his regiment would be filed by the Secretary of War, that no time should be lost. As the Walker tariff bill promised to emerge as a strong free-trade measure, and therefore a realization of his own tariff ideas, and as he knew that certain advantages might be secured by remaining, he consented. The chief advantage for which he hoped was to have his regiment equipped with the newly-invented percussion rifles. Later he wrote in his autobiography, that General Winfield Scott, the veteran head of the army, "endeavoured to persuade me not to take more rifles than enough for four companies, and objected particularly to percussion arms as not having been sufficiently tested for the use of troops in the field. Knowing that the Mississippians would have no confidence in the old flintlock muskets, I insisted."

In the end the colonel-elect won over the general, and the regiment of Mississippi volunteers were promised the new type of gun, then known as Whitney rifles; but later as Mississippi rifles. It was, however, a costly victory for Davis, as it started a conflict with the powerful head of the army which became more bitter with the passing years, and was bitterest in the first days of the Civil War when Scott, still head of the army, helped to give a sinister interpretation to Davis' actions as leader of the South.

Before starting to join his regiment, Davis sent to the Vicksburg *Sentinel* a letter designed first, to justify the war; second, to explain to his constituents why he was leaving Congress before the end of the session; and third, to account for his stewardship. The war, he declared, was unavoidable. "The minister sent . . . with full powers to treat on all questions, was rejected, without even being allowed to present his credentials. It could not be permitted to our rival claimant thus to decide the question and, though the insult would have justified an immediate declaration of war . . . the Administration refrained from recommending this measure, and merely moved forward our troops to take possession of the entire territory claimed as our own, when there was no longer a prospect of adjustment by negotiation." Apparently it escaped Davis' notice that there was scant difference between Mexico's desire "to decide the question," and America's act in "merely moving forward our troops to take possession of the entire territory claimed as our own."

"Those of our fellow countrymen," he continued, "who in answer to a call of the President have volunteered to serve the United States in the existing war with Mexico have elected me for their colonel . . . Believing that my services were due to the country . . . I could not delay until the close of the congressional session, though then so proximate that it must occur before a successor could be chosen and reach the city of Washington.

"It was my good fortune to see in none of the measures likely to be acted on at this session such hazard as would render a single vote important, except the bill to regulate anew the duties upon imports. The vote on this was to occur very soon [in two days] after the receipt of my commission as colonel, and I have the satisfaction to announce to you that it passed the House the evening before I left Washington; and I entertain no doubt of its passing through the Senate and becoming the law of the land. An analysis of the votes . . . will show that its main support was derived from the agricultural and exporting states. . . .

"In adopting the *ad valorem* rule and restricting its operation to the revenue limit, the great principle of taxing in proportion to the benefits conferred is more nearly approximated, and the power to lay duties is directed to the purpose of raising money, for which alone it was conferred in the Constitution of our Confederacy. . . . The collection of revenue has been the subordinate; the benefit to particular classes, the main object of duties. . . . I trust we shall never again witness the spectacle, so revolting to the idea of self-government, of a law in which . . . the purpose and effect are as absolutely concealed as in the edicts of the ancient tyrant, which were written in a hand so small and hung so high as to be illegible to those upon whom they were to operate." That this was a misplaced trust, the history of American tariff legislation since that day has abundantly shown. The letter further explained that the controversy with England over Oregon was at last settled. "The exact terms . . . have not yet transpired; but . . . it may be stated as settled on the basis of the 49th parallel," giving the United States, "nearly all which would have been valuable to us."

On July 21st Davis joined his regiment at New Orleans; and five days later embarked them on the steamer, *Alabama*. Without significant incident they were duly landed at Brazos, St. Iago, seven miles from Point Isabel, where they encamped, and remained until August 2nd, when he started the march to the mouth of the Rio Grande, where he expected to find transports. During the journey he received from General Taylor the following letter:

HeadQrs. Ary. of Occupation or Invasion
Matamoras, Mexico. Augt. 3d, 1846.

My dear Col.

I heard with much pleasure of your safe arrival at Brazos
Island, with your excellent Regt. of Mississippi Volunteers, &
very much regret I cannot at once order your Comd. to Camargo,
where the greater portion of the army will be concentrated,
which is impracticable at the present time, but will do so as soon
as possible with our limited means of transportation; the want of
a more ample supply has embarrassed us not a little, & I fear will
continue to do so to some extent. I propose bringing up the
Regts. from their encampments on the banks of the Rio Grande,
where I flatter myself they will be pleasantly situated, as regards
pure air, health, wood & water, pretty much in the order in
which they arrived in the country, & must say it is a source of
mortification that yours was not among the first which reached
Brazos Island, as I can assure you I am more than anxious to take
you by the hand, & to have you & your command with or near
me, & flatter myself if we are not disappointed in the arrival of
several boats which are daily expected from N. Orleans and elsewhere, in addition to those now here, we will very soon be able
to bring you up ——

I expect to leave by the first boat which reaches here from below on her way to Camargo, & should have been highly gratified
could I have seen you before my departure for that place, but
trust it will not be long before I shall have that pleasure—
Wishing you continued health & prosperity I remain,

Truly & sincerely
Your Friend
Z. Taylor.

Col. Jefferson Davis
    Comdg. Mississippi Vols.
        Brazos Island.

Greatly encouraged, Davis led his command forward, reaching the mouth of the Rio Grande on August 12th, but found there no transports, nor any indication of their early arrival. The war had come suddenly, and the United States, little addicted to military operations, was in the throes of unpreparedness. He was therefore compelled to wait, with such patience as he could command, for several weeks, which he employed in drilling his undisciplined volunteers into the semblance of soldiers. No system of tactics adapted to the regiment's new-fashioned equipment existed, and Davis himself supplied the need by preparing a manual of arms for his troops. He personally instructed his officers, and they instructed their men, in the new system. "As he took his officers out for their daily drill," says Walthall, writing under Davis' personal supervision, "it became an habitual joke with the soldiers looking on to exclaim, in tones just loud enough to be overheard, 'There goes the colonel with the awkward squad!'" But he persisted, knowing that he must drill the amateur out of his volunteers if he wished them to find favour in the eyes of Zachary Taylor. He, however, chafed at the delay, and from time to time sent not too diplomatic complaints to Washington which doubtless came to the eyes of the Commander-in-chief, little disposed to favour the Mississippi volunteers armed by their colonel with the new arms. On August 24, 1846, for example, Davis wrote to Secretary Walker: "We have met delay and detention at every point. The quartermasters at New Orleans have behaved either most incompetently or maliciously, and I am now but two days in possession of the rifles ordered forward before I left Washington."

What had happened at the front, in the meantime, is available to us through Davis' own description. "The Mexicans [had] evacuated Matamoras, and General Taylor took peaceable possession, May 18th. Though responsibility for the war might still be debated, the fact of its existence could not be disputed, and as the Rio Grande, except at time of flood, offered little obstacle to predatory incursions, it was obviously sound policy to press the enemy back upon the border. General Taylor [had] moved forward to Camargo, on the San Juan, a tributary of the Rio Grande."

Davis' immediate problem was to reach Taylor at Camargo: and he might have been more patient of the delay, which meant drill for his volunteers, had he seen Taylor's comments upon the volunteers who had already joined the "Army of Occupation." "What is to be done with them . . . I am unable to say. I fear they are a lawless set," the General wrote to Dr. Wood, on June 20th, and added the next day: "There are now 10,000 men here, and in the vicinity, waiting and a portion of them a month, for a few small steamboats, and wagons to carry their provisions & c. toward the enemy . . . time enough to have sent to Liverpool for them. . . . Were I a prominent or ambitious aspirant for civil distinction or honours, I might really suppose there was an intention . . . to break me down."

This suspicion deepened as the weeks passed and the Democratic administration, with two Whigs, Scott and Taylor, as its chief commanders in the field, failed to bring order out of chaos. Only a few days before Davis' arrival at his headquarters, Taylor again relieved his feelings by a letter to Dr. Wood, complaining of this chaos, and adding: "I know but one way to correct the same, which is to remove Qt. Masters, not from one station to another, but to civil life." "Major-General Butler, and Brigadiers Hamer and Shields," he wrote later, "have just arrived . . . and Br.-Gen¹. Marshall is expected by the first boat from below; so there will be no lack of Genlˢ. I could have myself wished they had not been quite so numerous."

When we compare these complaints concerning volunteers with what he had written twenty days earlier, to Davis concerning the Mississippi volunteers, it appears evident that Taylor relied upon Davis' skill to give the latter something of professional training, and in this he was not disappointed. When at last Davis presented his men, they were received almost as though they had been professional soldiers. Davis was welcomed as an officer, trained and tried; doubtlessly also as a fellow hater of "Old Fuss and Feathers" (the soldiers' nickname for General Scott) and as a public man who had recently defended Taylor in the Halls of Congress. Here, too, Davis met once more Major Bennett Riley of Fort Crawford days. "Well, my son," said Riley, "here we are again. Good luck to you, boy! As for me—six feet of Mexican soil, or a yellow sash!" And this, the distinguishing mark of a general officer, Riley got before the war ended.

Soon after the arrival of the Mississippi volunteers, General Taylor, dispairing of that perfection of supplies which a cautious soldier desires when invading an enemy country, decided to move westward from Camargo, equipped as he was, to prosecute the war, although he really longed for peace. "No one," he wrote to Dr. Wood, "can desire peace more than I do, and notwithstanding all the honours which have been conferred on me . . . I would willingly forego them all, could peace be restored to our country."

Although the last volunteer regiment to arrive, Davis' Mississippi Rifles were selected to move with the advance upon Monterey. "The want of transportation," comments his autobiography, modestly, "prevented General Taylor from taking the whole body of volunteers who had reported there for duty."

The "Army of Occupation" now numbered about 6,000 men, an absurdly small number to ears accustomed to the figures of later wars. There were two divisions of regulars, under Brigadier-Generals Twiggs and Worth, and one of volunteers under Major-General Butler. Davis' Mississippi Rifles became part of Butler's division, being one of two regiments known as Quitman's Brigade. As Taylor advanced, he was joined by the Governor of Texas, J. Pinckney Henderson, who led a formidable brigade of Texas Rangers and wore the uniform of a major-general. As thus constituted, the army was half regular and half volunteer, a fighting force of doubtful competency in view of the problems which lay before it, and of the politics which lay behind. To overcome the enemy with such an army, Taylor was determined; but he knew, and Davis, fresh from Washington, knew even better, that success would give scant satisfaction either to President Polk, fearful of Whig rivals, or to General Winfield Scott, eager to qualify as his Whig rival.

No serious obstacle was encountered until the middle of September when the army approached Monterey, a strongly fortified city on the slope of the mountain, and commanded by General Ampudia. After three days' careful study of his problem, Taylor moved forward his main army to San Francisco, twelve miles from Monterey: and the next morning, September 18th, advanced to the top of a long hill, whence he got his first view of the city nestling in the mouth of a great gap of the Sierra Madre. Its garrison, as was later learned, was larger than Taylor's army. Its strength was such that the Mexicans believed it impregnable, and during all the domestic struggles, Indian incursions and other wars, it had remained so. As Taylor measured its defences, its "new citadel," now grim and dusty with age, which the Americans christened "the Black Fort"; its massive stone walls, three or four feet thick, and estimated its strength, he must have revised an a priori opinion which he had expressed a few hours earlier: "It is . . . doubtful whether Ampudia will attempt to hold Monterey." Indeed, even as he gazed, a puff of white smoke from one of its defences changed doubt into certainty. Monterey would yield only to force; and Taylor knew that victory here would be far more difficult than at his earlier engagements of Palo Alto and Resaca de la Palma.

On the 19th of September the American army was encamped in the wood of San Domingo, a league from the city, and by the 20th Taylor had planned his assault. Texas Rangers under Captain McCulloch were to occupy Marín, an important town lying a few miles to the north. This point secured, General Taylor hoped to capture the city by attacking its main defences. General Worth was to lead an assault upon the west, while Butler's and Twigg's divisions, under his own personal direction, were to make a diversion on the eastern and northeastern sides of the city. Davis' Mississippi Rifles and Campbell's Tennessee Rifles, being of Butler's division, thus remained under General Taylor's direct command, and in the end saw the fiercest fighting, which was at the east end of the town. Apparently Taylor had foreseen this, for, as Davis later assured the Senate, "He always went where the hardest blows were to be given and received."

It is unnecessary to narrate in detail the fall of Monterey. "To place the position and trace the action of battalions and batteries," says Captain Liddell Hart, an English expert military critic, "is only of value to the collector of antiques, and still more to the dealer in faked antiques." But in so far as such details serve to illustrate the qualities of Jefferson Davis as a military leader, they are necessary to this narrative.

General Taylor's further study of the terrain had led him to the conviction that he would gain great advantage by making a flank movement and cutting Monterey's communications with Saltillo. This necessitated the capture of La Teneria (The Tannery), a stone building defended by infantry and covered by a redoubt with artillery. It had been attacked and the assailants repulsed before Davis arrived, but in a letter of November 16th, he tells the story of how his Mississippi Rifles turned defeat into victory:

"In the forenoon of the 21st of September, a part of General Twigg's Division made a demonstration upon the advanced work at the east end of Monterey. General Butler's division . . . heard the firing of small arms, but were not in sight of the combatants, when three regiments, to wit, the Tennessee, the Mississippi and the Ohio, were put *en route* in the direction of the firing, which was obliquely to our left and front.

"After we had proceeded a short distance, the Ohio regiment

was diverged to the front, and the Tennessee and Mississippi regiments continued their line of march in the order named, and moving by a flank.

"During the whole march we were exposed to a cross fire of artillery. A round of shot raking the Tennessee regiment made great havoc, but did not check the advance.

"The firing of small arms which had attracted us ceased, and when we halted before the fort and fronted it, a small body of troops in the undress of our 'regulars' was standing in such a position as to mask the right companies of the Mississippi regiment. I pointed out the fact to Brigadier-General Quitman, commanding in person, and, the closing or other movement of the Tennessee regiment having created an interval on our left, it was agreed that I should occupy it. We were within the effective range of the enemy's fire but beyond that of our Rifles. I therefore executed a movement which gained ground to the front and left, and when the regiment was again formed into line the troops who had stood upon my right were gone.

"The attacking force now consisted of the Tennessee and Mississippi regiments. The latter, on the right, was directly in front of the fort."

Although, as he says, "I had no instructions, no information as to the plan, no knowledge of any sustaining troops except the Tennesseeans on our left," Davis decided to charge the fort. "I announced to the men my conviction . . . that twenty men . . . could take the place." Captain J. L. McManus later declared that he heard Davis shout: "Now is the time. Great God! if I had thirty men with knives I could take the fort." Lieutenant-Colonel McClung, formerly captain of one of Davis' companies, from Tombigbee Valley, now challenged the latter with the words, "Tombigbee boys, follow me!" The men eagerly responded and were led against the fort, closely followed by the rest of the regiment, and by Colonel Campbell's Tennessee Rifles. McClung was the first to mount the wall: but Davis followed immediately.

Indeed, Lieutenant Daniel R. Russell later said in his report to Davis: "I think you passed Colonel McClung before he left the wall." Davis, however, never made this claim, content to leave the credit to McClung, who had paid for his bravery with his life.

To the calm observer reading the records after three quarters of a century, it seems madness for Davis to have ventured upon such an assault without orders; but he won the fort. Even while he and McClung balanced themselves upon the parapet, the defenders of the fort began to abandon it, crowding through the sally-port at the other side, to seek refuge in Fort el Diablo, some seventy-five yards beyond. They were closely pressed; so closely, indeed, that "we reached the gate . . . before it was secured, and upon forcing it open the men inside fled behind the pilasters of the portico and held up their hands in token of submission," declares Davis' official report. But before the surrender could be completed, Lieutenant Nichols appeared with an order from General Quitman to retire. This was a hard test of discipline: but Davis obeyed. "Had your command advanced fifty yards farther," wrote James H. R. Taylor, commander of Company I, of the Mississippi Rifles, "the fort would have been at your mercy." Under such circumstances, it is not surprising that, according to Russell's report, Davis cursed bitterly.

Davis made camp that night at Walnut Springs, and early on the following morning (September 22nd), being warned that his regiment would be required for action, mustered them upon the parade-ground. They saw little, however, of the action of the second day. Sent to relieve the guard left at Fort Teneria, they passed "so near the enemy as to hear his guard calls," as Davis said, but only later learned that "our force on the west side carried successfully the height on which stood the bishop's palace which commanded the city."

The victory of Monterey, however, was still to be won; and Davis' description of the third day's battle throws further light

upon his methods of leadership. "At dawn of the 23rd, our senti-
nels on the housetop reported that very few persons were visible
in the fort 'El Diablo.' My own observations . . . induced me to
believe that the greater part of the garrison had been withdrawn.
I communicated these things to General Quitman, commanding
the post, who authorized me to make a sortie with four companies, two of Mississippi Rifles and two of Tennessee infantry.
We entered the suburbs of the city, and saw the enemy retreating rapidly before us." At this point, Davis was joined by Major
Bradford, with four companies, and, a little later, by the eastern
regiment of Texas Rangers. "As we advanced into the town," he
reported to Quitman, "armed bodies of men fled through the
streets. . . . Having turned the flank of the fort, we found it
evacuated and the artillery removed, as I suppose under cover of
the night. We took possession of it, but as it was commanded by
the forts in the rear of it, and the *têrra pleine* exposed to their
fire, it was necessary to take shelter upon the outer side."

The fifteen prisoners who were taken informed Davis that the
enemy had retired to the main plaza, and Lieutenant Scarrett was
dispatched to report to General Taylor, and "to apply for sapping
tools to advance into the city." Circumstances prevented his return; and Davis led his men back to "El Diablo," from which
point he reconnoitred the positions to the left.

Satisfied with the situation, Davis decided to force his way to
the cathedral area and encounter the enemy. "We continued to
advance until abreast of the cathedral of the main plaza. Here
we seized a two-storey house and maintained a contest, under the
converging fire of the enemy, which lasted several hours. We
were finally driven from every exposed position within the range
of our rifles."

Davis soon discovered, however, that he had pushed too far to
the right, and decided to seize "an unusually high house from
which it seemed a plunging fire could be thrown into the plaza."
"I had sent the Sergeant-major of the Mississippi regiment back

to find General Quitman and . . . to enquire also what had become of the piece of artillery which had been sent to co-operate with me. He returned and informed me that orders had been sent some time before, to General Henderson and myself to withdraw and that all the troops in our rear had retired. . . . We were engaged in forming a barricade to cross the street which was literally swept by the fire of both artillery and small arms." This was almost completed when the order to retire arrived. "It had been agreed between General Henderson (commanding the advance of Colonel Wood's Texas regiment) and myself . . . that we would take possession of a stone house in our front, which from its height would enable us to fire down into the main plaza, in which the great body of the enemy's troops had been collected. In that building we had determined to pass the night. . . . We were so far in advance that but little was known of the advantages we had gained." To this ignorance Davis attributed the order to retire. Retirement made it necessary to cross the street, and at great risk. Davis himself took the part of chief danger. "The arrangement made by me for crossing it," he declared, "was that I should go first; if only one gun was fired at me, then another man should follow; and so on, another and another, until a volley should be fired, and then all of them should rush rapidly across before the guns could be reloaded. In this manner the men got across with little loss."

Davis' part in this famous three days' battle had not been a decisive part, but it had proved his daring and resourcefulness, and had won the praise of General Taylor, and of Albert Sidney Johnston, whose praise was hard to win, but impossible to forget.

The heights had been taken by Worth's division, but the plaza remained in Mexican hands when, on September 24th, General Ampudia sent a flag of truce and requested a conference with a view to surrender. General Taylor readily consented and sent General Worth, Governor Henderson, and Colonel Davis as commissioners to arrange the terms. Davis prepared the memorandum of conditions. The city with supplies was to be surrendered, the enemy being granted the privilege of retiring peacefully, "a privilege," says Davis' autobiography, "which, if it had not been accorded, they had power to take by any one of the three roads open to them." The Mexican officers were to be allowed to reserve their side arms, "the infantry their arms and accoutrements, the cavalry their arms and accoutrements, the artillery one field battery, not to exceed six pieces, with twenty-one rounds of ammunition." The Mexican forces were to have seven days within which to retire "beyond the line formed by the pass of the Rinconada, the city of Linares, and San Fernando de Pusos." The citadel of Monterey was to be evacuated and occupied by the American forces on the following day at ten o'clock. The American forces were pledged not to advance beyond the line above described before the expiration of eight weeks, or until the orders of the respective governments should be received. And, as a final concession to Mexican pride, it was agreed that "the Mexican flag, when struck at the citadel, may be saluted by its own battery."

Governor Henderson had urged that "surrender at discretion" should be the demand, but his opinion was overruled by Worth and Davis, the latter insisting that the terms offered were, under the circumstances, "expedient, honourable, and wise." It was his opinion that, with forces "less than half the forces of the enemy," a demand for "surrender at discretion" would have been folly, especially in view of the fact that the attacking force was without siege artillery or entrenching tools.

After the terms, which were certainly generous, had been agreed upon in conference with General Ampudia, Davis left the document with him. "Have the articles signed," he said, "and I will call for them in the morning." Early the next day, as he passed the American headquarters on his way to Monterey, General Taylor halted him with the question, "Hello, Davis! Where are you going?" and when Davis explained, the general protested. "Not by yourself," he said. "One man is as good as twenty," was Davis' reply. "If they mean foul play, they would destroy twenty as well as one, and if there is danger, nothing but an army will do." Taylor, however, insisted that Davis should dismount, and talk the matter over. While they talked, the acting Inspector-General, Colonel Albert Sidney Johnston, came in and declared that he would accompany Davis. Reassured by this arrangement, Taylor offered no further objection and the two started. When they reached the Mexican lines, signs were far from reassuring. Artillery guarded the entrance, the men standing at their guns, with port-fires open, while on the roofs of houses were infantrymen, standing also at their guns. The scene presented so ominous an appearance that at Johnston's suggestion Davis raised a white handkerchief, to show that they travelled under flag of truce, and proceeding thus, they were conducted to Ampudia, who delivered the signed articles of surrender without delay. That the fear of treachery had not been wholly on the American side is evident from the fact, later recorded by him, "on our return, in jumping the ditch, the flap of my holster flew up, and I found that my pistol had been stolen by his orderly while I was with the Mexican general. . . . It had been given to me by Colonel Johnston, my companion during the Black Hawk war, and I prized it highly." Needless to say he did not return to recover it, however.

General Taylor officially approved the terms of surrender, declaring in General Orders No. 123, under date September 27, 1846, "Such terms have been granted as were considered due to the gallant defence of the town, and to the liberal policy of our own government," and he ventured the prediction that "our government will be pleased with the terms." Governor Henderson in the end declared his willingness to sign, and his purpose to defend the treaty against criticism. General Worth expressed the thanks of the commission "to Colonel Davis for having thrown together the material and the facts."

In Washington, however, the document met with censure, and the government, a few days before the end of the armistice, flatly disapproved the terms of capitulation, and ordered the truce terminated at once. There was no possible course but obedience, and thus, after many months' delay, General Taylor found himself still deep in the enemy country, and with a sense of having been sacrificed, for he considered the terms of the truce advantageous to the United States. By this rejection, Davis wrote, "we lost whatever credit had been given to us for generous terms in the capitulation, and hostilities were to be resumed without any preparation having been made to enable General Taylor, even with the small force he had, to advance farther into the enemy's country."

Considering such an advance as along the line of his duty, despite the difficulties which it now presented, Taylor made such preparation as was possible; among other things he requisitioned rubber bags in which to carry provisions and which, being emptied by the time they reached the sixty miles of desert could be filled with water to enable the troops and horses to cross.

While these and other preparations were in progress, Davis obtained a sixty-day leave, and started for Mississippi, riding "Tartar," the horse which had carried him through Monterey and which, when left to shift for himself, had chosen to advance alone "into a re-entering angle at Fort Teneria," and watch the battle. Arrived at "Brierfield," he made his will and consulted his faithful slave and friend, James Pemberton, concerning the latter's future in case his master should not return. Then, having disposed of such other plantation matters as demanded his personal attention, he mounted a new charger, "a noble bay with black points," and returned to Mexico, reaching Saltillo on January 4, 1847, there to resume command of the Mississippi Rifles, which Major A. B. Bradford had officered in his absence.

Shortly before Davis' return to headquarters General Taylor received from the President a request for advice as to the best method of prosecuting the war. Although smarting from a sense of injustice at the hands of General Scott, Taylor, as Jefferson Davis later declared, "recommended that a portion of his own command be sent to reinforce the southern column." This having been done, Taylor retained only a force sufficient to escort him back to enforced inaction; Davis' regiment was among those retained.

"For the good of his country," comments Davis, "he sacrificed his long-deferred hope of an advance, at the moment of its fulfilment and doomed himself to the worst punishment of a soldier —inactivity on a line of defence. . . . He gave his vest also to the man who had taken his coat." Later, however, when bitterness had passed, Davis acknowledged that this apparent injustice to Taylor "was more than compensated by the gain to the general cause."

To the Mexican General Santa Anna, to whom Taylor's apparently helpless condition had been reported, this seemed the moment to recover all the country down to the Rio Grande; and with confident expectation he advanced upon Taylor's small army. Colonel May reported the movement, and General Taylor, "as sage as he was brave," wrote Davis, made his dispositions as well as the small force at his command allowed. With only some forty-six hundred effective troops, his position seemed desperate indeed; and he might well have regretted his failure to accept General Scott's advice and retire to the shelter of Monterey.

As Santa Anna moved forward, Davis, unconscious of impending battle, wrote to his wife: "We are here on the tablelands of Mexico, at the foot of the Sierra Madre. We came expecting a host and battle; have found solitude and, externally, peace. . . ."

This solitude and peace did not last long, however, for General Santa Anna, the self-styled "Napoleon of the West," was approaching, to enforce an unequal battle. In view of his overwhelming numbers, estimated as high as 20,000, defeat of the American forces seemed inevitable, and the correspondents in

Taylor's camp warned the country that it must expect this result. But Taylor was by no means of that opinion, as he prepared for the greatest battle of his life. "Had it been known . . . that Santa Anna would come from Encarnacion, . . . through the pass of Carnero," said Davis, to the United States Senate, on August 5, 1850 "General Taylor would probably, with his tents standing, have fought the battle on that field." Not knowing this, as there were two passes in his rear, he decided to fall back to Buena Vista, and give battle there. "I was ordered to strike my tents, and hold myself in readiness to march to Buena Vista."

Early on the morning of February 23rd, Davis led his regiment towards the scene of the renewed battle, meeting on the way fugitives from the second regiment of Indiana volunteers. Major Bradford annexed some of these, who became members of his command for the day. At first the outlook seemed black; for, as Major Bradford reported to Davis, they were confronted with "a heavy column of infantry of about 4,000 of the enemy that had completely turned General Taylor's left and were moving to fall on his rear." "Many think," he adds, that "if it had not been checked by the Mississippi Rifles, [we] might have lost . . . the brilliant victory which followed. You perceived the critical position in which the army at this crisis was placed and determined to move forward upon them. . . . You gave the word and like veterans the regiment moved off, under one of the heaviest fires I ever saw, which was returned by our regiment with equal spirit."

Despite their superiority of numbers, the Mexicans were forced to give way, seeing which, a heavy body of Mexican lancers bore down upon the Mississippians on their left, and had almost overwhelmed them, when Colonel Davis ordered his men to fall back to a point where the plain was narrower, so as to have a ravine on each flank. "In this position," wrote Davis, "the second demonstration of the enemy's cavalry was received. They were repulsed, and it was quiet in front . . . until an aide . . . called from the other side of the ravine . . . that General Taylor wanted support . . . for the protection of the artillery on the right flank." At this point, as Davis wrote later, "we came suddenly on a gulch or chasm, apparently about fifteen or twenty feet across, and of about the same depth, and the sides almost precipitous. There was no chance to flank it in time for the occasion, and so it had to be crossed. I had to cleve it *en volt* . . . Ordinarily, I would have had confidence in my mount to clear it, for he was of blood and mettle. But that day I had but one spur available. But crossed it had to be; so, giving orders for the command to scramble down and up . . . as best they could, I went back some fifty yards for . . . impetus, and went for it full tilt, and cleared it in fine style. In the instant that I was in the air, I saw beneath a four mule team with the driver in the agonies of death. A minute later my men were crawling up the bank and we were soon in line and prepared to receive our visitors in a proper manner." "The necessity now was to prevent the cavalry from passing to the rear of our line of battle, where they might have attacked, and probably carried, our batteries, which were then without the protection of our infantry escort. It was our country's necessity, and not our own, which prompted the service there performed. For this the regiment was formed square across the plain, and there stood motionless as a rock, silent as death, and eager as a greyhound for the approach of the enemy, at least nine times, numerically, their superiors. Some Indiana troops were formed on the brink of the ravine with the right flank of the Mississippi regiment, constituting one branch of what has been called the 'V.' When the enemy had approached as near as he dared and seemed to shrink from contact with the motionless, resolute, living wall which stood before him, the angry crack of the Mississippi rifles was heard, and as the smoke rose and dust fell, there remained of the host which so lately stood before us but the fallen and the dying."

Bragg's and Thomas' batteries now opened upon them, firing

grape, and the rout was complete. "When the hostile demonstrations had ceased," adds Davis' report to Major Bliss, "I retired to a tent upon the field for surgical aid, having been wounded by a musket ball when we first went into action." He was confident, and he never afterward wavered in the conviction, that the First Mississippi Rifles, and their V formation, had rendered a service which, as he later assured the Mississippi Legislature, "in no small degree contributed to the triumph which finally perched upon the banner of the United States."

Caleb Cushing later expressed his agreement with this opinion, in words addressed to the "Expatriated Irish" of Boston: "In another of the dramatic incidents of that field, a man of Celtic race (Jefferson Davis) at the head of the Rifles of Mississippi, ventured to do that of which there is, perhaps, but one other example in the military history of modern times. In the desperate conflicts of the Crimea, at the battle of Inkermann, . . . a British officer ventured to receive the charge of the enemy without the precaution of having his men formed in a hollow square. They were drawn up in two lines, meeting at a point like an open fan, and received the charge of the Russians at the muzzle of their guns, and repelled it. Sir Colin Campbell, for this feat of arms, among others, was selected as the man to retrieve the fallen fortunes of England in India. He did, however, but *imitate what Jefferson Davis had previously done in Mexico*, in that trying hour, when, with one last desperate effort to break the line of the American army, the cavalry of Mexico was concentrated in one charge against the American line; then, I say, Jefferson Davis commanded his men to form in two lines, . . . and receive that charge of the Mexican horse, with a plunging fire from the right and left from the Mississippi Rifles, which repelled, and repelled for the last time, the charge of the hosts of Mexico."

Eye-witnesses are prone to exaggerate the relative importance of what they have witnessed, especially in the case of a battle; and the careful study of the documents relating to all parts of the field is equally prone to alter proportions, if not details. Such was the case as regards Davis' report. A succession of historians, after such study, have reduced the importance which he honestly attributed to the movements of the Mississippi Rifles, and to his much-praised "V." But, when all modifications have been made, it is agreed that at Buena Vista, as at Monterey, Davis displayed both courage and ability. To prove this it is only necessary to quote the words of General Taylor, whose responsibilities covered the entire battlefield. "The Mississippi Rifles under Colonel Davis," he wrote in his official report, "were highly conspicuous for their gallantry and steadiness. . . . Brought into action against an immensely superior force, they maintained themselves for a long time unsupported . . . and held an important part of the field until reinforced. Colonel Davis, though severely wounded, remained in the saddle until the close of the action. His distinguished coolness and gallantry, and the heavy loss of his regiment on this day, entitle him to the particular notice of the government." To this testimony may be added the remark reported from the same source by General Colquit: "Napoleon never had a marshal who behaved more superbly than did Colonel Davis that day, and Reagan, later Postmaster-General of the Confederacy, says that Taylor, as he congratulated the wounded Davis, remarked, "My daughter was a better judge of men than I."

CHAPTER VI

IN THE SENATE

WITH the battle of Buena Vista, the time of the First Mississippi Rifles expired; and, still led by Davis, they left Brazos on May 29th, and landed at New Orleans eleven days later, where enthusiastic crowds paid tribute to the Mississippi hero; and Sergeant S. Prentiss, his former political antagonist, welcomed him in a fervent address. He received also a letter from President Polk, announcing his appointment as brigadier-general, and continuing: "Your distinguished gallantry and military skill while leading the noble regiment under your command, and especially in the battles of Monterey and Buena Vista, eminently entitle you to it." In reply, Davis thanked the President, but declined the appointment upon the ground that the constitution gives the President no power to appoint militia officers, and that "volunteers are militia." He then lent his now powerful assistance to the raising and equipping of a Second Regiment of Mississippi Rifles, with elected officers, which was soon on its way to the front.

Scarcely was this task accomplished, when Davis received from Governor Brown, of Mississippi, the notification of his temporary appointment as United States Senator, to fill the vacancy occasioned by the death of General Speight. The Governor added the gratifying comment that in offering the commission he was fulfilling the popular demand for this testimony of "our high appreciation of your valuable services as a member of the Twenty-ninth Congress, and your more valuable and distinguished services as the head of the First Mississippi Regiment in Mexico. . . .

It is the tribute which a grateful people . . . pays to heroic deeds of disinterested patriotism. . . . In returning to the arena of politics you may have it in your power to counsel your government in regard to a people whom you have aided in conquering, whose weaknesses and follies you have learned to appreciate from personal observation, and to whom I am sure you are willing to give an honourable peace whenever they and their rulers shall have the good sense to accept it."

The appointment was to hold only until the next session of the State legislature: but it offered Davis a chance to return to a work which he loved only next to that of the soldier, and with increased prestige, and elevated rank. In accepting, he wrote: "You have justly anticipated my views in relation to a peace with Mexico, an event to be desired not merely from its influence on our domestic policy, but also to save from monarchical alliance, or entire prostration, a republican confederacy, which, despite our caution and magnanimous forbearance, has forced us into war."

Immediately after posting this reply, Davis received a letter informing him that Colonel Reuben Davis had resigned his post as leader of the Second Mississippi Rifles and urging him to return to Mexico as its Colonel. At once he wrote: "I have not so far recovered from my wound as to be able to travel immediately," and added ". . . before the receipt of your letter I had accepted a commission to fill a vacancy in our representation in the United States Senate."

This incident was most unfairly ridiculed by Davis' political enemies as "staged for political effect," but while resenting the charge as "deliberate slander," he did not allow it to change his plans: but set his face the more uncompromisingly toward political service, to which he adhered to the end of his public career. It served, however, to make him abnormally sensitive to criticism, or even implied criticism, of his military service or that of his regiment; and he was always ready to carry such criticism to the "field of honour." Most of all he resented any question of the

originality of the "V" formation which he believed to have turned
the tide at Buena Vista, and it was a source of intense gratification
when the exploit was praised by Wellington, the "Iron Duke,"
and more than one European expert. From his writings, one
might compile a small volume of comments bearing upon that
cherished formation, for, as the years passed, he saw it in ever
larger perspective. "The most marked compliment ever paid by
one general to another [he told the Mississippi legislature in
1858], was that of Napoleon to Caesar, when he halted on his
encampments without a previous reconnaissance," and explained
how he himself had formed his "V," a juxtaposition of ideas
which may have caused Grant's later remark that Davis regarded
himself as a military genius.

On December 6, 1847, Senator Sevier, of Arkansas, presented to
the Senate the credentials of Davis' appointment, and he took the
oath to defend the Constitution of the United States. How he
understood the oath is shown in a letter written a month later to
C. J. Searles, and designed for the public press, in which he declared: that "it might become necessary to unite us Southern men
and to dissolve the ties which have connected us to the Northern
democracy, the position recently assumed in a majority of the
non-slaveholding states has led me to fear." The South should
"demand of their political brethren of the North a disavowal of
the principles of the Wilmot Proviso, an admission of the equal
right of the South with the North to the territory held as the
common property of the United States, and a declaration in
favour of extending the Missouri Compromise to all states to be
hereafter admitted into our confederacy.

"If these principles are recognized, we will happily avoid the
worst of all political divisions—one made by geographical lines
merely. . . . If, on the other hand, the spirit of hostility to the
South, that thirst for political dominion over us, which, within
two years past, has displayed such increased power and systematic
purpose, should prevail, it will only remain for our delegates to

withdraw from the convention. . . . We shall then have reached a point at which all party measures sink into insignificance under the necessity of self-preservation; and party divisions should be buried in union for defence."

Davis' return to politics coincided with the appearance of General Taylor in the rôle of Whig candidate for the Presidency. The surprising victory of Buena Vista, coming when the nation feared news of disaster to his little army, had made him available, though to Taylor himself, the idea of standing as a rival to the great Whig leader, Henry Clay, appeared absurd and he had written to the latter, describing a conversation with a friend, upon the subject: "I said to him specifically that I was ready to stand aside if you or any other Whig were the choice of the party, and that I sincerely hoped such might be their decision."

The suggestion of Taylor's nomination, of course, invited political criticism of his career, and shortly after Davis took his seat in the Senate, although himself a loyal Democrat, he was vigorously engaged in defending the actions of his old chief; and his speeches inevitably added to the latter's availability. As military operations had not yet ceased in Mexico, it was natural, furthermore, that Davis, a veteran, should assume the rôle of champion of the army and appeal for reinforcements to make safe and effective the men in the war zone.

On March 21st he took the floor in defence of the administration, facing Webster and even Calhoun with an insistence that its course had been constitutional, right, and patriotic. "The whole of Texas . . . was included in this disputed territory," he said, in answer to Calhoun's declaration that the President had had no right to order an army into "disputed territory": "and if the President had no right to march the army to the Rio Grande, he had no right to order it across the Sabine. Mexico claimed the whole of Texas. . . . The question was not whether the Nueces or the Rio Grande was the boundary, but whether Texas was a part of the United States," after it had been solemnly annexed by joint resolution. "In a just war we conquered a large portion of Mexico. . . . To it we have a title which has been regarded as valid ever since man existed in a social condition—the title of conquest. . . . The question is now how much we shall keep, how much we shall give up. . . . Mexico cedes nothing."

An interruption from Webster drew from Davis the declaration: "As a moralist I would not undertake to defend the seizure of a country from the inhabitants, but the question was settled long before the oldest member of the Senate entered it. These very Mexican people settled it when they conquered the ancient Aztecs. If they had the right to take the territory from that people, who did not cultivate it, the argument is equally good against them now. They produce little . . . and year by year the amount is steadily decreasing. The country is going to waste, villages are depopulated, fields once highly productive . . . now lie uncultivated, and marked only by the remains of the irrigatory ditches by which they were formerly watered. . . . Tell me whether all the arguments of utilitarianism and of humanity may not now be more successfully applied to the Mexican than by them against the Aztec population."

The argument that a strong and efficient nation may properly seize and make economically productive a country that is "going to waste" is still heard in the twentieth century, and it cannot be denied that in some cases the use subsequently made of such conquests has softened the verdict of history, if, indeed, it has not justified the seizure. There is a right anterior to the right of self-government, and that is the right to some kind of orderly and effective government, capable of protecting the "life, liberty, and property" of the individual, to quote from John Locke's famous *Second Treatise on Government*. And no one can deny that the inhabitants of the regions taken from Mexico have been better served than they were, or were likely to be, under Mexican rule.

Such discussion showed that already the political issues which grew out of the Mexican war were beginning to supplant the

82362

EMORY AND HENRY LIBRARY

conflicts over the conduct of the war itself. It was also apparent that although the war had given America a vast new territory, it had not decided the question of what was to be done with it. The anti-slavery men were determined that the principles of the Wilmot Proviso should keep slavery out of all the newly acquired territory: the slave-holding section was determined to maintain "equal rights" there. Davis' hope had been early expressed in the words: "I think the Wilmot Proviso will soon be of the things which were. Cass is heartily with us, and says he always was, but saw the necessity last spring of caution." So marked did Cass' caution become during his candidacy for the presidential nomination in the approaching contest, that Lincoln characterized him as "the ox that retreats while the farmer flourishes the goad."

The political outlook placed Davis in a difficult position. As a consistent Democrat, who had always followed the party ticket, he felt that he must support Cass if nominated: although the increasing likelihood of such an event had caused Taylor to write to Clay that he now considered himself in the hands of the people.

On May 22nd the National Democratic convention nominated Cass on the fourth ballot, while intimating their sense of Davis' popularity, by giving him one vote for the Vice-Presidency, and on June 7th the Whig convention nominated Zachary Taylor. On July 10th Taylor wrote to Davis: "I feel under, my dear General, the greatest obligations for the continued interest you feel and have taken in my reaching the first office in the gift of the American people, in which you and other dear friends, I am confident, take much more concern than I do. The statement you made to the Honorable Senator from New Jersey, Mr. Dayton, in regard to my course in the event of my election has added another to the many acts of kindness [for which] I am indebted to you; the smallest portion of which I greatly fear I will never have it in my power to repay. . . . I have your own advancement more at heart than my own. You are now entering on the stage of action, while I must soon retire from it; you must therefore pursue that course which your good judgment will point out, as far as your honour and the good of the country are concerned, without regard to my advancement. It is sufficient to me to know that I possess your friendship, which is all I ask or wish."

In the presidential contest, Davis followed the candidate of his own party, although with personal regret. "We are called to choose between the Whig and Democratic parties," he wrote to a committee which had invited him to speak at a political meeting, "and, as there is no well-founded personal objection to either of their candidates for the Presidency, we are . . . left to decide upon the measures and principles they avow. Separating myself as far as possible from the prejudice I may very naturally feel for the creed of my entire political life, it seems to me evident and demonstrable that the South should fraternize with the Democracy. This is the party of strict construction, of checks and balances, and constitutional restraints. We of the South are the minority, and such we must remain. Our property, our security in the Union, depend upon the power of the constitutional curb with which we check the otherwise unbridled will of the majority."

One of the fruits of Cass' caution was the doctrine of squatter sovereignty, destined to play an important part in the history of the next dozen years. Davis later claimed that the theory was born in 1848. "It was ushered in," he said, "by a great and good man [Lewis Cass]. He brought it forward because of that distrust which he had in the capacity of the Government to bear the rude shock to which it was exposed. His apprehensions no doubt to some extent sharpened and directed his patriotism, and his reflection led him to a conclusion to which, I doubt not, today he adheres as tenaciously as ever; but from which it was my fortune, good or ill, to dissent when his letter was read to me in manuscript. . . . I thought it a fallacy which would surely be exploded. . . ."

From the moment when he first saw Cass' Nicholson letter, Davis considered its meaning perfectly clear. To him it proved that Cass wished "to limit the action of Congress, in relation to territories, to the creation of proper governments, . . . leaving the people inhabiting them to regulate their own concerns in their own way." From the first, he saw inevitable controversy in such a doctrine, especially as Cass, intentionally or unintentionally, had failed to make clear just when the people inhabiting the territory in question were to declare how they would regulate their own concerns. The letter left the reader to answer that question in the way most satisfactory to himself, its purpose being not to decide the matter, but to win votes. At once, as Davis later declared, "it became a question in the South whether General Cass meant to assert that the inhabitants of a territory, prior to their admission into the Union as a state, could prohibit slavery, or whether he meant that this right could only be exercised when they changed their relation of territories for that of states. The latter construction was most consonant with the feelings and views of Southern Democrats, and they generally adopted it; whilst the former suited the purpose of the Southern Whigs the best, and they accordingly adopted it."

The fact that Cass, after the campaign, interpreted his Nicholson letter as Davis interpreted it during the campaign, did not affect the fact that Cass' followers at the time interpreted it, each as he saw fit. And when at last the ambiguity became clear to them, he was charged with deliberate deceit, a charge which he bitterly resented. And Davis, who supported him despite his objection to what was to him Cass' clear meaning regarding "Squatter Sovereignty," sympathized with the resentment. "Had I believed him guilty, or capable of such a crime," he said, "I would neither have advocated his claims nor have given him my vote."

Whatever Cass intended to convey in his Nicholson letter, there is no doubt concerning Davis' views. On June 23, 1848, while the Oregon bill was pending, he proposed an amendment that "nothing contained in this act shall be so construed as to authorize the prohibition of domestic slavery in said territory, whilst it remains in the condition of a territory of the United States." And in defending this amendment he made one of the most comprehensive declarations of political faith of his whole life, a speech full of illumination regarding his views upon law, government, and property, especially property in slaves. He argued that before the constitution was adopted, slavery was local: and had been made national by the very terms of the Constitution which recognized its rights. "In accepting the limitations upon its rights imposed by the Missouri Compromise of 1820, the South, in the spirit of concession . . . surrendered their unquestionable right to extend slavery over the whole of that territory which had been acquired under the name of Louisiana, and agreed, except within the limits of Missouri, to confine it to the south side of . . . 36° 30′ north." He was unwilling to have this restriction placed upon the Territory of Oregon, in view of the fact that the North was unwilling to allow the line 36° 30′ to be extended to the Pacific. "Who does not see the purpose, by forbidding the growth of the slave-holding states, and devoting all our vast territorial domain to the formation of those in which slavery is forbidden, to obtain in the future such preponderance of free states as will enable them constitutionally to amend the compact of our Union, and strip the South of the guarantees it gives." He argued, then, and he never ceased to argue, that neither Congress nor the inhabitants of a territory had power to prohibit within territories property rights recognized by the Constitution which covered the entire country. "To leave the whole subject to the territorial inhabitants," he said, "is equivalent to acknowledging them to be sovereign over the territory." "My argument will of course be understood to apply to the Mormons, and I . . . ask if anyone is prepared to welcome the consequences . . . which would flow from the exercise of sovereignty by them over the country of which they may take possession?"

Davis claimed, as Jefferson had claimed, that spreading slaves over larger areas, while not increasing their numbers, would alleviate their condition. "Nothing can be more plain than that, if confined to a small space, they must accumulate in the hands of a few, and if dispersed they must have many masters. Whatever there is of harshness arises from their accumulation, so that the master and slave are necessarily separated, and the latter placed under the authority of his agent. . . . To confine slavery to a small district would go farther than any other means to strip it of its kind, paternal character." "A large community of freemen would have the pecuniary ability to emancipate a small number of slaves; the reverse would be beyond their power. Upon a large territory, a few blacks might be turned loose without injury . . . ; but in a small territory a large number . . . could only be released by surrendering the country to them." The restriction of slavery "to the states in which it now exists, [would mean] not its extinguishment, but its perpetuation." "Involuntary service is less profitable than voluntary labor; and there is a singular uniformity in the degree of density at which, in different countries, it has been abandoned. . . . With what justice or propriety do those who have availed themselves of the demand for their slaves in the more Southern and sparsely settled states now insist upon closing the door against their egress to newer countries? . . . They sold their slaves when they ceased to be profitable, and slavery became to them a sin of horrid enormity when the property was transferred from themselves to their brother."

It is only fair to say that Davis, while defending slavery as a necessary stage in the progress of the negro race toward ultimate freedom, never looked upon it as a final solution of the problem of the race. In this same speech he declared that American slavery "may have for its end the preparation of that race for civil liberty and social enjoyment." "Leave natural causes to their full effect, and when the time shall arrive at which emancipation is proper, those most interested will be most anxious to effect it." "Leave the country to the south and west open, and speculation may see in the distant future slavery pressed by a cheaper labor to tropical regions where, less exertion being required to secure support, their previous preparation will enable them to live, in independent communities." And he faced the non-extensionists with the solemn prophecy: "If the principles of the Constitution are to be disregarded by a self-sustaining majority, the days of the confederacy are numbered. . . . If this amendment be rejected, I shall view it as ominous of the future, and stand prepared for whatever consequences may follow."

On August 10th, the Senate, by a vote of 33 to 21, approved a resolution of Stephen A. Douglas, "that the line 36° 30' of north latitude, known as the Missouri Compromise line . . . be, and the same is, hereby declared to extend to the Pacific Ocean," Davis and Calhoun voting with Douglas in the affirmative. On August 11th the House of Representatives rejected the measure by 121 to 82, and on August 12th the Senate accepted the evident wish of the House by receding from its previous affirmative vote and the proposal to share the new Western territory between the sections was lost.

In the November elections, Zachary Taylor was chosen President of the United States, but neither Davis' very real affection for his former father-in-law nor his lack of any great personal enthusiasm for Cass had been able to induce him to desert his own party. "To sink personal hostility . . . ," he told the Mississippi State Convention, on July 31, 1849, "is an easy task compared with its opposite, the sacrifice of personal ties because of political differences. Of this I can speak from experience, having been subjected to the test in the late presidential canvass; and though in my course on that occasion I find nothing to regret or repent, it was not permitted to pass without misconstruction and misrepresentation. . . . In the candidate of the opposite party, I recognized a personal friend to whom gratitude was due for his public services, and who had claims upon myself . . . which, if they were not of a higher, were of nearer and more binding character than those. Honoured as a patriot, admired as a soldier, trusted and loved as a man, yet I opposed him as a political candidate, and as the leader of our adversaries feared his success, in proportion to the influence which his military services, his elevated qualities, and many virtues would give him for the advancement of a policy which I believed to be wrong. Therefore whenever I addressed the people during the canvass, whilst I acknowledged the debt of gratitude which was due to General Taylor . . . and admitted all which his political supporters said of his private virtues, I, nevertheless, warned the Democracy against trusting political power to their adversaries because of the personal confidence they might feel in him who would thus become the head of the administration." And a few days later he wrote to his friend, Stephen Cocke: "I wonder how many of my opponents standing in the relation I did to General Taylor would have endeavoured to defeat him for Democracy's sake, and have refused to walk in the broad way and to the open gate of self-preferment."

Meanwhile the Mississippi legislature had met and elected Davis Senator for the remainder of Senator Speight's unexpired term, namely until March 3, 1851. He therefore resumed his seat on December 4, 1848. The record of debates show him very much in evidence; now, in hot discussion with Sam Houston over the accuracy of certain maps of the Texan territory; now, engaged with Senator Douglas concerning the question of postponing the discussion of California's application for statehood. Early in January, 1849, he took occasion to denounce the anti-slavery activities of "individuals whose piety is so great that they must always be appropriating to themselves other men's sins." "When," he demanded, "did the South ask for this vicarious repentance, and whence do you derive your power to instruct her in her moral duty? . . . Of all the claptrap that ever issued from the lips of advocates of such a policy, that which relates to the question of the right of petition is the greatest. . . . What grievance is there

to any non-slave-holding state if other communities think proper
to keep slaves? . . . Shall we receive, entertain, and discuss petitions upon a subject which everyone recognizes we have no right
to grant, upon which we have no power to grant anything? It is
an idle waste and a base abandonment of the duties of members
. . . to squander the time which should be devoted to some useful
purpose."

Two days later, with the aforesaid petitions in mind, he turned
again to the defence of slavery, with the words: It would be
better "if, instead of indulging in lamentations about the evils
resulting from slavery, they were to look upon the other side of
the picture, and ascertain if it has not prevented evils. Has it made
any man a slave any more than he was a slave without this institution, or reduced any man from liberty to slavery? This is the
question; and I answer, it has not. Under laws older than the
records of history men were taken captives in war, and held as
slaves. These slaves were purchased from contending, warring
bands who held their captives in slavery, and the slaves thus purchased were saved from a more ignominious and degrading slavery than they would be subject to on this side of the Atlantic. It
benefits them, in removing them from the bigotry and heathen
darkness which hangs like a cloud over the interior of Africa, to
the enjoyment of the blessings of civilization and Christianity."

Of this, as of many of Davis' speeches on slavery, we may say,
in the words of Carlyle: "Have a false opinion and tell it with the
tongue of angels! . . . The better you tell it, the worse it becomes." But in them all there clearly appears the influence of the
years spent at "Brierfield" and "Hurricane," working out, with
his brother, plans for the welfare of their slaves. His arguments,
however, like those of other ardent slaveholders who had seen the
institution only at its best, were such as the twentieth century can
hardly understand; defending as they did the lowest of social institutions, though holding the loftiest of political ideals.

The opening of the next session of the Thirty-first Congress found Davis in his place: and the historian, Prescott, surveying the Senate as then constituted, wrote of him as "the most accomplished" of its leaders, although Webster, Calhoun, Benton, and John A. Dix of New York were among the number. Another critic declared: "It is but simple justice to say that, in ripe scholarship, wide and accurate information on all subjects coming before the body, native ability, readiness as a debater, true honour and stainless character, Jefferson Davis stood in the very first rank, and did as much to influence legislation and leave his mark on the Senate and the country as any other who served in his day." And Senator Henry Wilson of Massachusetts with scant tendency toward prejudice in favour of a slaveholder, called him "the clear-headed, practical, dominating Davis."

There can be no doubt that Davis' position on the floor of the Senate was now an important one. He was there as a chosen advocate of a definite cause, and his service in the war which had brought that cause to the forefront of politics gave a somewhat personal character to the bitter criticisms levelled at the campaign by such giant opponents as Daniel Webster.

Davis' stand was clear and explicit. He was the sincere and unwavering exponent of the doctrines of state sovereignty and the legal rights of slaveowners. He held uncompromisingly to the view, inherited from his ancestors, reinforced by his study of constitutional law, and deepened by his eight years at "Hurricane," that the American Union was composed of separate, sovereign, and independent states, which had voluntarily confederated, and were free to resume their sovereignty, whenever their interests demanded it. He held always that the Federal Government was the product of a compact between these sovereign states, and had only such powers as were specifically delegated to it. He insisted that the Federal Government should respect the right of property in slaves with the conviction that interference with such property was an exercise of undelegated power, and as such dangerous to the sovereignty of the state.

These views he was ready at any moment to defend by citation of chapter and verse, and his knowledge of American history and American political theory made him a formidable antagonist in debate, for any one who accepted the premise that, in dealing with slavery, law and the precedents of the past must of necessity bind the statesmen of the present. For generations, this premise had been tacitly accepted on both sides of the line which separated the free states from the slave states, and for generations the South had had the better of the debate. Bishop Galloway was therefore right when he said, in an address on Davis in 1908: "Having read and re-read, with great diligence and no less delight the whole history of the fierce controversies that culminated in the war between the states, including the ablest speeches of our profoundest statesmen on both sides, and with all my genuine pride in a restored Union, I am bound to say that the Southern position was never shaken, and that the overwhelming weight of argument was on the side of John C. Calhoun and Jefferson Davis. And further, it was by surrendering the constitutional argument and resorting to what was denominated 'the higher law' of political conduct and conscience, that the North found apology or defence for its attitude towards the inalienable rights of the Southern states."

In the last analysis, this northern change of base is strikingly analogous to that by which our Revolutionary fathers improved their position in the long argument with George III. They pleaded rights under charters, but a supreme Parliament could not be stopped by charters which it had made and could unmake. They pleaded the inherited rights of Englishmen, until they saw that they themselves already had more advanced representative government than had Englishmen at home. They drew a distinction between external taxes which Parliament could legally impose and direct taxes which it could not impose, forgetting that they were arguing with a supreme Parliament. In the end, they took Aristotle's advice: "If unable to win your case by pleading the law of the land, plead natural law." The Declaration of Independence embodied this new argument, and it won.

Similarly, the North had for generations agreed with the South, first, that the Union could be abandoned by a state, and both sides at times had threatened such abandonment; and second, that slavery must exist because it was legal. In the end, the North abandoned both positions, and placed the slavery question where advancing civilization in other enlightened lands had already placed it, among the things which even law could not justify, or make binding upon the conscience of men. The result of the impact of the new basis against the old basis made inevitable the "impending crisis."

Had Jefferson Davis' career fallen a generation earlier, he would probably have lived and died a master in national politics. But law and precedent were not sufficient for the great questions which the Mexican War had forced to the front. The man who, in 1849, continued to debate as statesmen of all parties had debated in the first fifty years of the Constitution, was certain to find himself ticketed "rebel," and accused of plotting to destroy the Union. And Davis had not gone far in his Senatorial career before he faced that charge, as Calhoun had long faced it, and with as little justice. Calhoun, now nearing the end of his brilliant but losing conflict for state sovereignty and the security of slave property, had never desired to destroy the Union. His tenuous philosophy aimed but to save an interpretation of the slave clauses of the Constitution which time and progress and an awakening conscience were rendering obsolete. When Davis took up the task it was still nearer obsolescence. And it is but fair to remember that, in his acceptance of slavery, his views were those of Washington, Jefferson, Hamilton, and many other Fathers of the Republic; and were held as honestly.

On January 30, 1849, uneasy at the news that Henry Clay was to return to the Senate, Davis wrote to Governor John J. Crittenden, of Kentucky, who had held Clay's seat after his retirement:

"I regret exceedingly to see that Mr. Clay is to return to the Senate. Among many reasons is one in which I know you will sympathize, the evil influence he will have on the friends of General Taylor in the two Houses of Congress. Many who would have done very well in his absence will give way in his presence. This will introduce a new element in the selection of the General's Cabinet. It must be composed of men of nerve and of no Clay affinities. . . . I hope you will talk fully with General Taylor. He knows little of our public men personally and will have little opportunity to observe them after his arrival. . . . The general will need you, and I hope to see you here." This letter shows that already, two months before Taylor's inauguration, Davis entertained the fear that the latter would prove unable to cope with the powerful Whigs whose evident intention it was to manage his administration.

As a prominent Democrat, Davis was made a member of the joint committee of notification which found Taylor at "Hurricane," discussing with Joseph Davis his plans for Cabinet appointments. On February 27th he reported to the Senate Taylor's acceptance, and his wish to have the inauguration on March 5th, and at the designated hour, with his committee escorted the general to the appointed place, where the latter took the oath to "preserve, protect, and defend the Constitution of the United States." And having taken it, with characteristic frankness soon made clear that, though elected as a Whig, he would be no puppet, with the real Whig leader, Henry Clay, pulling the strings. He made it equally clear that, though a Southerner, and a slaveholder, he did not see eye to eye with Davis and his followers upon pending issues involving slave property.

Events soon showed that Davis' fear of the Clay influence had not been groundless. The Whig party was already split by faction, and when, towards the end of July, Davis appeared before the Mississippi Democratic Convention, assembled to nominate candidates for the coming state elections, he reviewed for its enlightenment the first five months of Taylor's administration, and reported disappointment. This disappointment he, however, attempted to turn to good account, by using it as an argument for party solidarity. Solemnly he warned his fellow Democrats against again being lured from support of their party ticket by promise of "a political millennium." Pointing to his own example of deserting a personal friend, in order to serve the superior claim of party solidarity, he urged upon them a united support of the Democratic ticket. Pointing to the historic case of 1840, when the Whigs, to gain temporary strength, had given their Vice-presidential nomination to John Tyler, a known Democrat, and, by the death of President Harrison, had seen him become President, he expressed the hope that they had reviewed that lesson and learned it so well that they would never again support the candidate of the opposing party. "I honour the Whig party," he said, when "openly avowing and supporting their creed, though I believe it to be wrong . . . but the 'no-party-party' I consider a cunning device to undermine the majority, and always to be regarded with . . . distrust." But he added: "Though one rises from the dead to testify, they will not believe."

Davis pointed out also the great opportunity offered the Democrats by the approaching congressional elections. "You have a majority in the Senate," he said, "and all you need is a gain of five members to give you a majority of the House of Representatives. Cannot Mississippi contribute one?" He warned them that the North and East, under the title of internal improvements at national cost, were systematically taxing the South for their own benefit. "It is the characteristic of all legislation for special interests," he said, "that the benefits inure to the strong; thence it has ensued that appropriations for internal improvements have mainly been made at the North and East. . . . Henceforth we must become relatively weaker in the national legislature, and therefore rather expect an increase than cessation of the unjust discrimination heretofore made against us."

The House of Representatives, based upon population, was certain of domination by the North, which received the vast majority of immigrants. These, more and more, tended to seek homes in free territory, where they would not have to compete with slave labour. Moreover the natural increase at the North was steadily more rapid as compared with the South. Davis saw that the chance of gaining the House of Representatives by electing five new members was one not likely to come again. He saw also that the scene was set for a party conflict, fiercer than the country had yet known, and to grow ever fiercer, and urged his fellow Democrats to prepare for it, by uncompromising loyalty to the party which represented state rights against the rising theory of consolidation.

The almost five months which intervened between this speech and the reopening of Congress offer no incidents of note in Davis' life: but on December 20, 1849, after he had resumed his seat in the Senate, his sense of guardianship for the institution of slavery caused him to rise in his place and protest when Senator Wm. H. Seward of New York proposed that Father Mathew, an ally of Daniel O'Connell, be admitted to a "privileged seat," in the Senate Chamber, because of his opinions relative to domestic slavery. "Even now," Davis said, "we see our Government seriously embarrassed by a dissention, the seeds of which were sown by the British emissaries, who assumed the false pretext of philanthropy to mask their unholy designs to kindle the fires of civil war among the United States. The good he [Father Matthew] has done to a portion of our race deserves the thanks of mankind. The heart pays a willing tribute to the benevolence of a labour like his; and who has not rejoiced in the happy influence his mission has exercised over his unfortunate countrymen. . . . The question is whether the Senate, partly composed of those who represent a slave-holding constituency, shall vote an extraordinary compliment to one known as the ally of Daniel O'Connell in his attempt to incite the Irishmen, naturalized citizens of the United

States, to unite as a body with the abolitionists in their nefarious designs against the peace, the prosperity, and the Constitutional rights of the Southern states. . . . Why, if he came purely as a missionary in the cause of temperance, should he have hesitated to disavow any purpose to interfere with the political relations of any portion of our citizens, or to assail any of the domestic institutions of our country? . . . In default of such disavowals, under answers which are said to have been evasive, and with such advocacy as we have just heard [namely, Mr. Seward's], his attitude is that of one who comes covertly as a wolf in sheep's clothing; and I hold the Senator from New York to be the very best authority on that subject. . . . I will say of the horde of abolitionists, foreign and domestic, that if I had the power to exclude them all from this chamber, I would not hesitate to do it."

This speech gives a vivid picture of the attitude of suspicion, fear, and whole-hearted determination to defend "Southern rights" in slave property, which, at the opening of the eventful year 1850, characterized Jefferson Davis, and the South, whose chief leader he was soon to become. Great issues, the results of the Mexican War, were clamouring for solution. Vast new territories were to be organized, and it was necessary to decide what should be the status of each with respect to slavery. On that decision, as Davis well knew, must depend the chance of the South to retain its control of the Senate, and through that control to prevent the precipitate overthrow of the institution.

In many of his speeches of the period appeared prophecies of inevitable civil war should the North continue to disregard the limitations which the Constitution had placed upon the powers of the central government. The South "will know how to sustain the institutions which they inherited, even by civil war," he said on January 10, 1850, in open Senate. The refusal of the free states, upon grounds of conscience, to return fugitive slaves, as the Constitution and the laws undoubtedly required, also drew from him such threats. And in this he had the sympathy of many

Northern leaders, as when Webster declared, at Capon Springs, Virginia, on June 28, 1851, "If the Northern states refuse, wilfully and deliberately, to carry into effect that part of the Constitution which respects the restoration of fugitive slaves, and Congress provide no remedy, the South would no longer be bound to observe the compact. A bargain cannot be broken on one side and still bind the other side. . . . You of the South have as much right to receive your fugitive slaves as the North has to any of its rights and privileges of navigation and commerce." And President Taylor went so far as to assure Davis that if any attempt should be made to deprive the South of her constitutional rights, he would be willing to see them "act promptly, boldly, and decisively, with arms in their hands if necessary, as the Union in that case would be blown to atoms, or be no longer worth preserving."

These questions, and many equally dangerous, were wrapped up in the most pressing question of 1850: What shall be done with the vast territory acquired from Mexico by the Peace of Guadalupe-Hidalgo? Should Congress apply to them the principles of the Wilmot Proviso, or should the people therein settled determine their own domestic relations in their own way? The imminence of the latter question was recognized, on January 21st, in a letter which Davis and five other Senators and Congressmen sent to Governor Quitman, of Mississippi, expressing the confident belief that California was soon to be admitted as a free state, and interpreting that fact as "an attempt to adopt the Wilmot proviso in another form." They requested the Governor to "submit the single fact to the people and the legislature," and ascertain what course they wished their representatives to pursue in that emergency.

This question was particularly difficult, as California, on account of the gold rush, had been settled so quickly that it was sufficiently populous to become a state before it had been organized as a territory. The fact that the ambiguity of Cass' popular-sovereignty theory had left unsettled the question of whether the people of a territory could choose between slavery and freedom, or must wait until a state government was formed, did not affect the situation; but Davis had often admitted that, on becoming a state, the settlers were competent to decide that question. It was, therefore, clear, according to his own arguments, that California must be allowed to exclude slavery.

CHAPTER VII

CONTESTING THE COMPROMISE OF 1850

IN INTRODUCING his compromise resolutions, meant to heal the controversies which slavery had produced, Clay made a series of comments, in one of which he said: "The North is contending for a mere abstraction, while with the people of the South it is a principle involving their property . . . their prosperity and peace." In a sense, this was true, as the North, having long ago sold their slaves to the South, could regard slavery from an abstract point of view. The South, with their 3,950,000 slaves, could not so view it. But most of these slaves were owned by a small body of great land owners, and Clay might justly have argued that it would be both undemocratic and unjust to allow the interests of so small a minority to dominate in a matter involving ownership in human beings. Instead, however, he sought to set one advantage against another, and, by mutual concessions, to reconcile two irreconcilable positions, the South's insistence upon her legal right to property in slaves, and the growing Northern view that slavery must be eliminated from the life of a Republic built upon the theory that "all men are created equal."

Clay's resolutions were ingenious, and comprehensive, so far as conflicting interests were concerned. They proposed that California, "ought, upon her application, to be admitted as one of the states of the Union, and that, as slavery did not exist by law in any of the territory acquired from Mexico, it was inexpedient for Congress to provide by law either for its introduction or exclusion, and that territorial governments ought to be established for all of said territories, not included within the limits of California, without any restriction or condition on the subject of slavery. That the western boundary of the State of Texas ought to be fixed on the Rio del Norte up to the southern line of New Mexico, and thence with that line eastwardly, excluding any portion of New Mexico. That it was inexpedient to abolish slavery in the District of Columbia, whilst that institution existed in the State of Maryland, without the consent of that state, without the consent of the people of the District, and without just compensation to the owners of slaves within the District. That it was inexpedient to prohibit, within the District, the trade in slaves brought into it from states or places beyond the limits of the District, either to be sold there as merchandise or to be transported to other markets without the District of Columbia. That more effectual provision be made for the restoration of fugitive slaves, and that Congress has no power to prohibit or obstruct the trade in slaves between the slave-holding states, the commission or exclusion depending entirely upon their own particular laws."

On February 5th Clay was assigned the floor, to defend his proposals. The vigorous constitution which had so long sustained him, was gone. He was so weak that he could not ascend the steps of the Capitol without assistance. He knew that his days were numbered, and the thirst for the presidency, which had plagued him so long, was gone at last. He had come to plead for the Union, endangered by the questions growing out of slavery: and he confessed that never before had he been "so oppressed, so appalled, so anxious."

As he spoke, his vigour seemed to return, and, hour after hour, he pleaded for compromise and peace. "What do you want who reside in the free states?" he asked. "You want that there shall be no slavery introduced into the territories acquired from Mexico. Well, have you not got it in California, already, if admitted as a state? Have you not got it in New Mexico, in all human probability, also? . . . You have got what is worth a thousand

Wilmot Provisos. You have got nature itself on your side. You have the fact itself on your side."

When Clay came to Article VII, the enactment of a more stringent fugitive-slave law, his remarks were as pleasing to the majority of slaveholders as though Calhoun himself had made them. "It is our duty to make the law more effective," he said, "and I shall go with the Senator . . . who goes farthest in making penal laws and imposing heaviest sanctions for the recovery of fugitive slaves and the restoration of them to their owners." This declaration seems inconsistent from a man who had declared, "No earthly power can ever compel me to vote for the positive introduction of slavery either north or south of the Missouri Compromise line." But, despite his outspoken detestation of slavery, Clay saw the problem through a lawyer's eyes. He knew that the Constitution made provision for the return of fugitive slaves, and that the law of 1793, passed to carry the provision into effect, had been practically nullified by hostile state action. He therefore desired the slave-catching machinery under the new law to be independent of state action; and in order to give control to national instead of state officials, federal courts and federal commissioners were empowered to hear pleas for the return of fugitive slaves and to decide their fate.

As they stood, the compromise proposals had behind them the best brains of the Senate, and were designed to give to each section enough to satisfy it. But the South was not satisfied. "With more than ordinary unanimity, and with far more than ordinary severity," as Davis later reported to his constituents, "these resolutions were opposed by the Senators of the Southern states."

While seeking by argument to overcome the South's objections, which he well understood, Clay turned towards Davis, now regarded as, next to Calhoun, the most powerful of the Southern leaders, and remarked that he would be glad, at some time, to debate with him upon the objections which his fellow Southerners had advanced. "Now is the time," was Davis' instant reply, but Clay, disregarding the challenge, continued his exposition. A week later, however, Davis found the opportunity, then denied him. His two days' speech, like the speeches of Seward, Chase, and Douglas, in the same debate, was overshadowed by the fact that "the Great Triumvirate," Clay, Webster, and Calhoun, were fighting their last three-cornered battle, and that each was the long recognized leader of a section. But there can be no doubt that each of these younger leaders made also a deep impression.

"The great part of the Senator's argument," said Davis, turning towards Clay, "has been directed against the right of the Southern states to that equality of enjoyment in the territories to which they assert they are entitled. He has rebuked the spirit of absolutism as the evil of the country, but, in doing so, instead of describing it as a factious, disorganizing, revolutionary spirit, he has only spoken of it as the offspring of party, the result of passion. . . . I contend that the reverse is true. . . . It is the want of party which has built up this faction and rendered it dangerous. . . . So long as party organization preserved its integrity, there was no place for a third party, and no danger from it." Clearly, he foresaw the dawning of a new party, made up of the anti-slavery elements of each of the existing parties, and bent, not upon the solution of an ethical problem, but upon the power to rule. "If this were merely the result of passion . . . I should have hopes which I cannot now cherish. If it were the mere outbreak of violence, I should see some prospect for its subsidence. But, considering it as I do, the cold, calculating purpose of those who seek for sectional dominion, I see nothing short of conquest on the one side, or submission on the other. This is the great danger which hangs over us—not passion—not party; but the settled, selfish purpose which alone can sustain and probably will not abandon the movement. That upon which it originally rested has long since passed away. It is no longer the clamour of a noisy fanaticism, but the steady advance of a self-sustaining power to the goal of unlimited supremacy."

He then turned upon Clay a fierce invective which must have reminded the Great Commoner of Andrew Jackson's denunciation of him as the Judas of the West who had closed the bargain for thirty pieces of silver. "Does he lend his own hand to arrest the progress of the flood?" Davis cried. "No, he comes here, representing the Southern interests which are at stake, surrenders the whole claim of the South, and gives a support to abolitionism which no Northern man—no, nor every Northern man in the Senate—could have afforded." Passionately, he demanded for slave property the continued protection which the Constitution was meant to give. "Less than that equal protection the South can never take, unless they are willing to become an inferior class, a degraded caste. . . . The Government is the agent of all the states; can it be expected of any of them that they will consent to be bound by its acts, when that agent announces the settled purpose in the exercise of its power to overthrow that which it was its duty to uphold? The essential purpose for which the grant was made being disregarded, the means given for defence being perverted to assault, state allegiance thenceforth resumes its right to demand the service, the whole service, of all its citizens."

This was a frank announcement that, should the course entered upon by the Federal Government be continued, the states whose legal rights were disregarded would call their sons to their service against the Federal Union.

After declaring that Clay's proposal of a stronger law for the return of fugitive slaves would prove "a dead letter in any state where the popular opinion is opposed to such rendition," Davis turned to the question, "Who constitute the communities which are to exercise sovereign rights over the territories?" Douglas, having borrowed Cass' vague answer, was fathering the view that it was "those who, in the race for the newly acquired regions, may first get there." Davis answered, that "the sovereignty rests in the states, and there is no power, save that of the states, which can exclude any property, in the territories so held by the states in common. That power the states have not delegated; it can be exercised rightfully only by compact or agreement of the states. . . . The Missouri Compromise derived its validity from the acquiescence of the states, and not from the act of Congress."

To the argument that slavery had been abolished in all Mexican territory, by the Mexican decrees of July 13, 1824, April 15, 1829, and the Mexican law of April 4, 1837, and must remain abolished until restored by act of American legislation, he replied by challenging the validity of these decrees and this law, and by pointing to the fact that Mr. Trist, acting for the United States in the negotiation of the Treaty of Cession, had specifically told the Mexican authorities that, if such a restriction were placed upon the purchased territory, "No President of the United States would dare to present such a treaty to the Senate; and that, if it were in their power to offer . . . the whole territory . . . increased tenfold in value, and, in addition . . . covered over a foot thick with pure gold, upon the single condition that slavery should be excluded therefrom, I could not entertain the offer for a moment, nor think even of communicating it to Washington." Davis added that Mexico could not "expect that their law shall be recognized by our Government," and that the territory, not taken by conquest, but purchased from Mexico for "much more than it was worth to them," was like all other American national domain, subject to the sovereign control, not of "the conglomerate mass of gold-hunters, foreign and native," which might invade it, as they had invaded California; not to the sovereign control of the Federal Government to which no such sovereign control had been delegated, but subject still to the sovereign control of the sovereign states which alone were competent to exclude slavery.

At this point, Douglas intervened, to reassert his belief that "all people have the right, derived from God Himself, to regulate their own institutions as they see fit." But Davis, having already paid his respects to this doctrine, of squatter sovereignty, refused to be diverted from his main theme, namely Clay's failure to offer anything substantial to the South. "The Senator from Kentucky," he continued, "has not only spoken repeatedly of these resolutions as resolutions of mutual concession, but on one occasion at least he spoke of them as concessions in which the North yields to the South far more than she receives. Where is the concession to the South? Is it in the admission, as a state, of California, from which we have been excluded? . . . Is it in the announcement that slavery does not and is not to exist in the remaining territories of New Mexico and Arizona? Is it in denying the title of Texas to one-half of her territory? Is it in insulting her by speculating upon her supposed necessities, and offering her a sum of money in consideration of a surrender of a portion of her territory? Is it by declaring that it is inexpedient to abolish slavery in the District of Columbia, unless this Federal Government make compensation to the owners of the slaves? . . . Are we to fill the Treasury, in order that it may be emptied for the purpose of abolition? . . . If this Federal Government had been invested with a trusteeship to take charge of the negroes of the United States and provide for their emancipation, then I would admit that appropriations of money might be made out of the Treasury for purposes of abolition in the District of Columbia, but not otherwise." And at this point he appropriately quoted the words of Clay himself, uttered in a previous Congress, "the abolition of slavery is not necessary to the enjoyment of this site as a seat of the general government."

It would be unfair to draw from this speech the inference that Davis' main purpose was the defence of slavery, although he declared that "through the portal of slavery alone has the descendant of the graceless son of Noah ever entered into the temple of civilization." His main purpose, as a careful reading of the speech clearly shows, was to compel the North to give to the South "equal rights" in the newly acquired territory. The right to property, including the right to slave property, he later declared, "comes from an authority above law; it precedes all law. The law only recognizes it. . . . We of the South have asked of the North the right to carry this question to the Supreme Court. That right has been denied us. We stand now, as we have always stood, upon the Constitution; and if there be no disposition to compromise, we have lived, and we will die, by the Constitution. If he [Mr. Badger, whom he was answering] supposes that the majority of this Congress shall construe the Constitution . . . then you may say the Union is at an end. . . .

"Lightly and loosely," he continued, "representatives of the Southern people have been denounced as disunionists by that portion of the Northern press which most disturbs the harmony and endangers the perpetuity of the Union. Such, even, has been my own case, though a man does not breathe at whose door the charge of disunion might not as well be laid as at mine. The son of a Revolutionary soldier, attachment to the Union was among the first lessons of my childhood; bred to the service of my country, from boyhood to mature age I wore its uniform. Through the brightest portion of my life, I was accustomed to see our flag, historic emblem of the Union, rise with the rising and fall with the setting sun. I look upon it now with the affection of early love, and seek to preserve it by a strict adherence to the Constitution, from which it had its birth, and by the nurture of which its stars have come so much to outnumber its original stripes. Shall the flag, which has gathered fresh glory in every war, and become more radiant still by the conquest of peace . . . now be torn by domestic faction, and trodden in the dust by sectional rivalry? Shall we of the South, who have shared equally with you all your toils, all your dangers, all your adversities, and who equally rejoice in your prosperity, and your fame—shall we be denied those benefits guaranteed by our compact, or gathered as the common fruits of a common country? If so, self-respect requires that we should assert them and, as best we may, maintain that which we could not surrender without losing your respect as well as our own."

It was inevitable that in such a discussion there would crop up some debate upon the Mexican War, its origin, its motive, and its conduct. It was also inevitable that some one would refer to the conduct of troops in the field, notably the heated controversy between the Indiana regiment and the Mississippi Rifles. Upon that subject Davis was supremely sensitive, and his wrath was certain to descend upon any one who ventured to side with the Indiana regiment. On February 21st the Honourable Colonel William H. Bissell offended; and on February 22d Davis sent him the following letter:

"Sir: I am informed that in yesterday's debate you asserted that at the time it was claimed for the Mississippi regiment, on the field of Buena Vista, to have passed through the scattered files of the 2^d Indiana regiment, and to have met the Mexican forces, who had routed and were pursuing that regiment, the Mississippi regiment was not within one mile and a half of that particular spot.

"Not having been able to find a 'report' of your remarks, and being the proper person to answer any charge which a responsible man may make against the Mississippi regiment referred to, I take this mode of asking whether the information I have received is correct?

Yours respectfully,
JEFF'N DAVIS."

Bissell replied, admitting that he had made the remark, that "at the time the 2^d Indiana Regiment gave way the Mississippi regiment was not within one mile and a half of the scene of action." He added, "I also said that the 2^d Kentucky, the 2^d Illinois, and a portion of the 1st Illinois regiments, were the troops that, at that time met and repulsed the advancing columns of the enemy," and explained that his statement was not meant as a charge against the Mississippi Rifles, but only "to do justice to the character of others, living and dead, whose conduct fell under my own observation on that occasion."

Davis, however, had not yet obtained the statement regarding the conduct of his regiment which he required. Accordingly, on February 23rd, he wrote again: "You state, . . . that you made no charge against the Mississippi regiment, but claimed that the 2^d Kentucky and 2^d Illinois regiments, and a portion of the 1st Illinois regiment, met and repulsed the advancing columns of the enemy at the place and time the 2^d Indiana regiment gave way. This would render it impossible that the Mississippi regiment could have met the Mexican forces who followed the retreat of the Indiana regiment, or that, in the language of the brigadier-general commanding the Indiana troops (General Joseph Lane) the 'regiment of the Mississippians came to the rescue at the proper time to save the fortunes of the day.'" To this Bissell replied: ". . . I did not mean to deny the correctness of General Lane's report."

Davis was not willing to accept this response, which left his regiment unvindicated, and after some verbal skirmishing between General Shields, who now undertook to look after Davis' interests, and Mr. Inge, "the friend" of Colonel Bissell, Davis wrote again, "I have to request that you will authorize a friend to arrange with my friend the necessary preliminaries." As the challenged party, Colonel Bissell had the choice of weapons and chose muskets loaded with ball and buckshot.

To the credit of the code of honour, however, it must be recorded that the seconds managed in the end to satisfy the honour of both colonels, by the simple expedient of revising the correspondence which had passed between them, and preparing a letter, dated February 22nd, and signed by Bissell, which was accepted as the answer to Davis' original letter. Its text was the same as Bissell's first letter with the following phrase added at the appropriate point: "but am willing to award them the credit due to their gallant and distinguished services in that battle."

Before the end of this correspondence, the Mississippi legislature re-elected Senator Davis for a term of six years, thus greatly strengthening his position in the Senate, and before the country. But the voice of the South was still John C. Calhoun, frail and broken in health though he was; and on March 4, 1850, he entered the Senate Chamber, swathed in flannels, and carrying a carefully written speech, his final plea for justice to the South. Too weak to deliver it himself, he handed the sheets to Senator Mason, with the request that he read them to the Senate; and as Mason read, Calhoun sat like a disembodied spirit, but marking every word. His main point was that the equilibrium upon which the safety of the Union depended had been broken by unjust encroachments of the Federal Government, by unjust tariff laws, and by the Ordinance of 1787 and the Missouri Compromise which had prevented the South from occupying vast areas of national domain. The cords of Union are snapping, one by one. To save the Union the North must yield equal rights in acquired territory, an effective fugitive-slave law, a pledge to cease the agitation of the slave question, and a Constitutional amendment calculated to restore the South to her old position of power for self-defence.

A posthumous essay shows that Calhoun had in mind an amendment which would establish two Presidents, one elected by the North and one by the South, each with a veto upon congressional legislation. "If," he concluded, "you of the North will not do this, then let our Southern states separate and depart in peace."

This speech was, as Davis later said, "the effort of a dying man whose affections clung tenaciously to the Union." Before the end of the month Calhoun's sad and disappointed life had ended, and Davis had begun to be recognized as heir to his leadership.

Two of the Great Triumvirate had spoken, with Davis occupying two days between them. But, on March 7th, the galleries were again crowded, for it was known that Daniel Webster, the third and greatest of the three, was to give his views upon the compromise proposals. Webster's age was that of Calhoun, sixty-eight years, but he was still vigorous in body and mind, and the vision of the presidency had not yet faded from his dreams. He had thought Clay's proposals through, and, despite the opposition which had met them in his own constituency, was prepared to defend them, and the speech in which he defended them ranks as one of the masterpieces of American oratory. It is the only speech in the nation's history which is known by the date of its delivery, "7th of March speech." Sweeping majestically along, deep and comprehensive in scope, and magnificent in delivery, it sustained Clay's compromise proposals by the unrivalled authority of the speaker, but it goaded his constituents to fury.

In referring to the plan for a convention at Nashville, which Davis had recently assured the Senate was aimed "to preserve, if possible, our Constitutional Union," Webster professed to accept this view of its purpose, but took occasion to warn the South that they should hold to it strictly. "If they meet for any purpose hostile to the Union," he said, "they have been singularly inappropriate in their selection of a place. I remember . . . that, when the Treaty of Amiens was concluded . . . a sturdy Englishman . . . said in the House of Commons that, if King William could know the terms of that treaty, he would turn in his coffin! Let me commend this saying . . . to any persons who shall meet at Nashville for the purpose of concerting measures for the overthrow of this Union over the bones of Andrew Jackson!"

During the debate which followed, Senator Douglas, already, though but thirty-seven years of age, one of the most commanding figures in the Democratic party, urged what Clay and Webster, the leading Whigs, had urged, the right of a territory, when applying for statehood, to exclude slavery if it so desired. He declared, furthermore, as plainly as later in his debates with Lincoln, the doctrine of unfriendly legislation; namely, that if a territorial legislature did not want slavery, it would simply neglect to make laws for the protection of slavery, and thus bar its entrance. He considered that the discussion of slavery extension was designed by politicians for partisan purposes, being purely academic, and unimportant, as it was his opinion that slavery could not find permanent footing in any of the seventeen states which he thought would emerge from the territory west of the Mississippi, "whether Congress shall prohibit slavery or not."

Davis countered with a resolution, "That nothing herein contained shall be construed so as to prevent said territorial legislature from passing such laws as may be necessary for the protection of the rights of property of every kind, which may have been, or may be hereafter, conformably to the Constitution and laws of the United States, held in or introduced into said territory," which resolution was rejected on June 5th by 30 to 25.

There were many other notable speeches during the debate, but the one which struck the deepest note was that of Senator William H. Seward of New York on March 11, 1850. Impatiently he brushed aside all legalistic arguments, and, with the words "There is a higher law than the Constitution," declared the moral law supreme. He pronounced the fugitive-slave clause of the Constitution invalid, as against the law of nations and the law of nature. He proclaimed the nation's right in the common domain, the right to form governments "for the security, welfare, and happiness of all who live under its protection," and denounced the opinion of the Supreme Court which, in the Prigg case, had sustained the fugitive-slave law, as "unjust, unconstitutional, and immoral."

Human beings suffer, and the world suffers in consequence, from any local complex. But Seward's "higher law" transcended all localism, all technical legalism, and declared in effect that laws can never invalidate "the Law." What is right must prevail over laws meant to shelter what is wrong.

The press, northern as well as southern, generally repudiated this attitude, and Mr. Justice McLean of the Supreme Court denounced it as "utterly destructive of all law." Even Clay and Webster ridiculed it, but none or all of them were strong enough to arrest it. In spite of opposition, it began to organize its battalions for the destruction of slavery, and Seward became at once the leader of the hosts opposed to both slavery and slave-extension.

These debates furthermore made clear the fact that vested interests had already changed what had been generally regarded as a voluntary Union, into a Federal Union, one and divisible only by force. Calhoun's failing voice, and Davis' rising one, might claim that each state was a sovereign unit, free to remain or to depart, in peace: but vested interests had already made peaceful secession impossible. "The peaceable separation of the states," said General Shields, Senator from Illinois, ". . . would be war. . . . Does any man suppose that the great northwest . . . will ever peaceably submit to see the mouth of the Mississippi River in the possession of a foreign government?" A rhetorical question, but one expressive of a truth. In all unions, it will always be true that peaceful secession will only be permitted until the time when its operation will destroy dominant, vital interests. Then will pass again the era of peaceful secession, as it had passed in America by 1850. Today, any nation may peaceably secede from the League of Nations, and some have done so; but once make the League a power, upon the maintenance of whose integrity vital interests of the majority of the member states are thought to depend, and the day of peaceable secession will be a thing of the past. A very few men in history have stood ready to fight for an abstract ideal; but all men, consciously or unconsciously, advance abstractions to justify them in fighting for what they want. The arguments upon the divine origin and sanctions of slavery came to the South with a new force after the cotton-gin; and even Webster's noble vision of "Liberty and Union, now and for ever, one and inseparable," was born after New England's interests in the Union had grown stronger than in the days of the Essex Junto, or the Hartford Convention, when nullification was her creed, and his own eloquent voice was raised in its favour.

Whatever else they had done, Clay's proposals had emphasized a new principle of action with respect to territories. Under the older system, as exemplified by the Ordinance of 1787, and the Missouri Compromise of 1820, Congress had decided by enactment where slavery should be allowed and where refused. But, by these proposals, the inhabitants of territories were to be free to decide the question. The change was the opening of Pandora's box, and the escape of Popular Sovereignty.

On the day following Webster's famous 7th of March speech, Davis had quoted himself as follows: "I stated . . . that, as there were two great antagonistic principles in this country, the one claiming that slavery shall be excluded from all the territories, and the other contending that slaveholders have a right to go with their property into all the territories . . . these two conflicting principles could not be reconciled," which statement meant just what Seward meant when later he spoke of the "irrepressible conflict," and what Helper meant when he entitled his epoch-making book, *The Impending Crisis:* and it is clear to any fair-minded student who examines the voluminous speeches of Davis that he no more desired that impending crisis to eventuate in secession and civil war than did either Seward or Helper. To him, then and later, secession was never desired, never "plotted," only accepted in the end as the alternative to what he considered majority exploitation of the minority. On June 27, 1850, he declared: "If I have a superstition which governs my mind and holds it captive, it is a superstitious reverence for the Union. . . . God forbid that the day should ever come when to be true to my constituents is to be hostile to the Union." But, "if there is a dominant party in this Union which can deny to us equality . . . this would be a central government raised on the destruction of all the principles of the Constitution: and the first, the highest obligation of every man who has sworn to support that Constitution would be resistance to such usurpation. . . . If, when thus fully warranted, they want a standard-bearer, in default of a better, I am at their command."

At this declaration, Davis' colleague, Senator Foote, rose and declared, "If the State of Mississippi should, under present circumstances, assume such a position, . . . whoever might hold the banner, I would not fight under it."

Davis replied, "I have no purpose now or at any other time to announce upon what I am ready to go to the ultimate resort of disunion. I have not spoken of disunion to the Senate . . . and whilst I hold a seat here, I shall make no such proposition. I shall never call on Mississippi to secede from the Union, but will remember that I am her representative on the floor of the Senate . . . and I shall ever leave it to her to judge how long she may require my services here, and when she may need them in a different field . . . I have nothing to say about disunion." He had said enough, however, to justify the belief that persistence along the lines laid down by Clay's compromise proposals would cause him to approve, if not to suggest, secession on the part of his sovereign state.

Conscious that his enemies interpreted his fight against centralized government as an effort to make the slaves' fetters everlasting, Davis protested, time and again, that he had no such desire. "There is," he said, "no policy which would perpetuate and rivet the institution for ever on this country so surely as that which confines the slaves to the present limits in which they are held. There must—to render emancipation practicable—be a door opened by which they may go out; and that door must be towards the equator. All who understand their habits and constitutional peculiarities, must admit this. And yet, the policy is here advocated, day after day, by those who claim to be the peculiar friends of emancipation, to draw around us a barrier to prevent the exodus of the slaves, and dam them up in the small territory which they occupy, where, increasing in numbers year by year, the impossibility of emancipation will augment also, until he only can deny that the system must be perpetual, who is prepared to see the slave become the master, to convert a portion of the states of this Union into negro possessions, or, to witness the more probable result, of their extermination by a servile war."

Towards the middle of April, Davis saw signs of a movement to postpone the Nashville convention, the purpose of which Webster had seemed to question in his 7th of March speech, but which he himself still enthusiastically advocated, as a movement towards peace and sectional accord. Out of sixty newspapers published in the ten slaveholding states, Mr. Rhodes calculated that not more than fifteen gave it decided support, at the end of March. Only in South Carolina and Mississippi remained any genuine enthusiasm for the plan. This alarmed Davis, and, on April 13th he wrote to F. H. Elmore: "My own view is, that the convention should meet for preventive purposes: that it is necessary to begin an organization of the South, the want of which has left us a divided people, when union and co-intelligence were necessary for our safety. The charge which has been made of a design to sever the Southern states from the confederacy has but increased the propriety of meeting. If we had no other purpose than to redress past wrongs it would be proper to wait . . . but to check aggression, to preserve the Union, peaceably, to secure our rights, requires prompt action. . . . A postponement is in my opinion equivalent to abandonment of the Southern convention and to being hereafter branded as disunionists who were arrested in their purpose."

Despite defections, under the spur of such charges, Mississippi continued to push the plans for the Nashville convention, since Davis' views were their views, and in state-wide convention, early in May, declared: "The Union must and will be preserved. The slave states, in resisting . . . usurpations of the Federal Government, are defending the Constitution and the Union." To that end, it urged a "regularly constituted convention of all the assailed states . . . to provide for their separate welfare by the formation of a compact and a union that will afford protection to their liberties and rights."

To protect these rights it declared: "It is the duty of . . . Congress . . . to provide the means of enforcing in said territories the guarantees of the Constitution of the United States in reference to the property of the citizens of any of the states removing to any of the said territories with the same, without distinction or limitation." These words present in essence the later famous doctrine of Congressional protection of slavery in the territories, which split the Democratic party and made possible the election of Abraham Lincoln.

In presenting these resolutions to the Senate, on May 8th, Davis explained that the ideas which they contained, including the idea of Congressional protection for slavery in the territories, probably originated in "the proceedings of the popular meeting which preceded" their adoption by the Mississippi legislature, and added that he fully accepted them. "Congress," he declared, "has failed to exercise what is an official, a moral, a Constitutional obligation. . . . And why? . . . because the power of fanaticism has interfered with our legislation; its influence has been sufficient to control the action of Congress. We have been unable to legislate, unless in accordance with the demands of the anti-slavery party. . . . Some have proposed to escape from this responsibility by allowing immigrants, drawn from all countries by the attractive force of gold . . . to execute those powers which it was the duty of the Federal Government in part to have exercised, and in the whole to have preserved as the property of the states, until surrendered on their part by competent authority. When we received the territory into the United States it was the acquisition of the states, and ours the obligation to secure it for the common benefit and to the common use: that we have failed to perform. There was a right in every citizen of the United States to go into that territory and to find for his property the protection of the law and the Constitution . . . that has been denied —denied for the express purpose of stripping the people of the South of the advantages which even the declaration that the Constitution extended to the territory would have given to the slaveholders. . . . Congress has thus indirectly done that which it has not dared directly to do. It has . . . excluded slaveholders from going with their property into the territories as effectively as it could have done by the odious, abandoned Wilmot Proviso. Need we graver or other causes of complaint to justify a Southern convention?"

On July 18th Davis presented to the Senate the proposition of the Nashville convention, "to divide the territory [of California] by the parallel of 36° 30′, with the right to carry slaves below that line." "We claim that the Federal Government shall provide means of enforcing our Constitutional rights, of protecting us in our property . . . within those territories to which the states have surrendered the control to the central government. This is not begging the Federal Government to come to the protection of the states. This is not inviting the Federal Government to infringe the limits of sovereign states; but demanding that she should perform those functions which have been confided to her in regions from which the states have withdrawn their right of control." In the end, the recommendations of the convention were rejected, and Davis observed that another effort at conciliation had failed.

It now seemed likely that Clay's compromise proposals, so long and so bitterly opposed by Davis and his Southern supporters, would suffer a similar fate, as President Taylor, feeling that California had a right to prompt admission with the Constitution which she had chosen, was proving an unexpectedly strong opponent. Had he lived, the compromise might have been defeated; but, on July 9th, Taylor died, and on the day of the funeral Clay wrote with ill-concealed satisfaction "today will witness the funeral ceremonies of General Taylor. . . . I think the event . . . will favour the passage of the compromise bill"— now called the "omnibus" bill, which had been constructed with the hope that, in this combination Clay's measures could be carried.

During the debates on the omnibus bill, Davis persistently urged the extension of the line 36° 30′ to the Pacific coast, as his ultimatum, the ultimatum of his constituents, and of the Nashville convention.

By August, the omnibus bill had been so denuded of provisions, that only the one providing a territorial government for Utah remained to be enacted into law. Clay's compromise proposals had been beaten, and Davis pointed with pride to his part in their defeat. Clay, however, deplored the ruin of his efforts to calm the country by compromises which he declared, "would have harmonized . . . all discordant feelings which prevail." Ill and discouraged, he left Washington, on August 2nd, in the hope that a brief visit to Newport would improve his physical condition. Here, he eagerly watched the vigorous efforts of his followers at the Capitol, who were bringing forward the defeated measures of the omnibus bill as separate bills, and were pressing them upon the Senate. Soon all of them passed that body but Davis still hoped that they could be beaten in the House. On August 15th, he reproved the Southern Senators who had failed to resist them, with the words: "The representatives of the Southern states here have but poor encouragement to struggle for what they believe to be the rights of their constituents; and can have but small hope of maintaining them when the greatest opposition comes from those representing the same interest as themselves. Our friends from the slaveholding states, if they did not choose to act with us, might at least have had the grace to keep their seats and let us have a fair, though unequal, contest with the Northern majority, known to be against us. . . . A common cause might have claimed toleration, if not favour. But, instead, their voices have been the first to be raised in opposition; have rung loudest in the conflict. . . . The South can never get her rights until represented by those who will unite in maintaining them. If she had been so represented at this session, we had friends from the non-slaveholding states who would have joined in giving us that to which we are entitled. I am weary of the complaint of the friends of the so-called compromise bill, this eternal wailing after its death, like Rachel weeping for her children, and would not be comforted because they were not. That measure met with the doom which I thought it deserved. I glory in being one of those who inflicted death upon it. . . ."

Senator Downs here interrupted to say: "The gentleman rejoices and takes great credit to himself for having assisted effectively in destroying the compromise bill. It seems to me that the exaltation of my friend is a little out of date. It might have been very well ten days ago. But I cannot for the life of me see how it has much application now, inasmuch as every single feature of the compromise bill, with no alteration, has obtained the sanction of the Senate."

The bills, however, had not passed the House, and shortly after this speech was delivered, Clay reappeared in the Senate, determined to devote his remaining strength to their passage through that body, and before September 30th, they had been enacted into laws. His compromise of 1850 was to have its trial, after all.

While stilling strife for a time, however, the compromise contained the seed of yet more bitter strife, as any state, formed from the newly acquired territory, might now decide for itself whether slavery should be allowed. Furthermore, California's two free-soil Senators would lessen the Senate majority of which Davis had boasted before the Mississippi legislature. So much was clear as soon as the bills were signed, and though few statesmen of the period marked the fact that determination by act of Congress is a principle at variance with determination by act of settlers (popular sovereignty), the conflict of these two principles dominated American politics for the next ten years.

From the moment when Mason of Virginia introduced the new fugitive-slave bill, to the moment when it became a law by Fillmore's signature, Davis had consistently sought to improve its provisions, believing that the methods of capture and adjudication which it provided were unworkable, with Northern sentiment. "Are the inhabitants of a city" [in which a fugitive slave has been captured], he asked, on August 19, 1850, "the best judges whether he is a slave, or the inhabitants of the place whence he is said to have fled? Let him be taken to the neighbourhood from which he is said to have escaped, and who is there who does not know whether he is a fugitive slave or not?" And he added, with a confidence not shared by his Northern hearers, "It is but justice to the South to say that in no community could stronger feelings exist than would be found there against him who would kidnap a freeman for the purpose of making him a slave."

He was, from the first, of the opinion that the regulations for the capture and trial of fugitive slaves tempted and would be met by nullification, which he disapproved as an illegal conception, equivalent to retirement from the Union, but without the sanctions possessed by the theory of secession. "I deny," he said in the Senate on February 24, 1851, "the power of Massachusetts to nullify the law and remain in the Union, but I concede to her the right . . . to retire from the Union—to take the 'extreme medicine,' secession." "If she has resolved to cast off the obligation of the Constitution . . . then she is, of her own free will and sovereign act, virtually out of it. I, for one, will never give a dollar to coerce her back." This prophecy of the nullification of the fugitive-slave law was the more confident as Davis knew, and indeed everyone knew, that it had been applied to its predecessor of 1793, as it was later applied by the people of the United States to the Eighteenth Amendment.

The few Northerners who had supported the South's demand for a more efficient fugitive-slave law soon felt the power of Northern sentiment. Webster was subjected to gross insult at the hands of his indignant constituents. Wendell Phillips said, "Nature has provided you a monster like Webster," you should "exhibit him—himself a whole menagerie—throughout the country." The legislature of Massachusetts named him, "the recreant son": and his fellow Whig Senators from New England shunned him as a man unclean. Horace Mann described him as "a fallen star, Lucifer descending from Heaven." Theodore Parker, in a speech in Faneuil Hall, compared him to Benedict Arnold after his betrayal of West Point. Garrison's *Liberator* referred to his defence of Clay's compromise measures as "the late Satanic speech of Daniel Webster." And Whittier pilloried him in "Ichabod," which was read to the House of Representatives on August 23, 1852:

> "So fallen! so lost! the light withdrawn
>   Which once he wore!
> The glory from his grey hairs gone
>   For evermore!
>
>   .   .   .   .   .
>
> "Let not the land once proud of him
>   Insult him now,
> Nor brand with deeper shame his dim,
>   Dishonoured brow.
>
> "But let its humbled sons, instead,
>   From sea to lake,
> A long lament, as for the dead,
>   In sadness make.

"Of all we loved and honoured, naught
　　Save power remains;
A fallen angel's pride of thought,
　　Still strong in chains.

"All else is gone; from those great eyes
　　The soul has fled:
When faith is lost, when honour dies,
　　The man is dead."

·　　·　　·　　·　　·

Davis, though not satisfied with the law, had voted for it, much to the satisfaction of the South. In his new capacity of Southern leader in the Senate, he laboured in vain to prevent California's two Senators, William M. Gwin and John C. Frémont, from taking their seats by questioning their credentials, and insisting that they "be referred to the Committee on the Judiciary." In debating the question of the abolition of the slave trade in the District of Columbia, "the only measure which the 'Compromise' Committee originated," according to him, he scornfully repudiated the picture, so often drawn, of gangs of manacled slaves bound for "slave pens" within the District. "I have never seen anything of the kind during the various sessions I have served here," he said. "I have asked some of the oldest inhabitants of the District if they had ever seen a gang of slaves passing manacled through the streets, and they have all answered me, 'No.'" He attempted no defence of slave-traders, "usually Northern men who come among us but are not of us"; but insisted that the law was an attempt "by one long stride to pass the barriers of the Constitution and cater to an anti-slavery feeling by tramping upon Constitutional rights in a species of property against which the Government seems now to be arrayed."

That his constituents approved Davis' position on the great issues of the day was shown, at this point, by a movement to elect him to succeed himself in the Senate, but to make assurance doubly sure, eight of his "Brierfield" neighbours published in the *Woodville Republican* the following questions, which Davis was asked to answer:

"1st—Are you in favour of dissolution of the Union now or hereafter, because of the legislation of the late session of Congress?

"2nd—Are you in favour of the establishment of a Southern Confederacy, now or hereafter, because of the late session of Congress?

"3rd—Are you in favour of a secession of the State of Mississippi from the Union, now or *hereafter* because of the legislation of the late session of Congress?

"4th—Are you in favour of resistance, of any and what kind, to the recent acts of Congress? If so, please state the character, the manner and time of such resistance."

Davis' reply, printed in the *Mississippi Free Trader*, was unequivocal: I. "If any have, falsely and against the evidences before them, attempted to fix on me the charge of wishing to dissolve the Union, under existing circumstances, I am sure your information and intelligence has enabled you to detect the shallow fraud." II. "If any have represented me as seeking to establish a Southern Confederacy . . . my whole life, and every sentiment I have ever uttered . . . gives them the lie." III. "If any have supposed, gratuitously (they could not otherwise), that my efforts in the Senate were directed to the secession of Mississippi from the Union, their hearts must have been insensible to the obligations of honour, and good faith which I feel are imposed upon me, by the position of an accredited agent from Mississippi, to the Federal Government.

"Your fourth question, therefore, is the only one which I feel you could have addressed to me, as your Representative, for any other kind of purpose, than to give me an opportunity thus summarily to dispose of baseless slanders." To that fourth question, as to whether he was in favour of resistance to the recent acts of Congress, he replied that the South should stand firmly upon her ancient constitutional rights . . . and should be prepared "to go out of the Union, with the Constitution, rather than abandon the Constitution, to remain in *an* Union." The result was his election, followed on December 30th, by Governor Quitman's approval of a resolution of the Mississippi legislature, commending his course and that of Congressmen Brown, McWillie, Featherston, and Thompson, "in their firm and consistent support, and able advocacy of the rights and honour of Mississippi and the South, in all the questions before Congress at its late session involved in the slave controversy," and highly disapproving that of the other Senator, Henry S. Foote.

On the 4th of March, 1851, Davis took the oath prescribed, and looked forward to six more years of service as Senator. From that day to the following September he was extremely active, speaking often upon the floor of the Senate, and highly content with a career in which he had won distinction and which he preferred to all others. Already the facts had confirmed his prophesies regarding the failure of the fugitive-slave law. The protests with which the North had greeted its passage had merged into action. The first arrest under the law had been made in New York, where a negro who had resided there for two years, apparently a freedman, was seized and carried to Baltimore. A purse had been raised and his freedom purchased. In Boston, in February 1851, a negro named Shadrach was imprisoned to await a hearing before the Commissioner: but the men of Boston defied both laws and police, and Shadrach, rescued by a mob which forced its way into his prison, was now safe in Canada. The alarming fact in these and other cases was that public opinion in the North seemed disposed to justify such methods of practical nullification. This angered Davis, who consistently held that nullification by a state was a violation of the very basis of sound government, and even President Fillmore's special message, which declared that he would compel obedience to the hated law, did not encourage him to hope that it would be observed; for he well knew that north of Mason's and Dixon's line the fugitive law had not public opinion behind it. Charles Sumner had been right when he had declared, in Faneuil Hall, "the public conscience will not allow a man who has trodden our streets as a free man, to be dragged away as a slave," and his subsequent election to the Senate had been a demonstration of the fact that he had spoken the mind of his constituents.

Since the law had come into existence, the number of fugitive slaves had considerably decreased: but Davis knew that the determination to protect them when once within the anti-slavery states had increased. He believed, as the historian, Rhodes, later believed, that the purpose of the law, in so far as the North had been responsible for it, was not so much to recover runaway negroes as to further irritate anti-slavery sentiment. And he could not close his eyes to the fact that, if this were its purpose, the law had done its work well.

To a man of Davis' convictions, such a situation seemed to offer a chance for effective work in the Senate. He knew that with the passing of Calhoun had passed a leader capable of defending the Union as it was, a union of sovereign states. He knew also that the eyes of the South had turned to him as Calhoun's successor.

At this point, however, came a call from Mississippi, an unwelcome call, since it involved resignation from the Senate and enlistment in the narrower field of state politics. Governor Quitman, "a man . . . grown old in honourable service, civil and military, and whose grey hairs had brought him accumulated honour," to quote Davis' description, had been "dragged from the duties of his station to answer the charge of aiding and abetting," the famous first Lopez expedition to Cuba, in 1850. In accordance with the dignity of his office, Quitman had resigned the governorship, being "unwilling to cause a possible collision between the state and the Federal Government in a case in which I am personally concerned." After his acquittal, some of the Democrats of Mississippi, Davis among them, had attempted to restore him to his post by making him again their candidate for Governor. Opposition within the convention, upon the ground that his nomination might fix upon the party the imputation of being a party of disunion had, however, rendered success doubtful, and an attempt had been made to persuade him to withdraw his name, and allow Davis to become the candidate, thus leaving vacant a place in the Senate to which General Quitman could be appointed.

Although preferring to continue in the Senate, Davis declared that he would accept the nomination, if his state wished, but only upon the understanding that Quitman should himself decide whether he would continue the fight. Quitman preferred to fight, and Davis at once joined actively in the campaign for his election. His opponent was Davis' detestation, ex-Senator Foote, who, although a Whig, was running upon a Unionist ticket, the Unionists, as a caustic observer declared, having taken the Foote of one party and made it the head of another. As the campaign progressed, Foote attacked Quitman so bitterly that the latter resigned his nomination.

Before the committee whose duty it was to fill the vacancy had time to act, the sentiment in favour of Davis was seen to be so strong that the chairman notified him that he had been nominated "by the people and the Democratic press of the whole state." This notification was brought to him while he was confined to his room by the condition of his left eye, which he eventually lost, and he answered at once: "It is not in an hour when clouds have darkened our fortune that I can refuse any poor service . . . still in my power to render." A few days later he resigned his seat in the Senate with the statement: "If elected [Governor] . . . I must necessarily vacate [the Senatorship]; if not elected, I should view it as such an evidence of the disapprobation of my public course by my constituents, as would require me to return to them the trust which has been confided to me."

The campaign, bitter before Quitman resigned, now grew more bitter. Davis was accused of having supported Cass in 1848, with the knowledge that the latter's Nicholson letter was meant to deceive the South, which groundless charge, combined with the burden of carrying the banner forced from the hands of Quitman, and the fact of his physical inability to carry on a vigorous campaign, rendered the verdict unquestioned from the first. He was defeated, but he had reduced the Union majority from 7,500 to 999; and enthusiasts were already elevating him to presidential possibilities. Even Foote's supporters, wrote one enthusiast, "are now for you for President. You are emphatically the head and front of the Democracy in this state and the whole South, without a rival."

To Davis, his defeat was a humiliation. Having declared that he would understand it as proof of disapprobation of his public career, he found no consolation in the fact that it had been only a slight defeat. He retired to "Brierfield" and devoted himself to its cultivation, until early in 1852, when he again left its seclusion to address the Mississippi Democratic convention, in the Presidential campaign of that year. He referred to his late defeat, in the words: "Fraud and falsehood, and Free Soil and Foote, and Fillmore have triumphed in Mississippi, but success thus acquired must be as temporary as its means were corrupt." Ardently, passionately, at times with eloquence, he pleaded with his fellow Democrats not again to be decoyed from their natural allegiance, by any alliance which treacherous Whigs might offer. "Who obstructed the prosecution of the war with Mexico?" he scornfully asked. ". . . Who burnt blue lights along the coast of New England in the War of 1812? Who nullified the recent law passed to carry the Constitution into effect? Was it your old friends, or new allies?" Boldly he proclaimed sympathy with Americans who had adventured with Lopez for the freedom of Cuba from the unbearable tyranny of Spain. "They went on such mission as brought La Fayette, Kosciusko, De Kalb, and a host of others to the aid of our fathers . . . ; and the President marked their devotion by a proclamation which branded them as pirates." "A gallant band of these brave youths, disappointed in the hopes and expectations which had induced them to land on the island of Cuba, abandoned the expedition and started for the United States. They were captured in open boats, upon the open sea, and, without the trial to which they were entitled, condemned as pirates to an ignominious death."

This denunciation of the President and his associates was well calculated to stir the pulse of his Mississippi hearers, and when he had finished, many were ready to revise the opinion that Jefferson Davis' sun had set for ever.

On May 1, 1852, the *Southern Standard* of Columbus, Mississippi, published a letter from Commodore Stockton in answer to a proposition advanced by John A. Whetstone and others, that the Democratic ticket for President and Vice-President, soon to be named, should read, "Stockton and Davis." "I entertain great respect for the character and public services of Colonel Jefferson Davis," it read, "and would feel honoured by being associated with him at any post to which the suffrages of the people might call us." But the call came not to them. The Democrats finding that no one of their four chief leaders, Cass, Buchanan, Douglas, or Marcy, could command the necessary two-thirds of the Baltimore convention, turned to Pierce as their dark horse; and selected King as his running mate. From the point of view of previous service, personal ability, or widespread popularity, it was a weak ticket: but the Whigs proceeded to make it strong by nominating General Winfield Scott, Davis' pet abhorrence, and Wm. A. Graham.

Both parties accepted the compromise of 1850 as a finality, and faced the country upon less important issues, chief of which was the personality of the candidates. Scott's personality was a doubtful asset, for, as was once said of another candidate, "his friends did not like him." Pierce was personally agreeable, but politically obscure, and Webster remarked that after the election the Whig party would be known only in history.

But Pierce and Davis were upon terms of close personal friendship, and it was with real enthusiasm that the latter volunteered his support in the campaign, declaring that with Pierce the Democrats could regain the Presidency. The result proved the soundness of this prophecy. Pierce received 254 votes to 42 for Scott, who was deserted by the Southern Whigs as not enough of a compromise man.

Although this election carried into the White House one of the least distinguished of American Presidents, the victory itself was one of the most important in American history, as it left the Free Soil party shattered beyond recovery, and carried Stephen A. Douglas back into the Senate, with presidential aspirations intensified. Chief of all its results, it marked the emergence of sectional parties which have lasted to the present day.

On December 7, 1852, Pierce, now President-elect, wrote to Davis, "I am not permitted to know that you would accept a place . . . and I do not ask an interview on the ground that I have arrived at a fixed conclusion upon the subject, but, because I wish to talk with you as a friend." Davis consented to "talk as a friend," but when offered the post of Secretary of War, at first declined upon personal grounds. Pressure from the President, persuasion from other friends, and a sense of fitness for the task of the office prevailed, however, and he accepted.

CHAPTER VIII

SECRETARY OF WAR

LIKE Turgot in France, or Hamilton and Calhoun in America, Davis entered executive office, a lover of abstract theory, and like them he proved in office that this quality may exist side by side with a high degree of executive efficiency. In debate he was bold, direct, and controlled more by knowledge than by sentiment; in administration, frank, open, and fearless. He early announced his intention to keep the military branch of the Government free from political influences, in spite of the many Democratic Senators and Congressmen who wished to pay campaign debts with official positions. The army and many influential civilians also had "deserving Democrats" for whom they desired posts, and Democratic machine men felt that such as received them should contribute to the party chest. With this policy the Secretary of War was not in accord, as shown by the following letter:

(Unofficial)

War Dept. *Oct. 17, 1853*

My dear Sir,

I have received your letter of the 13th inst. in relation to the attempt made by certain political committees in Philadelphia to levy assessments upon the salaries of the clerks in the Department of the service under your charge.

I entirely approve of the course you have taken in the matter by refusing to allow your clerks to submit to the imposition of this tax. Their salaries are paid to them for a different purpose—

and ought not to be subject to a diminution by a forced contribution.

It is my desire to keep the military branch of the government free from political influences—and your employees need have no apprehension that they will suffer in my estimation from unfriendly reports of their conduct in failing to comply with the requisitions of political committees.

Yours truly & Respectfully

JEFF'N. DAVIS

Maj. G. H. Crosman.

From the pen of Carl Schurz we have the following description of Davis as he saw him upon a visit to the War Department at the beginning of his term:

"His slender, tall and erect figure, his spare face, keen eyes, and fine forehead, not broad but high and well shaped, presented the well-known strong American type. There was in his bearing a dignity which seemed entirely natural and unaffected, that kind of dignity which does not invite familiar approach."

James Campbell, Pierce's Postmaster-General, draws an equally pleasing picture: "I know that Jefferson Davis is not popularly known as a socially genial man, but he was, as I came to know him. . . . He was very quiet and domestic in his habits, correct in his private life, and exceedingly temperate in both eating and drinking. These abstemious habits he must have kept up all his life, or he could never have lived to be eighty-one years of age. . . . [He] was the best educated man whom I ever came in contact with. His acquirements were broad and often surprised us. . . . He was famous for his retentive memory and the extent and range of his knowledge that was encyclopædic. . . . On one occasion we were talking about a certain medicine—Mr. Davis went into a minute analysis and scientific description of its nature and effects. . . . I asked . . . 'where did you learn all that?' 'Judge,' he replied, 'you forget that I had to learn something of medicine to take care of the negroes on my plantation.'" And Senator Sumner said of him: "No one ever yet has found his judgment and taste at fault." He never lost his interest in Greek and Latin, and spoke several modern languages with ease if not exactitude. Mrs. Hezekiah Sturges, herself half German, tells of a dinner party at which Mr. Davis discussed the military history of the Mexican War with "a distinguished German army officer . . . in the stranger's own language," and told amusing stories of Santa Anna "in the Mexican patois." French he spoke also, though so imperfectly that, when he visited France in the days following the war, the papers declared: "he stumbles much in our language."

The post of Secretary of War demanded no great qualities, and offered no opportunities for proving their possession. But Ingersoll, in his history of the War Department, states that Davis conducted it "with notable success, and with great acceptability to the army." Later propaganda depicted him as using the office for treasonable plots, which charge Ingersoll dismisses with the curt sentence: "Whatever faults Mr. Davis had to answer for, this is not one of them," a statement which President Pierce supported, in the words: "If treachery had come near him, it would have stood abashed in the presence of his truth, his manliness, and his confiding simplicity."

Among his routine duties were making estimates for constructing a system of water supply for Washington and Georgetown; for the extension of the capital toward the east; plans for wars against Indian tribes who refused to be bound by treaties; reforms in the military machines of destruction; and the enlargement of the Nation's fighting force. Another task, the plans for which had been bequeathed to him from the Fillmore administration, was the building of a bridge over Cabin John Creek, near Washington, later described as one of the largest spans in stone which the world had seen. The work was begun under Davis, and when it was finished in 1861, his name was quite properly inscribed on the tablet which read:

WASHINGTON AQUEDUCT
Begun A. D. 1853
President of the United States
Franklin Pierce
Secretary of War, Jefferson Davis
Building A. D. 1861
President of the United States
Abraham Lincoln
Secretary of War, Simon Cameron

In 1862, when the passions of war were at their zenith, Caleb B. Smith being then Secretary of the Interior, some one, said to have been acting by his orders, chiseled out Davis' name. When Lincoln was informed of this action, which has never been actually traced to his Cabinet Councillor, Smith, he expressed disapproval, but the tablet remained defaced. At the end of the war, the Daughters of the Confederacy erected the demand for the restoration of Davis' name into what was very nearly a crusade, but still nothing was done until Theodore Roosevelt, who in 1885 had coupled Davis' name with that of Benedict Arnold, and who had unjustly branded him as the father of repudiation in Mississippi, took the responsibility, as President of the United States, of ordering that his name be reinscribed upon the tablet of Cabin John Bridge, an order which was executed in 1909.

But of all the tasks which Davis accomplished as Secretary of War perhaps the most important was a series of reconnaissances of routes for the construction of railways to the Pacific coast. Detailed plans were made for no less than four such routes between the years 1853 and 1856, and the skill shown in the work is evidenced by the fact that they correspond, approximately, to the lines since actually built, with governmental assistance, namely, the Southern Pacific, the Kansas Pacific, the Union Pacific and the Northern Pacific. Ingersoll, in his *History of the War Department*, describes the work done in preparing for these roads as, "the most valuable contribution to commerce and to science that had ever been prepared from actual surveys and reconnaissance in the field," and it is significant that Davis supported his recommendations for railway extension upon the ground of "the need of safe and rapid communication with the Pacific slope, to secure its continuance as part of the Union." Among his earliest selections for this work was the gifted young Captain George B. McClellan; destined to become one of his own most formidable opponents.

Davis' determined efforts to keep party politics out of his department did not prevent his close watch upon political developments in Mississippi, where Foote, now Governor, was making plans to return to the Senate. The letters which arrived were eagerly read, some of them not without difficulty, as the following example will show:

> "Tatesville Desoto Miss
> *July 10, 1853.*

". . . as politics is Be coming som what acsited in my county I feel ansious for you to Be in formed of som of the planes plans and skeams of Gov⁰ʳ Foot. he has Bin with the people at hernando and at last has gotten up considerable excitement, I, was in formed a few Days ago By a Whig who was a mem Ber last session from this County that foot Says that he never intends to Sleep a hole night So help him god until he Slays Davis, Brown & McRay, this conversation he had privitly he alsoses that if he is Ellected to the U. S Sinet that he can have influence anof with Presi Dent Peirce to hav a new cabinet mad ther's menny other things I could in form you of though noing that you have menny friends that is fully competant to keep you fully acquainted with the sines of times in our State, this you can keep to your Self hoping that you may not take no of fence at me for addressing you those few lines if we ar not personly acquainted I give you this for what it may Be worth to you wishing you Success in all your

under takings &c I predict from the present that we ar going to
have quit a warme an election this fall. Yours & C.

J. Mitchell"

Endorsed
    Important
    about Mi. politics
    In De Soto County.

One wonders much about this letter; chiefly, perhaps, where
Mr. Mitchell had learned to spell; but condemnation of Governor
Foote was pleasing in any orthography; and warning concern-
ing his wiles most welcome.

About the middle of July, 1853, Pierce, with certain members
of the Cabinet, made a whirlwind tour northward, stopping at
various points to receive the applause of assembled multitudes.
As a leading Cabinet official, Davis spoke frequently on the trip,
touching always upon some point of history which would appeal
to national pride, and to the feeling of state sovereignty, which
he ever kept to the fore. In Delaware, he recalled the fact that
Napoleon had been born in the tiny island of Corsica: and that
Delaware, though small, had "given heroes enough . . . to silence
vain speculation as to the amount of respect due to her," as a
sovereign state. At Trenton, New Jersey, he declared, "well may
you assert your sovereignty as a state, which you notably achieved
when you were but an infant colony"; and warned his hearers
against "the danger . . . of consolidation, centralization, and the
re-establishment of despotism." At Princeton, "ground consecrated
by the Revolution," he invoked the shade of Mercer to "teach a
lesson." At Philadelphia, he painted a picture of "the smoke of
Pennsylvania coal [which] might later be seen on the desert
waste, and beneath the snow-capped mountains [the Rockies],
and of her iron, . . . reaching in long, serpentine tracks to the
slopes of the Pacific." He then stated the reasons why a Democratic administration, strict constructionist in its view of the Con-

stitution, and opposed to internal improvements at national cost, had yet pressed forward the project of binding east and west, ocean and ocean, by a transcontinental railway, justifying such construction upon the ground of national defence, and national unity. With these words, he struck a sympathetic chord in the hearts of Pennsylvanians and the President's manifested approval and assent greatly enhanced the effect of the speech.

On July 19th, the party was entertained at the Crystal Palace, in New York, where an international scientific conference was in session. The occasion called for an address upon international themes, and Davis was asked to furnish it. "I most cordially rejoice," he said, "in the manifestations around me, which seem to indicate an increase of the fraternity of nations. For such must be the effect of bringing together men from every quarter of the civilized globe, to compare with each other what each has been doing for the advancement of science. . . . These are contributions to that bond of peace which will hold men together as one brotherhood. . . . The earth was given to man for his domination. It has been perverted from the great object of the Creator by vice and ignorance of men, who, warring one with another, have forced nations to employ their industry upon things not adapted to their condition, climate, and soil, at the sacrifice of all the loss of time and productiveness which belong to this want of adaptation." A burst of applause interrupted. When it subsided, Davis continued: "Throw open the ports of all the world. Let the civilized nations represented here declare that we are one brotherhood, and that whatever can be produced more cheaply in another country shall be brought thence. Thus we will have a bond of peace that will not be in the power of unwise rulers ever to break." Men had said this before, men have said it since, and are saying it still: but tariff walls rise ever higher and higher, more and more separating men into air-tight compartments, inducing foolish dreams of peace, but breeding wars.

In defending his free-trade theory, Davis pointed out that "free trade was a corner stone in the foundation of our political temple. It was placed there by the hands of sages, philosophers and patriot soldiers. . . . And has it not redounded to the benefit of the American people? You of New York, . . . because belonging to this union of states, have entire free trade with all the states of the Union. This is to you a great blessing. But suppose you had free trade with all the civilized nations of the world, would not your advantages be magnified? . . . I believe that the sun of truth has risen upon the globe, and will, in time, lead man to see . . . that it is for his comfort, and for the peace and salvation of the civilized earth, that there shall be untrammelled, unbroken free trade." This speech shows us a man thinking in terms of the skyline, with visions of "that far-off divine event to which all nations move."

The news which most pleased Davis, upon his return to the War Office, was that Governor Foote had retired from the canvass for Senator, and would leave Mississippi at the end of his term as Governor, to practise law in New Orleans or California, a decision which Davis considered highly advantageous to Mississippi.

On December 1, 1853, Davis sent to the President his first annual report as Secretary of War. Like many which had preceded it, and more which have followed, it is a dreary recital of military details, much needed by the President, no doubt, but of no possible value to the present generation. At intervals, however, there are references to questions of permanent interest. The army at that time, as now, was in charge of many constructive works, such as the improvement of rivers and harbours. The cost of such works was therefore charged to army expenses. Today, the same system of bookkeeping places the United States before the world as spending upon its armies vast sums which have little relation to the actual military budget. Thus Europe is often led to overestimate America's military expenses, greatly to the detriment of the movement for international limitation of armaments. In another section of the report Davis said: "Napoleon when in Egypt used with marked success the dromedary . . . in subduing the Arabs whose habits and country were very similar to those of the mounted Indians of our Western plains. . . . France is about again to adopt the dromedary in Algeria. . . . For like military purposes, for expresses and for reconnaissances, it is believed, the dromedary would supply a want now seriously felt in our service."

Davis had made a most searching investigation of the history of camels in connexion with military activities in many lands and in many periods, and had convinced himself of their adaptability to American problems. A. C. Bancroft records a conversation with Major William B. Lee, who served under Davis in the War Office, and who declared him "a regular bulldog when he formed an opinion, for he would never let go." It was so in this case. In the face of opposition, obstruction, and ridicule he pressed his idea until thirty-four camels were landed at Powder Horn, Texas, on May 14, 1856. Later importations followed, and the experiment was still in progress, and showed promise, when the Civil War cut it short. It was never thereafter revived.

Davis' conclusions upon the question, so conspicuous in later American discussions, of whether the nation should manufacture its own arms, or secure them by contract from private producers are convincingly in favour of the former alternative. "Under a proper administration of a national armory," he said, ". . . arms can be obtained cheaper by government manufacture than by contract. . . . In the case of the private contractor there must be a profit on the manufacture, not only sufficient to cover the interest on the investment, but also the hazard which will attend a contract necessarily made for a short period. . . . Since 1840 the contract price for rifles based on the cost at national armories has been reduced from $14.50 to $11.62½ each, which exceeds the cost of that arm at Harper's Ferry . . . by $1.60." He considered also that the government-made rifle was of higher standard, as to both material and workmanship.

With the explanation that it was not within his province to discuss this question in the light of "political considerations," he passed over in silence a phase of the subject which today (1937) so much occupies the attention of a world seeking methods of reducing armaments, i.e., the lobbying, corruption, and enlistment of the sympathy of a public drawing dividends from investments on private establishments for the manufacture of arms. But, in view of the fact that, by political opinion he was little disposed to favour the introduction of Federal Government into business, his conclusions upon the desirability of the Federal Government's making its own war equipment are highly pertinent to twentieth-century problems.

Late in December Davis was proclaimed by the Democrats of Yazoo County, Mississippi, as their candidate for United States Senator. They gave as their reason his pre-eminent abilities as a statesman, and the fact that he had been defeated in his race for the Governorship by "a caucus, which many of us considered, and do now consider, unjust and unfair." As he had declared two days earlier, in a letter to Stephen Cocke, that he would never "return to public life until called by the people of Mississippi," who had rejected him, this mark of affection and regard deeply gratified him: but the records show no reply, and the matter passed as an act of courtesy on the part of his friends. Apparently at the moment, he was not interested in a return to the Senate, and the reason may perhaps be found in a visit which he made with President Pierce to Fortress Monroe. Mrs. Clay, in *A Belle of the Fifties*, writes:

"At night the fort and the waters beyond were lit up by a pyrotechnic display . . . and enthusiasm rose to its highest when, amid the booming of cannon and the plaudits of happy people, an ingenious device blazed across the sky the names of Franklin Pierce and Jefferson Davis." But if Davis cherished vice-presidential ambitions, he has left no indication of it in his papers.

While making one of the many journeys which the duties of

his office, and his interest in Mississippi politics, made necessary, the Secretary of War had one very unpleasant experience. Accompanied by his private secretary, he boarded a train at Branchville, S. C. The train consisted of an engine and one coach and was bound for Augusta. Its only passengers when the strangers entered were James Noble, his wife and children, who had with them a small trunk, containing, among other things, a considerable sum of money in cash. At the end of the journey the money was missing, and the two strangers were suspected. They were handed over to the police, who released them when convinced of their identity. Mrs. Noble, however, was not easy to convince, and insisted that they must be guilty. The story leaked out, the press took it up, and the Secretary of War suffered embarrassing publicity. In later years the conductor of the train was hanged for a graver crime, and on the scaffold confessed to the robbery.

For the remainder of the year, and the year 1854 which followed, the routine of the War Office apparently consumed all of the Secretary's energies. There is scarcely a political reference in the letters and papers surviving from this period. His second annual report offers no items of general or lasting interest, though occasional references mark the fact that his heart was turning again to the Senate. His friends in Mississippi failed to move effectively in his behalf, however, and he was unwilling to become an active candidate. On January 13, 1855, John J. McRea, the recently elected Governor of Mississippi, wrote: "Your friends," in the late campaign, "had their silent sentiment, but your name was not used as a candidate, while the names of others became familiar with the people, and now, Colonel, if you are not returned to the Senate, as you know I think you ought to be, by this legislature, it will be for this very reason, operating upon many members of the legislature. . . . You know how anxious I was for you . . . to avow your position openly as a candidate. Now see how much you risk, when if you had done so there would be no doubt or danger. . . . One-third of the members of the legislature . . .

did not know that your term in the Cabinet expired the same time that the senatorial term begins. For myself, I have had but one sentiment in reference to your position since you resigned your seat in the Senate and gave your name to us for Governor and that is that you ought to be reinstated."

But Davis was still determined not to re-enter politics until his fellow Mississippians voluntarily summoned him, and in silence saw others take the prize which he coveted. Even Governor McRea's assurance added in a postscript, "Since writing this letter, I have seen Col. Torpley, and he says that I may assure you that you have forty-nine votes certain in the caucus, which gives you a majority of six," failed to draw from him any open announcement of his desire.

An acid test of executive ability is to live in harmony with one's higher subordinates, a test to which Davis at times responded unconvincingly. His term as Secretary of War brought many controversies, the most violent of which was, unfortunately, with the active head of the army, General Winfield Scott. The two had been covertly hostile since Mexican War days, and their new official contact made open controversy inevitable.

There can be no doubt that Scott was a man difficult to deal with. His military record bristles with controversies. As early as 1809, when Davis was only a year old, Scott was court-martialled for remarks about the conduct of a superior officer, and suspended for one year, and his controversy with Trist, at the end of the Mexican War, is one of the curiosities of American history. But his long military career had given him a high place in the nation, and, in 1852, the Whig party had presented him as their presidential candidate. The preceding year, a resolution had been introduced into Congress reviving in his interest the long-lapsed rank of Lieutenant-General, and Davis, as chairman of the Military Committee of the Senate, had offended him by opposing the measure. While this bill awaited its third reading, Scott, according to his own statement, informed Senator Foote who was supporting the measure, that if it should pass, it would involve a handsome addition to the salary which Scott was receiving. Davis later claimed, however, that Foote had told the Senate that Scott's note had stated that the additional pay would not be large, and he quoted the *Congressional Globe*, p. 533, to prove the point. After long delay the bill was passed, on February 15, 1855, Davis having meanwhile become Secretary of War; and Scott then put in a claim for $30,000 back pay, a claim which Davis hotly protested. In a letter to Scott, dated December 30, 1855, Davis reviewed the history of the case, and argued: "Had the grade of Lieutenant-General been *created* anew, no pay would have attached without express provision of law. . . . The necessity for express legislation was avoided by changing the word *'created'* in the original bill to *'revived,'* so as to enable you to claim by construction the pay and allowance which had been attached to that grade when, at a former period, it existed in the army," and added the highly offensive statement, "Here, I think, may be detected the same crafty hand that *sketched* the instructions to the commission of the Cherokee removal." Not content with this, he accused Scott of having also "wrongfully realized an emolument at the expense of the old and crippled soldiers."

Whatever the legal interpretation of this very intricate case—and the letter of the law appears to favour Scott—such an accusation against the head of the army was most unwise, unless he intended to take action, nor do the unbelievably bitter letters of Scott appear to justify the personal retorts of a Secretary of War. To this correspondence, furthermore, Davis devoted an entirely unreasonable amount of energy with no compensating advantage; for Scott continued at his post, and was now added to Andrew Johnson in the list of men who were to make bitter the pathway of Davis' later life, the one as commander of the Federal armies when the first shot was fired at Fort Sumter; the other as

President when Davis was captured and imprisoned at Fortress Monroe after the war.

These matters, while important for the light which they throw upon Davis' character and executive capacity, pale into insignificance in comparison with the great problem of President Pierce's administration, the problem of "Bleeding Kansas," which, emerging out of the uncertainties left by the so-called "Compromise settlements of 1850," was bound to enlist the pro-slavery sympathies of the Secretary of War, who had so ardently opposed those proposals.

When Pierce's administration began on March 4, 1853, all of America's public domain, not included within the territory of any sovereign state, had been divided, apparently finally, between the pro-slavery and the anti-slavery sections of the nation. The line of the Ordinance of 1787, joined by the line of the Missouri Compromise, 36° 30', divided the area into two parts; all territory to the north, with the exception of Missouri, was devoted to freedom; all to the south had been supposed, until 1850, to be open to slavery, though there had been those who disputed its rights, even there. To the North the situation was highly satisfactory. They had control of both houses of Congress; and, with the exception of the small group called "Abolitionists," no one felt it necessary to challenge the generally accepted theory that the sovereign states of the South were free to keep their "peculiar institution," provided they kept it at home. Furthermore, it was evident that, if forced to keep it at home, the slave states would never be able to dominate any state which in future might be formed from the national territories. This would inevitably mean a steady increase of the control which the free states already enjoyed over both houses.

On January 4, 1854, Senator Douglas, as chairman of the Senate Committee on Territories, proposed a plan for organizing Nebraska, a territory, to quote Senator Sumner, "larger than the original thirteen states, vying in extent with all the existing free states . . . only a little smaller . . . than Italy, Spain and France combined." At the time it contained less than 1,000 white inhabitants. In explaining the plan of the committee, Douglas declared that one of the primary purposes of the Compromise of 1850 had been to take from Congress whatever power it had over slavery in the territories, and to give it to the people settled therein. There was nothing novel in this idea. Cass had advanced it in his Nicholson letter. Douglas had himself defended it and Davis had opposed it during the debates on the compromise proposals. Cass and Douglas had called it popular sovereignty, and Davis and his associates had given it the contemptuous name of squatter sovereignty. The Committee of Thirteen had defined it in the words: "The true principle which ought to regulate the action of Congress in forming territorial governments for each newly acquired domain, is to refrain from all legislation on the subject in the territory acquired, so long as it retains the territorial form of government, leaving it to the people of such territory, when they have attained to a condition which entitles them to admission as a state, to decide for themselves the question of the allowance or prohibition of domestic slavery."

The meaning of these words is unmistakable, and it is difficult to believe that Clay's keen mind had failed to see that squatter sovereignty was wholly at variance with the earlier principle of Congressional control of slavery in the territories. His views upon the effect of this inconsistency, however, did not become significant during the brief remainder of his life. But in the hands of Senator Douglas, squatter sovereignty was now shrewdly interpreted as repealing settlements based upon Congressional control.

Cautious at first about disturbing the old Compromise adjustment, but determined to conciliate the South by removing the restrictions upon slavery extension north of 36° 30', Douglas reported his committee as desiring that Nebraska, when admitted as a state, should be received as a free state or a slave state, as its Constitution should provide.

As both parties had, in their platforms of 1852, declared the Compromise settlements of 1850 a finality, it seemed politically safe to assume that Nebraska was to be organized as a territory upon this basis. Douglas, therefore, had chosen an impregnable position, but the pro-slave Senators were not satisfied. They wished the bill to declare that the Compromise of 1850 had in effect repealed the Missouri Compromise of 1820, and thereby obliterated the old line 36° 30', north of which slavery might not go. When this was suggested to him, Douglas had visions of Northern rage, should it be adopted, and of protests from his Free-soil constituency which might endanger his political future. He therefore refused, whereupon Clay's successor, Archibald Dixon, announced that he would offer an amendment to the Nebraska bill, declaring the Missouri Compromise repealed. This would have been to allow Dixon to capture the gratitude of the South, which Douglas was far too keen to permit. He therefore, himself, prepared a substitute for his earlier bill, and sought the help of the administration to pass it. In a memorandum dated Beauvoir, June 13, 1886, Davis adds this item to the story: "Two committees of Congress came to me to obtain for them an interview with President Pierce . . . concerning this Kansas-Nebraska bill. . . . The President knew nothing of the measure until it was explained to him in that . . . interview. Then he gave his assent because it was in conformity with his opinion of the constitutional power of Congress, and because the Missouri Compromise was regarded as virtually repealed by the refusal to recognize its binding force in the division of recently acquired territory in 1850. To this extent, and this *only*, was it an administration measure, and the committees left the President with the ability to say that he concurred in the propriety of the measure."

Davis knew that such a bill would make easier the task of railway-building in the West, in which he was deeply interested, and it is clear from his own statements that he preferred the adjustments offered by the bill to the *status quo*. He declared, in a speech at Portland, on August 28, 1858, that if he had been a member of Congress at the time, he would have voted for the repeal of the Missouri Compromise, on the ground that equality of right demanded that the Government leave the territories open. He denied that Congress had the power to extend slavery into the territories; which meant a denial of its power to exclude slavery from the territories. As Secretary of War, however, he was in no position to press his views, and was content to use his efforts with the President, that the latter's influence might be given to Douglas' new bill.

On January 30, 1854, Douglas took the floor to explain the meaning of his bold proposal. He declared that the Compromise of 1850, based upon popular sovereignty, had repealed the Missouri Compromise, based upon Congressional action. The debate which followed was of unprecedented bitterness. But, despite opposition, strengthened by a flood of protests from individuals, and state governments, it was evident that Douglas had a majority sufficient to pass his bill through the Senate: and when on March 3rd he rose at 11.30 P.M. to close the debate, his words were designed less for his immediate audience than for the members of the House of Representatives and the public. He declared that the object of his bill was not the repeal of the Missouri Compromise, which had already been superseded by the later Compromise of 1850, but to make clear the principle of the latter, now accepted as "a finality" by both parties. That principle, he said, is "that Congress shall neither legislate slavery into any territory or state, nor out of the same, but the people shall be left free to regulate their domestic concerns in their own way, subject only to the Constitution of the United States." Douglas spoke until daybreak; and the vote was then taken, showing 37 Senators in favour of his bill, and 14 against it.

As Chase and Sumner, who had led the opposition, left the Capitol, they heard the firing of cannon, and Chase remarked: "They celebrate a present victory, but the echoes they awake will never rest until slavery itself shall die." And Davis later wrote: "Out of this bill arose a dissension which finally divided the Democratic party and caused its defeat in the presidential election of 1860. And from this empty, baseless theory grew the Iliad of our woes."

In the House of Representatives the debates on the bill continued, at intervals, until May 22nd, when it passed the Committee of the Whole by 113 to 100. Its final passage followed almost immediately, and amid wild applause from the gallery, the Missouri Compromise was repealed so far as the legislature could accomplish it. The votes, which repealed it were made up in part of representatives who held their seats by virtue of the "Federal Ratio" which allowed representation to three-fifths of the slaves, but of course votes to none. If all of these, some twenty in number, had voted in the negative, the Kansas-Nebraska bill, as it was now called (a clause having been inserted separating the region into Kansas and Nebraska), would have failed in the House. Thus, in effect, the slaves had been used to pass a measure allowing them, for the first time since 1820, to be taken by their owners into regions north of 36° 30′.

On May 30, 1854, Pierce's signature made the bill a law—a law, as Senator Sumner predicted, which paved "the way for that hereafter when slavery must disappear. It annuls all compromises . . . makes all future compromises impossible. . . . It puts freedom and slavery face to face and bids them grapple. Who can doubt the result?"

The immediate result was that from that moment, American party politics became almost exclusively a conflict leading towards civil war. By it the North was made more determined in its efforts to nullify the fugitive-slave law. By it, New England was largely cut loose from the Democratic party. By it the Whig party was destroyed, the Southern Whigs tending to become Democrats, while the Northern Whigs drifted towards the new combination which, in 1856, became the Republican party. By it, Abraham Lincoln was recalled to an interest in politics which had deserted him for a season. In view of which facts, we may accept Mr. Rhodes' opinion that it was the most momentous measure passed between the adoption of the Constitution and the Civil War.

In the grim contest between free-state and pro-slavery settlers which caused Kansas to be known as Bleeding Kansas there is little that can properly be traced to Jefferson Davis. There is no proof that he encouraged his fellow Southerners to join the crowd, some 20,000 in number, which waited on the Missouri and Iowa frontiers, ready to rush into the new territory as soon as it was opened, and take up claims in order to make it safe for slave property. If he knew of their plans, he doubtless approved them on the ground that other bands, equally large, waited also on the borders, determined, by the same method, to make the new territory Free Soil. It is true that his sympathies with the pro-slavery immigrants were shared by President Pierce; but by no means certain that he imposed them upon his chief, as has been often intimated. It is true that the men from Missouri earned their name of "border ruffians" in their efforts to prevent the New England Emigrants' Aid Society from effectively reinforcing the free-state settlers, but no sign of the hand of the Secretary of War appears in the struggle. When Governor Reeder was removed by Pierce, his friends sought to make a martyr of him by charging that he had been removed "by advice of Jeff. Davis" because of his heroic stand against the border ruffians, a charge which Davis denied.

"The Friends of the South," "the Sons of the South," "the Blue Lodges"—organizations formed to make Kansas a slave state were as little the result of Davis' planning as was "the New England Emigrants' Aid Society" itself. The famous black code by which, as Lincoln remarked, it was "a felony even to tell a negro in that territory that he was free," bears no indication of his influence, and is as far as possible removed from his oft-repeated view that it was the duty of Congress, not of the chance inhabitants of a territory, to make laws for the protection of slave property therein. And it would require a mad flight of imagination to see the hand of this legalist in the work of the lawless bands who, "by the sharp logic of revolver and bowie knife," to quote Edward Everett's phrase, made Kansas into another "dark and bloody ground."

He might, consistently with his character and his known views, have encouraged President Pierce to send to Congress his special message of January 24, 1856, which denounced the Topeka free-state movement as a lawless attempt of persons "not constituting the body politic," to transform the territory of Kansas into a state, and declaring the whole free-state movement, from the organization of the New England Emigrant's Aid Society to the Topeka convention, a treasonable and unwarrantably partisan movement which must be suppressed by Federal intervention should it dare to proceed to organized resistance against the constituted authorities—which were, in Pierce's view, as in Davis', the Shawnee Mission pro-slavery legislature. But no evidence appears in his papers, or elsewhere to prove that he did. Indeed, existing evidence shows that he disapproved the President's order to Federal troops to disperse the so-called Topeka legislature, which the free-state men had set up. But he himself later boasted, that this was the only act performed by Federal troops which he found it necessary to disapprove.

President Pierce's next step was to advise the inhabitants of Kansas to frame a Constitution and ask admission to the Union as a state—an unfortunate move, being in effect, a presidential invitation to any detached body of squatter sovereigns to unite in a new movement, to defeat the aims of both the Shawnee Mission pro-slavery legislature and the Topeka anti-slavery state government, by drafting a third state Constitution and demanding executive recognition. Eventually it called into being the Lecompton pro-slavery state Constitution for Kansas, but before

the movement had time to take shape partisan activities had led
to civil war in Kansas. They had led also to what was danger-
ously near pandemonium in Washington, and Davis' urgent desire was to be free again to take part in the debates of the Senate
upon these stirring questions.

Already, on January 6, 1856, he had written to his friend,
Stephen Cocke, regarding the coming Mississippi election of a
United States Senator: "Should the choice fall upon me, it will
for special reasons be very gratifying to me." But he declined
to return home and seek election, although warned that his
presence was essential. He could not forget his declaration that
he would wait until Mississippi, which had rejected him as candidate for the governorship, should summon him of her own
accord. In spite of his absence, however, when the legislature at
last voted, Davis was its choice for Senator.

In the Presidential elections of 1856, Pierce did not fare so well.
"Bleeding Kansas" was excellent campaign material for his enemies, both inside the party and in the camps of the Whigs.
Sumner's bitter speech of May 20, 1856, Lawrence, burned the
next day, and the brutal attack on Sumner the day after, by two
Congressmen from South Carolina, drove men into still stronger
sectional partisanship: while John Brown's mad revenge in his
atrocious "Pottawatomie massacre" tended to feed the flames of
fanaticism. In Kansas, affairs had reached such a state that Redpath, then a newspaper correspondent, declared: "Whenever
two men meet here the first question is: 'Free soil or Pro-slavery?'
The next is the report of a pistol."

It is, therefore, not surprising that in Washington, contact with
recent events in Kansas was a distinct political liability, and that
the Democrats were afraid to go to the country with a candidate
held in some sections responsible for the troubles. They therefore
looked round for one who had been in no way connected with
them. They found him in the minister to the Court of St. James's,
James Buchanan, and on June 2d the Democratic national con-

vention, meeting in Cincinnati, after expressing unqualified admiration of Pierce's administration, nominated Buchanan unanimously, as its candidate for the Presidency.

During Buchanan's residence in England, Davis had helped to keep him aware of the progress of southern Democracy, as shown in the following letter:

Washington, D. C.
23rd July, 1855

My dear Sir;

It gives me real pleasure to present to you my friend W. E. Starke of New Orleans. He visits Europe on commercial business but like Mrs. Gilpin on pleasure bent will probably go to, as she went out, of Londontown. Among those things which he will desire for the gratification it will give him will be an interview with you. He is a zealous, state-rights Democrat and always shares the toil of a canvass when Democracy gives her banner to the breeze.

The little carking cares which you know visit a Secretary have prevented me from writing to you sooner and replying to your very kind and interesting letter, I will write to you very soon at more length and for news from the Southwest refer you to my friend Starke who bears this.

You need not have regretted the necessity of referring inventors to me, for the war in the East has given such impulse to domestic as well as foreign destructiveness that weekly sometimes daily projects are presented for the more rapid and certain killing of our fellow men. Even the Clergy engage in this, a Rev'd parson sometime presented a breech loading rifle with which he said he could kill a man at eighteen hundred yards, but seeing my surprise, he corrected himself by saying "a good shot who had tried the gun could do so." Our trouble however in this connection is very small compared with that of our friend Stoeckel.

The formation of a secret political organization extending over the Union is one of the events in our country which presents a new era. Its contemplation is both saddening and disgusting. I hope never to despair of the Republic or to lose confidence in the people, yet such things do inevitably shake confidence in the sober thought of our masters.

In haste I must conclude & hoping to write again soon remain very truly yours

JEFFERSON DAVIS

HON. J. BUCHANAN.

The South was at first disappointed at Buchanan's nomination, but an inspection of his record showed that he had never voted against slave interests, nor spoken a word which could wound the delicate sensibilities of slaveholders. Henry A. Wise assured his fellow Virginians that Buchanan's career was as spotless, regarding slave property, as that of John C. Calhoun himself.

Furthermore, the Democratic platform, with its support of the Kansas-Nebraska bill, popular sovereignty, the fugitive-slave law, and state rights; and its declaration against all future slavery agitation, had been accepted by Buchanan before his nomination, and was in general pleasing to the South, although Davis resented the countenance given to popular sovereignty. As a Democrat, however, he had no choice but to accept his party's leader, who was ardently pressed forward on the ground that the election of Frémont and Dayton, the first purely sectional presidential ticket ever presented, would mean a dissolution of the Union. Indeed, Davis later interpreted the formation of this "purely sectional party," as itself secession. "We [of the South]," he said, "are represented as secessionists, whilst they [the Republicans] seceded in the last presidential election, went off as a section, organized for themselves and attempted to force a sectional candidate, supported exclusively by a sectional vote. That was secession, practical secession." His letters and speeches, in the campaign, however, show no evidence that he considered the

Union in serious danger, although Senator Toombs of Georgia shouted the warning: "The election of Frémont would be the end of the Union, and ought to be. The object of Frémont's friends is the conquest of the South. I am content that they own us when they conquer us, but not before."

As the campaign progressed, it became daily more evident that the issue was Buchanan or Frémont, protection for slavery in the territories, or no protection. Against the issue of protection for slavery in the territories, the Republicans were united, for it was that issue which had called their party into being. The Democratic platform, however, chose to be ambiguous, hoping thereby to hold its northern members, and declared only that the territories should themselves determine whether they would have slavery, leaving out the question of when and under what conditions the determination should be made. This ambiguity doubtless did much to hold together the Northern and the Southern Democrats who differed radically upon this question.

In the election, Buchanan was chosen President. His popular vote, however, was less than the total popular vote cast for his opponents. Frémont secured 1,341,264, Fillmore 874,534, and Buchanan 1,836,169. And so it came about that a minority President, the last Democrat elected until Grover Cleveland, faced problems difficult enough to tax a far abler man, and to defy solution by a far more united party.

In Pierce's Cabinet, Davis, now recognized as the leading southern statesman of America, had been, according to James G. Blaine, "the guiding and controlling force," but the restraints imposed by his Cabinet post now chafed him and he longed for the Senate's open forum where he could speak as a leader rather than whisper, however effectively, as a subordinate counsellor.

His final annual report as Secretary of War, dated December 1, 1856, is packed with details of army changes. He assured the President that his faith in the project of introducing camels as beasts of burden in the Southwest had been proven sound. He reported the Capitol extension roofed in, the ceilings of the House and the Senate completed; and the aqueduct for the Capitol's water-supply "suspended . . . for want of means."

Amid such duties, it was doubtless a relief to turn to that of answering a friendly letter from Buchanan, expressing a desire to renew the "old relationship of friendship and confidence." In reply to which Davis urged the President-elect to "fly away and be at rest, if indeed there be a place of rest, where your ears will not be reached by the continual cry of those who would be remembered 'when thou comest into thy kingdom.' "

Davis now turned to the task of terminating his connexion with the administrative department, and the camels followed him to the end, his last official document as Secretary of War being an order to Lieutenant D. D. Porter to assemble the materials necessary for "a full explanation of all matters connected with them." He could thus close the book of the camel experiment, but he knew that no one could close that of the dire experiments in popular sovereignty. That problem he must take with him to the Senate, where the echo of John Brown's voice had not died away: "Without the shedding of blood there is no remission of sin," Brown had cried, and by "sin" he meant slavery.

As we review, after a lapse of more than three-quarters of a century the achievements of Davis as Secretary of War, we find them creditable. He had marked the pathway of future railways across the continent, had introduced an improved system of infantry tactics, substituted iron gun-carriages for wood, introduced rifles, muskets and pistols and the deadly Minié ball into the service; added four regiments to the army; strengthened the seacoast and frontier defences, made common the practice of casting heavy guns hollow, and had adopted large-grain powder. These and many other important technical improvements in the service brought forth the appreciation of George B. McClellan, later reported by his son: "Colonel Davis was a man of extraordinary ability. As an executive officer he was remarkable. He was the best Secretary of War—and I use best in its widest sense—I have ever had anything to do with"; and that of another contemporary who wrote: "So wonderful was Mr. Davis' oversight of the Department of War that it would have been impossible for the Government to have been cheated out of the value of a brass button."

CHAPTER IX

THE SENATE AGAIN

WHEN on the fourth of March, 1857, Pierce moved out, to make room for Buchanan, he bade Davis an official farewell in words too warm to be *merely* official: "I can scarcely bear the parting from you who have been strength and solace to me for four anxious years, and have never failed me."

Two days after Davis resumed his seat in the Senate, the Supreme Court took the action which he had long predicted, declaring, in the Dred Scott decision, that slavery existed in all national territories by virtue of the Federal Constitution, and that the Missouri Compromise was "not warranted by the Constitution," which implied, as the *Edinburgh Review* later commented, that slavery could exist everywhere in the Republic, except where locally repudiated. This view, Davis had always held and he applauded the decision as the "rule of right" which "claims the respect and obedience of every citizen of the United States." "It fully sustains our position." The latter claim was well justified, for certain paragraphs of the Dred Scott decision might have been written with his own hand, for example:

"If Congress itself cannot do this [prohibit slavery in a territory], if it is beyond the powers conferred on the Federal Government—it will be admitted, we presume, that it could not authorize a territorial government to exercise them. *It could confer no power on any local government established by its authority, to violate the provisions of the Constitution.* . . . And if the Constitution recognizes the right of property of the master in a

174

slave; and makes no distinction between that description of property and other property owned by a citizen, *no tribunal,* acting under the authority of the United States, whether legislative, executive or judicial, has a right to draw such a distinction, or deny to it the benefit of the provisions and guarantees which have been provided for the protection of private property against the encroachments of the Government. . . . No word can be found in the Constitution which gives Congress a greater power over slave property, or which entitles property of that kind to less protection than property of any other description. The only power conferred is the power, coupled with the duty, of guarding and protecting the owner in his rights.

"Upon these considerations, it is the opinion of the Court that the act of Congress which prohibited a citizen from holding and owning property of this kind in the territory of the United States north of the line therein mentioned, is not warranted by the Constitution, and is therefore void; and that neither Dred Scott himself, nor his family, were made free by being carried into this territory; even if they had been carried there by the owner, with the intention of becoming a permanent resident."

This decision left no doubt about the limitations upon popular sovereignty. Any decision against slavery in any Territory must await the formation of a State Constitution, and the lawless bands which were seeking to abolish slavery in the Territory of Kansas must be curbed by Federal authority. It also made probable Kansas' early admission into the Union as a slave state; for, as Charles Eliot Norton remarked, "the President's present latitude is a far southern one."

The attempt of the Shawnee Mission Legislature of Kansas to make Kansas into a slave state had failed: but the Lecompton Constitution awaited the new President's action. It had not long to wait. On February 2, 1858, Buchanan sent to Congress a special message, urging that Kansas be at once admitted as a state, and that her Lecompton pro-slavery Constitution be accepted as satisfying the requirements laid down in the Federal Constitution. "Kansas," he declared, "is at this moment as much a slave state as Georgia or South Carolina. It has been solemnly adjudged by the highest judicial tribunal known to our laws, that slavery exists in Kansas by virtue of the Constitution of the United States."

Douglas at once declined to followed the President, and from that moment the Democratic party became a house divided against itself, thus giving new hope to its chief rival, the new Republican party, that the history of 1856 would not be repeated in 1860.

On February 8th, Davis discussed Buchanan's message in the Senate, announcing his concurrence with its suggestions and his "hearty approbation of its high motives." He discussed also the relationship of a Senator to the Federal Government, declaring it to be the same as that "of a minister to a friendly court." "The moment he sees this Government in hostility to his own," he said, "the day he resolves to make war on this Government, his honour compels him to vacate the seat he holds."

"Why should we [of the slave states] care," he asked, "whether they [the slaves] go into other territories or not? Simply because of the war that is made against our institutions. . . . Had you made no political war on us, had you observed the principles of our confederacy . . . that the people of each state were . . . to be left perfectly free to form and regulate their institutions in their own way, then, I say, within the limits of each state the population would have gone on to attend to their own affairs, and have little regard to whether this species of property or any other was held in any other portion of the Union. You have made it a political war. We are on the defensive. How far are you to push us?"

To his mind, the North was making war on the South: and the South was rallying to the defence of the Constitution. "I have given evidence in every form in which patriotism is ever subjected to a test," he said, "and I trust that, whatever evil may be in store for us by those who wage war on the Constitution and our rights under it, I shall be able to turn at least to the past and say, 'up to that period when I was declining into the grave, I served a Government I loved, and served it with my whole heart.' . . . Violent speeches denunciatory of people in any particular section of the Union; the arraignment of institutions which they inherited and intend to transmit, as 'leprous spots on the body politic,' are not the means by which fraternity is to be preserved, or this Union rendered perpetual."

When the bill for the admission of Kansas was presented to the Senate, it passed, but with a proviso that after admission it must relinquish its claim to all the land asked for in its ordinance, except 5,000,000 acres, "that being," as Davis later explained to the Mississippi legislature, "the largest amount which had been ever granted to a state at the period of its admission." It also contained a provision declaring the right of the people to change their Constitution at any time; though the instrument itself had restricted them for a term of years. "I considered both these provisions," Davis added, "objectionable; the first, because it was directory of legislation to be enacted by a state; and the second, because it was inviting a disregard of the fundamental law, and had too much the seeming of a concession to the anti-slavery feeling which was impatient for a change of the Constitution."

In the North, on the other hand, Buchanan was accused of having sold himself to the South and of having attempted to bribe the people of Kansas to accept a pro-slavery Constitution which they did not desire. There is, however, no evidence to justify the accusation. He wished to settle the Kansas question in the easiest and quickest possible way: and that way seemed to him to lie in accepting the Lecompton Constitution.

Davis warmly defended the President against the charge of bribery and coercion in connexion with the Kansas land claims. " 'Bribery,' " he scornfully said, later, "to give less, by twenty millions of acres of land, than was claimed." " 'Coercion' to leave them the option of receiving the unusual endowment, or waiting until they had an amount of population which would give some assurance of their ability to maintain a state government. . . . Not for all the land of Kansas, not for all the land between the Mississippi and the Pacific Ocean, not for all the land on the Continent of North America, would I agree that the Federal Government should have the power to coerce a state." Douglas he denounced as a double dissembler, "one of whom asserts the power of Congress to deprive us of a Constitutional right, and the other only denies the power of Congress, in order to transfer it to the territorial Legislature. Neither the one nor the other has any authority to sit in judgment on our rights under the Constitution."

During the remainder of his term, Davis, though in bad health, stuck to his post, speaking often upon boundary questions, river and harbour bills, and other domestic problems which crowded the closing days of the session. He repeatedly made clear his faith in free trade, denouncing "every duty . . . imposed as protection" as "on the same footing of class legislation." He pled for world markets, "so that consumption . . . may keep pace with . . . increased production, or, if it exceed it, may enhance the value of it to those who produce." He met in debate the ablest of the Senators, and so successfully that even so judicial a witness as Mr. Justice Lamar declared, "I never saw him worsted in a debate. He was an off-hand speaker and debater, and always thoroughly up on every question that he discussed. I once heard him debate with Mr. Benton . . . Mr. Benton was made to acknowledge that he was mistaken—the only acknowledgment of the kind I ever heard of his making." And an even less partisan witness, Horace Greeley, of the New York *Tribune*, wrote: "Mr. Davis is unquestionably the foremost man of the South at the present day. Every Northern Senator will admit that from the Southern side of the floor the most formidable adversary to meet in debate is the thin, pale, polished, intellectual-looking

Mississippian with the unimpassioned demeanour, the habitual courtesy, and the occasional unintentional arrogance which reveals his consciousness of great commanding power. . . . He belongs to a higher grade of public men in whom formerly the slaveholding democracy was prolific."

Davis' reputation had been won, however, at the sacrifice of health, and his physicians had repeatedly warned him that rest was essential to its recovery. His eyes also were troublesome; and E. M. Hitchcock, in urging upon him a certain professional consultation, wrote, "We look to you to sustain the South, and you can't see through any eyes but your own." But such suggestions were disregarded for the time, and Davis remained at his post until Congress adjourned. He then started east in the hope of finding rest and freedom from political excitement. But he approached New England with misgiving: "The political position which I had always occupied," he later said, "justified the expectation that . . . I should be left in loneliness. In this I was disappointed; courtesy and kindness met me on my first landing, and attended me to the time of my departure."

On July 9th he answered a serenade in Portland, Maine, with a speech longer than even a well man should have delivered but which delighted his audience by its praise of the country's unity, and its defiance to outside nations to test it by refusing justice to an American citizen in any part of the world. Sectionalism he denounced in unsparing terms: "Representatives and Senators are chosen by districts and by states, but their acts affect the whole country, and their obligations are to the whole people. He who, holding either seat, would confine his investigations to the mere interests of his immediate constituents would be derelict to his duty, and he who would legislate in hostility to any section would be morally unfit for the station. . . . Has patriotism ceased to be a virtue, and is narrow sectionalism no longer to be counted a crime?"

He pictured American territorial expansion as a brilliant triumph of definite principles—"Whatever fears may have once existed as to the consequences of territorial expansion, must give way to the evidence which the last affords. [With] the general government strictly confined to its delegated functions, and the states left in the undisturbed exercise of all else, we have a theory and practice which fits our Government for immeasurable domain and might, under a millennium of nations, embrace mankind."

In August he visited Brunswick to receive an honorary LL.D. from Bowdoin College, the leader of the Slaveocracy honoured in the village where Harriet Beecher Stowe had lately written "Uncle Tom's Cabin." On August 24th he addressed the Maine Democratic Convention at Portland, and praised the Federal Government for its refusal to join the European governments in the prohibition of privateering. Such an arrangement, he declared, would be to "give the whole privateering to those governments which maintained a large naval establishment in time of peace." We should rely "upon the merchant marine to man whatever additional vessels we should require, and upon the bold and hardy Yankee sailor . . . [to] go forth like a knight errant of the sea in quest of adventure against the enemies of his country's flag."

He spoke as boldly and as specifically, in defence of slavery, and its right to protection, as though he had been addressing a Southern audience. "We of the South," he said, "on a sectional division, are in the minority; and if legislation is to be directed by geographical tests—if the Constitution is to be trampled in the dust, and the unbridled will of the majority in Congress is to be supreme over the states, we should have the problem which was presented to our fathers when the Colonies declined to be content with a mere representation in Parliament. If the Constitution is to be sacredly observed, why should there be a struggle for sectional ascendancy? The instrument is the same in all latitudes, and does not vary with the domestic institutions of the several states." Frankly, he faced the fact, unpopular in Maine, that slavery was the outstanding domestic institution of the South; and declared himself a believer in that institution.

"When Republicans . . . introduced the subject of slavery," [in Senate debates] he said, "I defended it, and answered pharisaical pretensions by citing the Bible, the Constitution of the United States and the good of society in justification of the institutions of the state of which I was a citizen; in this I but exercised the right of a free man and discharged the duty of a Southern citizen." He might as truthfully have mentioned, instead, the fact that he had claimed to be a disciple of the only feasible method of ultimate abolition.

Having thus "brushed away the cobwebs," as he said, he entered upon the discussion of the still burning question of Kansas. "The Federal Government has no power to declare what is property, anywhere. . . . Whatever is property in any of the states must be so considered in any of the territories. If Congress had the power to prohibit the introduction of slave property into the territories, what would be the purpose? Would it promote emancipation? That could not be the effect. . . . Would it promote the civilization and progress of the negro race? The tendency must be otherwise. By the dispersion of the slaves, their labour would be rendered more productive and their comforts increased. . . . In every way it would conduce to the advancement and happiness of the servile caste. No, no—it is not these. . . . 'Tis for sectional power, and political ascendancy. . . . For what patriotic purpose can the Northern mind be agitated in relation to domestic institutions for which they have no legal or moral responsibility, and from the interference with which they are restrained by their obligations as American citizens?

"When it was declared that soil, climate, and unrestrained migration should be left to fix the status of the territories, and institutions of the states to be formed out of them, no one probably anticipated that companies would be incorporated to transport colonists into a territory with a view to deciding its political condition. The movement of the Emigrant Aid Society of the North was met by counteracting movements in Missouri, and other Southern states, and thus opposing tides of emigration met on the plains of Kansas. The land was a scene of confusion and violence. Fortunately the murders, which for a time filled the newspapers, existed nowhere else; and the men who were reported slain, usually turned up after a short period to enjoy the eulogies which their martyrdom had elicited. But arson, theft and disgraceful scenes of disorder did exist, and bands of armed men indicated the approach of actual hostilities. . . . It was necessary to have a force—one which would be free from . . . partisan zeal and under executive control. The army fulfilled these conditions. It was therefore employed. It . . . disarmed organized invaders, arrested disturbers of the peace, gave comparative quiet and repose to the territory, without taking a life, or shedding a drop of blood. . . ." He blamed both sides for the fact that Kansas had not gained admission to the Union, a fact which he personally did not regret, as he felt that she was still "wanting in the essential characteristics of a community."

This was a bold speech, but the hostility which he had been warned to expect did not manifest itself. The people of Maine heard him, with interest, but maintained their own views on the slavery question and the Kansas crisis.

Davis' next address was in the capital city of Augusta, where he was received as an honoured guest, although the papers had made known his views as declared at Portland. On September 29th he spoke to a large audience in Representatives' Hall, in which he again declared his uncompromising nationalism, and his hatred of sectional partisanship. "If I know myself," he said, "I have never given a vote from a feeling of hostility to any portion of our common country; but have always kept in view the common obligation for the common welfare, and desired, by

maintaining the Constitution in each and every particular, to perpetuate the blessings it was designed to secure."

The crowning achievement of his journey was an address in
Faneuil Hall on October 11th; the occasion, the ratification of
the candidates of the Massachusetts Democracy, many of whom
were present on the platform. The hall was packed to the doors.
His first tribute was to Caleb Cushing, the "great statesman . . .
who has introduced me, and long association with whom has
caused me to feel that a Massachusetts Democrat has a heart
comprehending the whole of our wide Union." His next was
for Franklin Pierce, "from the neighbouring State of New Hampshire," who during four years of Cabinet association, in the intimate relationship of a President to a trusted adviser, had proved
that he knew "no north, no south, no east, no west, but sacred
maintenance of the common bond." "Never," he said, "in the
history of our country . . . did a man of higher and purer patriotism, a man more devoted to the common weal of his country,
hold the helm of our great ship of state, than that same New
Englander, Franklin Pierce. . . . When I heard your statesman
[General Cushing] say, that a word once here spoken never died,
that it became a part of the circumambient air, I felt a reluctance
to speak which increases upon me as I recall his expression. But
if those voices which breathed the first instincts into the colony
of Massachusetts, and into those colonies which formed the
United States, to proclaim community independence, and assert
it against the powerful mother country—if those voices live here
still, how must they [the Abolitionists] feel who come here to
preach treason to the Constitution, and assail the Union it
ordained and established."

Turning to the portraits which lined the walls, he continued:
"Highest among them all you have placed Samuel Adams and
John Hancock. You have placed them highest, and properly; for
they were the two, the only two, excepted from the proclama-

tion of mercy, when Governor Gage issued his anathema against them and their fellow-patriots."

He interpreted the American Revolution as centring about one great ideal, "Community independence." "If I were selecting," he said, "a place where the advocate of strict construction of the Constitution, the asserter of democratic state rights doctrine, should go for his text, I would send him into the collections of your historical association. . . . He would find here, in bounteous store, that sacred doctrine of states rights, which has been called the extreme and ultra opinion of the South. He would find among your early records, that, at the time when Massachusetts was under a colonial government, administered by a man appointed by the British crown, guarded by British soldiers, the use of Faneuil Hall was refused by the town authorities to a British governor, to hold a British festival, because he was going to bring with him the agents for collecting, and naval officers sent here to enforce an unconstitutional tax upon your commonwealth.

"Such was the proud spirit of independence, manifested in your colonial history, such the great stone your fathers hewed with sturdy hands, and left, the fit foundation for a monument to state rights! And so, throughout the early period of our country, you find Massachusetts leading, most prominent of all the states, in the assertion of that doctrine which has been recently so much decried."

Moving onward to the days of Confederation, he said, "Your fathers had sacrificed too much to claim as the reward of their trials that they should merely have a change of masters. And a change of masters it would have been had Massachusetts surrendered her state sovereignty to the central government, and consented that that central government should have the power to coerce a state. But if this power does not exist, if this sovereignty has not been surrendered, then, I say, who can deny the words . . . spoken by your candidate this evening, when he pleaded to you the cause of state independence, and the right of every community to be the judge of its own domestic affairs? This is all we have ever asked—we of the South. . . . Your candidate for Governor has asserted tonight everything which we have claimed as a right.

"You did not surrender your sovereignty. You gave to the Federal Government certain functions. It was your agent, created for specific purposes. It can do nothing save that which you have given it power to perform. Where is the grant of the Constitution which confers on the Federal Government a right to determine what shall be property? Surely none such exists; that question belongs to every community to settle for itself: you judge in your case; every other State must judge in its case. . . . Why then," he asked, entering at last upon the most dangerous of themes, "in the absence of all control over the subject of African slavery, are you so agitated in relation to it? With pharisaical pretension it is sometimes said it is a moral obligation to agitate. . . . Who gave them the right to decide that it is a sin? By what standard do they measure it? Not the Constitution; the Constitution recognizes the property in many forms, and imposes obligations in connexion with that recognition. Not the Bible; that justifies it. Not the good of society; for if they go where it exists, they find that society recognizes it as good. . . . Is it in the cause of Christianity? It cannot be, for servitude is the only agency through which Christianity has reached that degraded race."

Rarely, if ever in history, have sound logic and compelling eloquence been combined more brilliantly to sustain so poor a thesis. Davis placed slavery not only "under the aegis of the Constitution," as Sumner complained; but under the aegis of the Bible. And this in Boston, in Faneuil Hall; and the people were applauding.

There is probably no one of his many speeches which more completely captivated the audience to which it was addressed. Any one wishing to know the orator, Davis, at his best should read it in its entirety. But it contains no sentence so eloquent as this of Abraham Lincoln: "I must fight this thing, until the sun shall shine, the rain fall and the wind shall blow upon no man who goes forth to unrequited toil."

After his New England vacation, where friendliness and hospitality met him "in every town and village," Davis started home, stopping at New York to appear in Palace Garden, where he defined the impending crisis as "a contest upon the one side to enlarge the majority it now possesses, and a contest upon the other side to recover the power it has lost." "If . . . one section should gain such predominance as would enable it, by modifying the Constitution and usurping new power, to legislate for the other," he said, "the exercise of that power would throw us back into the condition of the colonies; and if in the veins of the sons flows the blood of their sires, they would not fail to redeem themselves from tyranny, even should they be driven to resort to revolution." And the great audience cheered this ominous pronouncement of the leader of the South.

At that time the question of excluding foreigners from the ballot was among the national issues; and Davis turned to it to show that his concern was not slave property alone, but any attempt of the national government to encroach upon rights reserved to the states. "Has Congress the right to say that foreigners shall not vote within the limits of your state?" he asked. "Are you willing to leave that to Congress?" A roar of dissent answered the question; and Davis added: "Go, look along your lines of internal improvements, where every mile has mingled with it the bones of some foreigner who laboured to create it. Go to your battle fields . . . and you will find the sand dyed red by the blood of the foreign born. . . . We do not advocate that any country shall empty its poor houses . . . and throw the charge upon us. . . . But we do war against the use of terms that delude the people, and are intended to exclude the high-spirited and hard-working men who contribute to the bone, the sinew, and the wealth of our country."

During the evening another speaker had made reference to Giddings, an outstanding abolitionist of the period: and Davis seized upon the reference as an excuse for elaborating the issues before the nation. Had Mr. Giddings, he said, known anything of the relations between the master and the slave, "he would not have talked of the slave armed with the British bayonet. Our doors are unlocked at night; we live among them with no more fear of them than of our cows and oxen. We lie down to sleep trusting to them for our defence, and the bond between the master and the slave is as near as that which exists between capital and labour anywhere. . . . The delusion which has always excited my surprise the most, has been that which has led so many northern men to strike hands with the British abolitionists to make war on their southern brethren. If they could effect their ends, and Great Britain could insert the wedge which should separate the States, what further use would she have for the northern section? You are the competitors of Great Britain in the vast field of manufacture, whom she most fears. . . . The moment that separation should be effected she would be, under the promptings of interest, your worst enemy. . . .

"You have among you," he added, "politicians of a philosophic turn, who preach a high morality; a system of which they are the discoverers. . . . They say, it is true the Constitution dictates this, the Bible inculcates that, but there is a higher law than those; and they call upon you to obey that higher law of which they are the inspired givers. [Loud applause.] Men who are traitors to the compact of their fathers—men who have perjured the oaths they have themselves taken—they who wish to steep their hands in the blood of their brothers; these are the moral law-givers who proclaim a higher law than the Bible, the Constitution, and the laws of the land. This higher-law doctrine . . . is the most convenient of which I have ever heard—for the criminal . . . The doctrine is now advanced to you only in relation to property of the Southern States . . . but it will react deeply upon yourselves, if you accept it. What security have you for your own safety if every man of vile temper, of low instincts, of base purpose, can find in his own heart a law higher than that which is the rule of society, the Constitution, and the Bible? The higher law preachers should be tarred and feathered, and whipped by those they have thus instigated. This, my friends, is what was called in the good old revolutionary times, Lynch Law. It is sometimes the very best law, because it deals summary justice upon those who otherwise escape . . . punishment."

This closing paragraph, impromptu, as was the entire speech, shows that Davis was at times carried away by his own eloquence. We must allow something, perhaps much, for the excitement of the moment, for the flash of anger, but after such allowance has been made, we must admit that his eastern speaking tour would have been more creditable without it.

It was impossible that a series of addresses, by a leader so dominant in the South and so prominent in Washington, should pass without criticism. Denunciation came from his own section, because Davis "had praised the 'Yankees'"; from the North because he was "a propagandist for disunion"; and most of all from the Abolitionists who bitterly resented his defence of the "accursed institution."

On November 16, Davis made a report to the Legislature of Mississippi, and as there had been criticism of his speeches here also, he defended himself against charges from both sides of the Mason and Dixon line; but took his stand squarely upon the proposition that, while never having advocated a dissolution of the Union, he was ready to follow his state should she decide that secession was necessary. And he warned the Legislature that at no distant time they might be compelled to make the decision.

Of the leading candidate for the Republican nomination for the Presidency, William H. Seward, Davis said: "The mastermind of the so-called Republican party, Senator Seward, in a recent speech at Rochester, announced the purpose of his party to dislodge the Democracy from the possession of the federal government, and assigns as a reason the friendship of that party for what he denominates the slave system. He declares the Union between the states having slave labour and free labour to be incompatible, and announces that one or the other must disappear. He even asserts that it was the purpose of the framers of the government to destroy slave property, and cites as evidence, the provision for an amendment to the Constitution. He seeks to alarm his auditors by assuring them of the purpose, on the part of the South and the Democratic party, to force slavery upon all the States of the Union. Absurd as all this may seem to you, and incredulous as you may be of its acceptance by any intelligent portion of the citizens of the United States, I have reason to believe that it has been inculcated to no small extent in the Northern mind.

"It requires but a cursory examination of the Constitution of the United States, but a partial knowledge of its history and of the motives of the men who formed it, to see how utterly fallacious it is to ascribe to them the purpose of interfering with the domestic institutions of any of the states."

Continuing, he declared that Seward misunderstood, and grossly misrepresented the slave-system, and that his election to the presidency would be the fulfilment of the condition which he had pictured as a just cause for secession. "Where he learned his lesson, I am at a loss to imagine; certainly not by observation, for you all know that by interest, if not by higher motives, slave labour bears to capital as kind a relation as can exist between them anywhere, that it removes from us all that controversy between the labourer and the capitalist, which has filled Europe with starving millions."

It was his opinion, based upon his recent experiences in the East, and upon the assertions of eminent northern men such as ex-President Franklin Pierce, "that whenever a Northern army should be assembled to march for the subjugation of the South, they would have a battle to fight at home before they passed the limits of their own state," and, he added, "our friends claim that the victory will at least be doubtful.

"I hold the separation from the Union by the state of Mississippi," he continued, "to be the last remedy—the final alternative. In the language of the venerated Calhoun, I consider the disruption of the Union as a great, though not the greatest, calamity. . . . I love the flag of my country with even more than a filial affection. . . . For many of the best years of my life I have followed it, and upheld it on fields where, if I had fallen, it might have been claimed as my winding sheet. . . . I glory in the position which Mississippi's star holds in the group; but sooner than see its lustre dimmed—sooner than see it degraded from its present equality—would tear it from its place to be set even on the perilous ridge of battle as a sign round which Mississippi's best and bravest should gather to the harvest-home of death."

He urged Mississippi to make needful preparation, for "whatever contingency may befall us. The maintenance of our rights against a hostile power is a physical problem and cannot be solved by mere resolutions. . . . Such preparation will not precipitate us upon the trial of secession, . . . but will give to our conduct the character of earnestness of which mere paper declarations have somewhat deprived us; it will strengthen the hands of our friends at the North, and, in the event that separation shall be forced upon us, we shall be prepared to meet the contingency with whatever remote consequences may follow it.

"It seems now probable that the Abolitionists and their allies will have control of the next House of Representatives, and it may be inferred from their past course that they will attempt legislation both injurious and offensive to the South. I have an abiding faith that any law which violates our constitutional rights will be met with a veto by the present executive. But should the next House of Representatives be such as would elect an Abolition President, we may expect that the election will be so conducted as probably to defeat a choice by the People and devolve the election upon the House.

"Whether by the House or by the People, if an Abolitionist be chosen President of the United States, you will have presented to you the question of whether you will permit the government to pass into the hands of your avowed and implacable enemies. Without pausing for your answer, I will state my own position to be that such a result would be a species of revolution by which the purposes of the Government would be destroyed and the observance of its mere forms entitled to no respect. In that event, in such manner as should be most expedient, I should deem it your duty to provide for your safety outside of the Union of those who have already shown the will, and would have acquired the power, to deprive you of your birthright and reduce you to worse than the Colonial dependence of your fathers."

As a military man, Davis believed that the best chance for peace lay in being prepared for war: and the advice which he gave to his state, he gave also to the nation. As chairman of the Senate Committee on Military Affairs during these last critical months he had made constant pleas for larger military appropriations, but, while pointing out that there were no armories south of Harper's Ferry, he had asked no appropriation for the purpose of supplying them—convincing proof that he did not seek to use his position at Washington to prepare the South for war, as his enemies later contended.

CHAPTER X

THE ELECTION OF 1860

AFTER his speech to the Mississippi legislature, Davis returned to Washington, to watch in the Senate the development of the scenes against which he had warned his fellow Mississippians. To most public men of the time Seward seemed the likeliest leader of the Republican party, and Davis looked upon the chance of such leadership with deep forebodings. To him the higher-law theory was a menace, not only to slavery, but to the Union itself. Had he been able to divine the near future, and to see Seward displaced by Lincoln, his forebodings would certainly have been lessened, for Lincoln was no believer in the higher-law theory. Often he had declared that with slavery in the states where it existed he did not wish to interfere, and that the Federal Government had no right to do so. But as yet Lincoln seemed hardly a possibility, especially to the man who remembered him in the Black Hawk War, the ragged captain of a ragged hoard called his company. It is true that since that time Lincoln had won local fame in Illinois, but he had recently been defeated for the Senatorship by Stephen A. Douglas, and there was as yet no reason to believe that this defeat had made him Presidential timber.

It was, therefore, in the possibility of Douglas' nomination and election in 1860 that Davis saw a menace almost as grave as would be precipitated by the nomination and election of Seward. To him the doctrine of squatter sovereignty, especially since it had been so interpreted as to enable the North to banish slavery from the territories, was still abhorrent, for so far as the South's hope of an equal share in the national domain was concerned, its ascendency would mean an inequality scarcely less galling than Republican supremacy. Yet, since his re-election to the Senate, Douglas had become almost fanatical in his devotion to it, and his outspoken championship had deepened the determination of Davis and his followers that, come what might, Douglas should not be the Democratic candidate for the Presidency in the next campaign. Therefore, as recognized leader of the South, Davis watched for an opportunity to face Douglas in debate on the floor of the Senate, and to interpret to the South the meaning of the latter's "Freeport heresy."

The contrast between the two men was marked: Douglas was the embodiment of expediency: while Davis referred his actions to set principles, sometimes to rather unsound principles. "My country always right, but right or wrong, my country," he once quoted, and added, whimsically, "it would require some modification for the legislator, and yet my sentiments, as an American, very much respond to that maxim." Douglas' aim was personal success; Davis', the success of the American government on the old lines.

A chance remark of Douglas on the danger of secession gave Davis his opportunity, and on February 23, 1859, he took the floor. "If, in the progress of our history, we have reached the point where it is necessary to part, as the Senator from Illinois [Mr. Douglas] says, or to adopt a creed like that which he has announced, I wish him God-speed and a pleasant journey. . . . Not the breadth of a hair would I follow the Senator in the career which he announces. . . ."

In the Lincoln-Douglas Debates of 1858, Lincoln had declared that Douglas was claiming that a thing may be legally driven away from a place where it has a legal right to remain. Davis' logic went beyond this passing witticism. "It is the duty of Congress to interpose," as he announced, ". . . to make that protection adequate. . . . The claim of the Colonies was that laws were passed in violation of their charters, and hence they were termed unconstitutional. . . ." Does the Senator hold that "a law pronounced unconstitutional by the Supreme Court is still to remain in force within the territory, Congress failing to provide any remedy which would restore the right violated by that unconstitutional act?"

Douglas replied, from his seat, "Clearly not."

"Then," continued Davis, "I ask him, what is the remedy? The law is pronounced unconstitutional, and yet the right which it has violated is not restored; the protection which is required is not granted; the law which deprived him of protection, though it may be declared unconstitutional, is not replaced by any which will give him protection. They [The Americans of 1776] had rights under the British constitution . . . those rights were violated; and the colonists rose . . . and asserted those rights, they asserted them by revolution." He announced himself ready to acknowledge the independence of the people of a territory if they should demand it by revolution, but "until they acquire the power of a sovereign state they remain the inhabitants of a territory belonging to the United States; they remain under the control of the Congress. . . ." Continuing, he took his stand boldly upon the Constitution, as recently interpreted in the Dred Scott decision, "that there is no power, either in Congress or in the people of a territory, during their territorial condition, to prohibit the introduction of slavery. . . ."

Douglas again interposed with the words, "men must come to one of two positions, and there is none other; either property is to be protected in those territories by the territorial laws, with the right of appeal to the Supreme Court to test their constitutionality, or by the intervention of Congress."

Davis answered: "What the Government owes to person and property is adequate protection"; as the Supreme Court had declared slaves to be property, which Douglas had acknowledged, it was fair to assume, as the South had assumed, that "Congressional legislation would follow . . . and secure to us the enjoyment of the right thus defined." Of the two possible alternatives which Douglas had just proposed, he unhesitatingly chose the second, "intervention by Congress." And he asked Douglas to state whether, in view of the Dred Scott decision, he was willing to "give that right [to hold slaves in a territory] the protection of Congressional legislation."

Douglas replied: "I am willing . . . to assume that the decision of the Supreme Court goes to the extent of the expression of opinion by Chief Justice Taney, that Congress could not prohibit a man from going into a territory with a slave, and therefore that the territorial legislature could not prohibit his coming in. . . . You have the same right to hold them [slaves] the same as other property, subject to such laws as the legislature may constitutionally enact. If those laws render it impracticable to hold your property, whether it be your horse or your slave, it is your misfortune."

Davis answered, at once: "The obligation is upon Congress . . . to protect the citizen who goes to this joint property, in person and property; and if the territorial legislature does not protect him in his mules, it is the duty of Congress to compel that territorial legislature to perform its proper function, and to enact the laws which are needful in the premises."

Douglas well knew what Davis had in mind. He knew that, as early as May 8, 1850, Davis had presented a resolution to the Senate, that: "It is the duty of the Congress of the United States to provide . . . the means of enforcing in said territories the guarantees of the Constitution in reference to the property of citizens of any of the states removing into any of the said territories." He saw that this doctrine was irreconcilable with Davis' other cherished theory of local autonomy, and decided to expose the inconsistency, and make clear the fact that what Davis demanded was not equal, but special protection for the South in the territories. "The Senator says," he cautiously began, "that there is something peculiar in slave property, requiring further protection than other species of property. If so, it is the misfortune of those who own that species of property. He tells us that if the territorial legislature fails to pass a slave code for the territories, fails to pass police regulations to protect slave property, the absence of such legislation practically excludes slave property as effectively as a constitutional prohibition would exclude it. I agree to that proposition. He says, furthermore, that it is competent for the territorial legislature, by the exercise of the taxing power, and other functions within the limits of the Constitution, to adopt unfriendly legislation which practically drives slavery out of the territory. I agree to that proposition. That is just what I said, and all I said, and just what I meant by my Freeport speech in Illinois, upon which there has been so much comment throughout the country. . . .

"The Senator from Mississippi says they ought to pass such a code; but . . . if they do not do it, there is no mode by which you can compel them to do it. He admits [this] . . . and . . . insists that, in case of non-action by the territorial legislature, it is the right and duty of Southern Senators and Representatives to demand . . . by Congress . . . a slave code for the territories. . . . I recognize slave property as being on an equality with all other property, and apply the same rules to it. I will not apply one rule to slave property and another rule to all other kinds of property." Davis replied that property was entitled to "*adequate* protection . . . the amount of protection which must be given will necessarily vary with the character of the property and the place where it is held."

When the debate was over, it remained fixed in the minds of the auditors that Davis, a life-long advocate of non-intervention, now demanded that Congress intervene in the territories, to give to slave property a kind of protection which it gave to no other property.

Lincoln, in his debates with Douglas, had skilfully side-tracked the Dred Scott decision, by declaring it improperly obtained, and a proper subject for revision in some tranquil period. Douglas had announced himself in favour of letting it stand, and of destroying its effect by unfriendly local action, and Davis had now put himself on record as accepting it as guaranteeing the special kind of protection required by the "peculiar institution."

No one of the three desired to conceal in any part his opinion: all were ready to face whatever consequences might follow. Lincoln knew that his view would offend the South; but his frankly anti-slavery sentiments had already placed him without the pale so far as the South was concerned. Douglas feared that his attitude would split the Democratic party and had so acknowledged during the debate. Davis agreed with that opinion, but remained unmoved by the danger. "What may be the fate of the Democratic party," he had said, "if it suffers that division to which the Senator refers, I cannot say. It has achieved many a glorious victory in the cause of its country. It can claim credit for the acquisition of every acre of territory which has been added to our original domain. It leaves behind it the legacy . . . of a glorious past. If it is to be wrecked by petty controversies in relation to African labor; if a few Africans, brought into the United States, where they have advanced in comfort and civilization and knowledge, are to constitute the element which will divide the Democratic party and peril the vast hopes, not only of our own country, but of all mankind, I trust it will be remembered that a few of us have stood by the old landmarks of those who framed the Constitution."

The issue of chief importance as the year 1860 approached was the question of restricting slavery to the territory already possessed by it: and upon that question Davis' views are recorded in his "Notes on the proposition to restrict the institution of African slavery . . . to its present limits," to be found in the Library of Congress. "The present number of African slaves in the Southern states," he wrote, "and the ratio of increase which has existed heretofore, show that the period is not remote when that point

will be reached at which they will cease to be valuable. . . .
Crowded to such an extent as to have become unprofitable, first
the comforts and then the necessities of life must be curtailed.
This contented, well-clothed, well-fed body of labourers must be
reduced to the want of the masses of overcrowded Europe and
in the descending scale may finally reach the end which pseudo-
philanthropy has indicated with a cruel indifference from which
the Southern slaveholder recoils with horror and disgust—the
reduction in the comforts of life to a degree so low that the further increase of the race would be checked.

"To this proposition, . . . there is an alternative, the abandonment of the country by the white race; the surrender to decay
and barbarism of the land where representative liberty has attained its highest perfection . . . are these the ends aimed at
when men prate of a higher civilization, a purer religion, a loftier
morality? . . . It is not by the arrogant interference of those who
would make a semblance of virtue by picking at the mote in their
brother's eye . . . that we are likely to be taught how to manage
our own household affairs."

He pointed to recent Northern "prohibitory enactments against
the immigration of free negroes" to prove that, when the pressure
of numbers within the areas to which the anti-extensionists were
seeking to restrict slavery should offer only a choice of starvation
or migration, the negroes, whether as slaves or as freedmen, could
not hope for a haven of refuge in the North. The South's solution,
Davis urged, was to allow slavery to spread and, spreading, to
gain new comforts for the slaves. But he knew while he urged
this policy that the Republican party had been formed for the
express purpose of preventing this "South's solution," and that it
would not consent to accept it now. Indeed, he believed, as he had
recently told the Mississippi legislature, that "a party too powerful
to be unheeded, and marked, . . . by territorial limits, is now organized for the destruction of the labour system of the South,
and seeks to obtain possession of the general Government, that

its machinery may be used in aid of their war upon our existence as a sovereign state."

In discussing the results of the law of 1820, passed to make more effective the law of 1818, and both aimed to stop the African slave trade, he declared, "It has magnified the horrors of the middle passage; it has led us to an alliance with Great Britain, by which we are bound to keep a naval squadron on the deadly coast of Africa, where American sailors are sacrificed to a foreign policy urged under the false plea of humanity; it has destroyed a lucrative trade for ivory, oil, and gold-dust, which our merchants had long conducted . . . and transferred it to our commercial rivals, the British." He repudiated the idea that the trade was inherently inhuman or selfish. "No consequence which would justify such denunciation," he said, "can flow from the transfer of a slave from a savage to a Christian master." He was employing arguments as old as Las Casas, to defend both slavery and the African slave trade, and employing them as honestly as that old churchman had employed them. He was as confident as Las Casas that God had made him a master and the same God had made the black man a slave. "It matters not," he said, "whether Almighty Power and Wisdom stamped diversity on the races of men at the period of the creation, or decreed it after the subsidence of the flood. It is enough for us that the Creator, speaking through the inspired lips of Noah, declared the destiny of the three races of men."

As the year 1859 drew to its close, Davis was wholly occupied with the problem of meeting Douglas' ingenious use of squatter sovereignty, and gaining for the South the special protection in the territories which the Dred Scott decision seemed to him to warrant. His papers contain no trace of an ambition to succeed Buchanan as President, although several extant documents show that he was regarded by competent judges as among the eligibles. One friend, resident in the West, assured him that "among all the prominent men before the country, you have the highest reputation for decision of character and unfaltering will. I sincerely hope that by the time the Charleston convention assembles, public opinion will fix upon Jefferson Davis as the man for the time." Closely following this, a letter from ex-President Pierce, Davis' personal choice for the Democratic nomination, expressed the same hope:

[New York.] Clarendon Hotel
January 6, 1860.

My dear Friend:

I wrote you an unsatisfactory note a day or two since. I have just had a pleasant interview with Mr. Shepley, whose courage and fidelity are equal to his learning and talent. He says he would rather fight the battle with you as standard-bearer in 1860 than under the auspices of any other leader. The feeling and judgment of Mr. S. in this relation is, I am confident, rapidly gaining ground in New England. Our people are looking for "the coming man"—one who is raised by all the elements of his character above the atmosphere ordinarily breathed by politicians—a man really fitted for this emergency by his ability, courage, broad statesmanship and patriotism. Col. Seymour arrived here this morning, and expressed his views in this relation in almost the identical language used by Mr. Shepley.

It is true that in the present state of things at Washington and throughout the country, no man can predict what changes two or three months may bring forth. Let me suggest that in the running debates in Congress full justice seems to me not to have been done to the Democracy of the North. I do not believe that our friends at the South have any just idea of the state of feeling, running at this moment to the pitch of intense exasperation, between those who respect their political obligations, and those who have apparently no impelling power, but that which fanatical passion on the subject of domestic slavery imparts. . . . I have never believed that actual disruption of the Union can occur

without blood, and if, through the madness of Northern abolitionism, that dire calamity must come, the fighting will not be
along Mason's and Dixon's line merely. It [may] be within our
own borders, in our own streets, between two classes of citizens
to whom I have referred. Those who defy the law and scout
constitutional obligations will, if we ever reach the arbitrament
of arms, find occupation enough at home. . . . I have tried to
impress upon our people, especially in New Hampshire and Con-
necticut, where the only elections are to take place during the
coming spring, that while our Union meetings are all in the right
direction and well enough for the present, they will not be worth
the paper upon which their resolutions are written, unless we can
overthrow political absolutism at the polls and repeal the unconstitutional and obnoxious laws which in the cause of "personal
liberty" have been placed upon our statute-books. I shall look
with deep interest and not without hope for a decided change in
the situation.

Ever and truly,
your friend,
FRANKLIN PIERCE

James G. Blaine, a man trained to measure presidential timber,
says in his *Twenty Years in Congress*, that Davis "had been growing in favour with a powerful element in the Democracy of the
free states, and but for the exasperating quarrel of 1860 "might
have been selected as the presidential candidate of his party." But
Davis himself understood national conditions too well to suppose
that he could be elected or even nominated, and his chief concern
was to make history of Lincoln's prophecy that Douglas, with the
Freeport heresy clinging to him, could never obtain that high
post. Conscious that he had by no means annihilated the "Little
Giant," during their recent debates, he was anxious for another
engagement.

The chance came on January 12, 1860, when Senator Pugh

quoted in Douglas' interest the following words from Davis' recent Portland speech: "If the inhabitants of any territory should refuse to enact such laws and police regulations as would give security to their property . . . the owner would be practically debarred . . . from taking slave property into a territory where the sense of the inhabitants was opposed to its introduction." "If," added Pugh, "the Senator from Illinois can be charged with such an offence by an expression of his opinion at Freeport, the same charge is equally good against the Senator from Mississippi . . . but I do not make the charge either against the Senator from Mississippi or the Senator from Illinois."

Here Davis interposed to explain that Pugh had quoted from a text which did not fairly represent Davis' statement, which was so badly reported that he had not attempted to revise the form in which the press had published it. Pugh incautiously answered, "I do not know whether the Senator revised the speech or not," and was instantly faced with this retort: "You do know. I *tell* you, I did not." Any further declaration of doubt would have been followed by serious consequences; for Davis was punctilious when honour was involved. "Now I do know," replied Pugh, and proceeded to criticize the speech upon the basis of an unrevised text.

It would be unfair to allow this incident to leave the impression that Davis was habitually overbearing. On the contrary, he was willing always to acknowledge a fault and offer an apology. Upon one occasion, in the heat of debate he lost his temper and used such insulting language that the offended Senator sent his second to demand "the satisfaction known among gentlemen." After reading the challenge, Davis said to its bearer: "Tell Mr. —— I will answer him tomorrow in the Senate." And he answered thus: "Yesterday I . . . used language concerning my colleague which I ought not to have used, and which no gentleman ought to use to another. . . . I desire in this presence where I did the wrong . . . to make him all the reparation that a man can make to another. I was wrong; I am sorry for it, and in this chamber I beg his pardon and yours." Had Alexander Hamilton so treated the demand of Aaron Burr, whose challenge he much desired to refuse, there would have been no tragic scene on the heights of Weehawken.

Senator Pugh had not got far in his speech, after Davis' interruption, before Douglas interposed to reaffirm his Freeport heresy which Pugh had sought to excuse as a declaration made in heat of debate. "At Freeport," he said, "in reply to a question, I did say that slavery might be excluded from a territory by non-action and also by unfriendly legislation. I had made the same remark in the Senate over and over again, in 1850, and during every session of Congress from that time to the period when I was removed from the chairmanship of the Committee on Territories. Every member of the Senate during that period knew that I held those sentiments. I had been eleven times appointed chairman of the Committee on Territories by the unanimous vote of this body, after I had repeated those remarks, over and over again." Later he added: "You can hardly open the Congressional debates of that period at any page without finding them [the Freeport opinions] expressed. . . . In 1852, in 1853, in 1854, in 1855, and in 1856, they were uttered in the presence of every Senator then in the Senate—not once, not twice, not ten times, but as often as the question arose." This avowal deals a fatal blow to the much-advertised theory that Lincoln had skilfully manœuvred Douglas into a fatal mistake, at Freeport. Douglas had but brought out in public debate an old heresy which when uttered in the Senate seems not to have attracted general attention.

On January 30, 1860, from his seat in the Senate, Davis wrote to Pierce: ". . . Nicholson, of Tennessee, is reading a speech, need I say on what? Do we ever speak of anything but that over which we have no control, slavery of the negro?

"The prospect . . . is not less gloomy than when you left. The condition in which General Cushing said men should provide for storm seems to be rapidly approaching—I will stand by the flag and uphold the Constitution while there is possibility of effecting anything to preserve and perpetuate the Government we inherited—beyond that my duty and my faith bind me to Mississippi, and her fortunes as she may shape them. I hope on for the kind providence that has preserved us heretofore and still labour at my post as a member of the general Government." While not considering it worth while to comment upon Pierce's suggestion concerning the Presidency, Davis assured him that he would rather see his party split than united upon a leader with the views of Stephen A. Douglas. The grim sincerity of this declaration was shortly provided by the preparation of a set of resolutions designed, as well as calculated, to make the doctrine of congressional protection for slavery in the territories the basic Democratic doctrine, and the test for the Presidential nomination. For the composition and presentation of these resolutions, he himself was responsible, though he had considered the opinions both of other Senators, and of the general public. He was, as Stephens later recorded, "but the instrument, the draftsman, through whom the overwhelming majority of the states announced for themselves the nature of the bonds of their union. This exposition," adds Stephens, "was . . . substantially the same as that given by the same august body of ambassadors [the Senate] . . . in 1838."

The text of these famous resolutions, as Davis presented them to the Senate, on February 2, 1860, is as follows:

1. *Resolved,* That in the adoption of the Federal Constitution, the States adopting the same acted severally as free and independent sovereignties, delegating a portion of their powers to be exercised by the Federal Government for the increased security of each, against dangers *domestic* as well as foreign; and that any intermeddling by any one or more States, or by a combination of their citizens, with the domestic institutions of the others, on any pretext, whether political, moral, or religious, with the view to their disturbance or subversion, is in violation of the Constitution, insulting to the States so interfered with, endangers their

domestic peace and tranquillity—objects for which the Constitution was formed—and, by necessary consequence, serves to weaken and destroy the Union itself.

2. *Resolved,* That negro slavery, as it exists in fifteen States of this Union, composes an important portion of their domestic institutions, inherited from their ancestors, and existing at the adoption of the Constitution, by which it is recognized as constituting an important element of the apportionment of powers among the States; and that no change of opinion or feeling on the part of the non-slave-holding States of the Union in relation to this institution can justify them or their citizens in open and systematic attacks thereon, with a view to its overthrow; and that all such attacks are in manifest violation of the mutual and solemn pledges to protect and defend each other, given by the States, respectively, on entering into the constitutional compact which formed the Union, and are a manifest breach of faith and a violation of the most solemn obligations.

3. *Resolved,* That the union of these States rests on the equality of rights and privileges among its members, and that it is especially the duty of the Senate, which represents the States in their sovereign capacity, to resist all attempts to discriminate either in relation to person or property, so as, in the Territories—which are the common possession of the United States—to give advantages to the citizens of one State which are not equally secured to those of every other State.

4. *Resolved,* That neither Congress, nor a Territorial Legislature, whether by direct legislation or legislation of an indirect and unfriendly nature, possesses the power to annul or impair the constitutional right of any citizen of the United States to take his slave property into the common Territories; but it is the duty of the Federal Government there to afford for that, as for other species of property, the needful protection; and if experience should at any time prove that the judiciary does not possess power

to insure adequate protection, it will then become the duty of Congress to supply such deficiency.

5. *Resolved,* That the inhabitants of an organized Territory of the United States, when they rightfully form a constitution to be admitted as a State into the Union, may then, for the first time, like the people of a State when forming a new constitution, decide for themselves whether slavery, as a domestic institution, shall be maintained or prohibited within their jurisdiction; and if Congress shall admit them as a State, "they shall be received into the Union with or without slavery, as their constitution may prescribe at the time of their admission."

6. *Resolved,* That the provision of the Constitution for the rendition of fugitives from service or labour, "without the adoption of which the Union could not have been formed," and the laws of 1793 and 1850, which were enacted to secure its execution, and the main features of which, being similar, bear the impress of nearly seventy years of sanction by the highest judicial authority, have unquestionable claim to the respect and observance of all who enjoy the benefits of our compact of Union; and that the acts of State Legislatures to defeat the purpose, or nullify the requirements of that provision, and the laws made in pursuance of it, are hostile in character, subversive of the Constitution, revolutionary in their effect, and if persisted in, must sooner or later lead the States injured by such breach of the compact to exercise their judgment as to the proper mode and measure of redress."

"I have presented these resolutions," Davis explained, "not for the purpose of discussing them, but with a view to get a vote upon them severally, hoping thus, by an expression of the deliberate opinion of the Senate, that we may reach some conclusion as to what is the present condition of opinion in relation to the principles there expressed. The expression even of the resolutions is, to a great extent, not new. The first and second are substantially those on which the Senate voted in 1837-38, affirming them then by a very large majority. I trust opinion today may be

as sound as it was then. There is also an assertion of an historic
fact, which is drawn from the opinion of Judge Story, in the decision of the ruling case of Prigg *vs.* the Commonwealth of Pennsylvania. It was my purpose to rest the propositions contained in
these resolutions upon the highest authority of the land, judicial
as well as other; and if it be possible to obtain a vote on them
without debate, it will be most agreeable to me. To have them
affirmed by the Senate without contradiction, would be an era in
the recent history of our country which would be hailed with joy
by every one who sincerely loves it."

These resolutions were a clear challenge to Douglas' theory of
"unfriendly legislation" by territorial legislatures; and Davis
knew that the latter would never accept them. His demand, therefore, sounded the death knell of Democratic unity in the pending
election. A Republican President was inevitable, and with Legislature and Executive both Republican, the condition long held as
justifying secession would have arrived, as a rapidly increasing
section of that party, headed by Seward, had made it clear that,
once in power, it would respect no law, whether of statute or of
the Constitution, which recognized rights in human property.
Sumner had declared that "the North would not and could not
obey the law as written, but must appeal to the law of justice."

It would still, however, be unfair to conclude that Davis' aim
was secession. His desire was rather to prevent secession by preventing Douglas and his followers from precipitating conditions
which would cause the south to secede. Stephens in his *War Between the States* wrote: "I never regarded him as a secession-
ist . . . but as a strong Union man in sentiment, so long as the
Union was maintained on the principles upon which it was
founded."

Eight days later Davis wrote from Washington to John R.
Pease: "I have an abiding hope that the coming Democratic
national convention will select a nominee who will receive the
united support of the Democracy and by his election secure peace

to the country, by maintaining to every section and to every citizen, all the rights and privileges which the Constitution was designed to perpetuate. Less than that would be an abandonment of the object for which the states united and would inevitably tend to their separation. . . . If the conservative feeling of our Northern brethren shall not be aroused by manifestations of hostility to the South, I shall be compelled to abandon that hope and feel that the time has arrived when we must look for our future safety to our own power to repel aggression."

That Douglas would reject the Davis resolutions as part of the platform, was certain. When asked whether he would be a candidate for the Presidency, he replied that if Davis' resolutions were to be the basis of the platform, he would not accept the nomination if offered. Davis, therefore, decided to press them, feeling that they would lessen Douglas' now rapidly diminishing chances —thus acting upon the French maxim: "Though your enemy seem as small as a rat, treat him like an elephant."

On April 23, 1860, the Democratic delegates arrived at Charleston, and the contest over Douglas was the dominating theme of conversation and caucus. It was soon evident that he controlled a majority of the delegates, but a mere majority cannot nominate, in a Democratic national convention. To succeed, a candidate must have a two-thirds majority; and Buchanan's influence had brought anti-Douglas delegates from Oregon and California, which, with the hostile Southern delegations, gave thirteen states against him, enough to prevent his nomination, should they remain united.

Davis had always felt that members of Congress should not seek to control delegates to conventions, and up to this time, as he had recently assured the Senate, had never, while serving in Congress, been in correspondence with one, or attended one. The present case, however, seemed to him to justify a departure from this rule, as he regarded Douglas as a menace to the unity of the party, and to the very Union itself. He therefore, though not attending the convention, exerted his influence with the Southern delegations to defeat him.

To the leaders in the convention, conscious of the danger of a split over Douglas' popular sovereignty and Davis' Congressional protection for slavery in the territories, it seemed wise to agree upon a platform before allowing the question of nominations to be formally introduced. A committee of thirty-three, one from each state, was therefore appointed for the purpose. "It seemed," says Rhodes, "as if the fate of the party lay in the hands of those thirty-three men, but they were really only representatives of Douglas and Jefferson Davis. The Southern delegates had in caucus determined to stand by the Davis Senate resolutions; the Northern delegates were committed to the position of Douglas."

On the fifth day the committee reported that no agreement could be reached and presented a majority, or Douglas, report, and a minority, or Davis, report. These were fiercely debated, recommitted, and rereported, in slightly altered forms, but still bearing the marks of Douglas and Davis.

On April 30th the convention adopted the Douglas platform, by a vote of 165 to 138, but it was evident that Douglas could not be nominated by such figures. The total vote was 303, and, under the two-thirds rule, it required 202 to select a candidate. Furthermore, the minority, who had stood for the Davis platform, considered that their ultimatum had been rejected, and seceded from the convention, Alabama leading, and Mississippi, Louisiana, South Carolina, Florida, Texas, and Arkansas promptly following. The delegates from Georgia remained until May 1st, when they too joined the secessionists. As the two-thirds rule had been interpreted to mean two-thirds of the convention as originally constituted, this made Douglas' nomination impossible; and Alexander H. Stephens prophesied that: "In less than twelve months we shall be in a war, and that the bloodiest in history."

The rump-convention balloted fifty-seven times, with Douglas always in the lead, but always lacking the necessary two-thirds.

Davis' strength was one and a half on the first ballot and one on the last, and the effect of his New England tour may perhaps be seen in the fact that Massachusetts' 49 votes, making one vote in the convention itself, were cast for him in unbroken succession. In each of the 57 ballots, Benjamin F. Butler, a delegate from Massachusetts, voted for Jefferson Davis as Presidential nominee, and later, when twitted for this in open Congress, replied: "I am proud of having voted as I did. Subsequent events have vindicated my judgment. I believed that Mr. Davis would be the strongest, most available candidate the Democratic party could run; and if nominated he would defeat the Republican candidate. He could unite the Democracy, North and South. . . ."

On May 3rd, weary of fruitless balloting, the rump of the Charleston convention adjourned, to meet again at Baltimore, on June 18th, after having sent an urgent appeal to the Southern states whose delegates had seceded to appoint new ones. The seceded delegates had, meanwhile, organized their own convention, adopted the Davis platform, and adjourned to meet at Richmond a few weeks later, if suitable agreements for harmony should not have been reached before that date.

Unmoved by the effect which his doctrine of Congressional protection of slavery in the territories had produced in the Charleston convention, Davis rose in the Senate, on May 8th, to press for a vote upon his resolutions. After expressing the hope that "Mississippi will never surrender the smallest atom of the sovereignty, independence, and equality to which she was born," he repeated the arguments for the compact theory based upon the complete sovereignty of each state separately, and amplified them, challenging contradiction. Later he turned to a consideration of what had happened at Charleston, where the "states met together to consult as brethren, to see whether they could agree upon the candidate as upon the creed, and it was apparent that division had entered into our ranks. After days of discussion, we saw that party convention broken up. We saw the enemies of Democracy waiting to be invited to its funeral, and jestingly looking into the blank faces of those of us to whom the telegraph brought the sad intelligence."

"I ask," he continued, "that when personal and property rights in the territories are not protected, then the Congress . . . shall intervene and provide such means as will secure in each case . . . an adequate remedy. I ask no slave code, nor horse code, nor machine code. I ask that the territorial legislature be made to understand beforehand that the Congress of the United States does not concede to them the power to interfere with the rights of person or property guaranteed by the Constitution and that it will apply the remedy, if the territorial legislature should so far forget its duty, so far transcend its power, as to commit that violation of right."

When the subject of his resolutions came again before the Senate on May 16th, as Douglas had made no satisfactory comments upon his theories, Davis ridiculed him upon his recent statement that he would not accept the Democratic nomination if coupled with the new doctrine of Congressional protection of slavery in the territories. "Does the Senator consider it modest," he asked, "to announce to the Democratic convention on what terms he will accept the nomination, but presumptuous in a state to declare the principle on which she will give him her vote? It is an advance on Louis Quatorze . . . The Senator tells us he will abide by the decision of the Supreme Court; but it was fairly to be inferred from what he said that in the Dred Scott case . . . they had only decided that a negro could not sue in a Federal court. Was this the entertainment to which we were invited? Was the . . . boon of allowing the question to go to judicial decision no more than that one after another each law might be tested . . . and that after centuries . . . we might hope for the period when, every case exhausted, the decision of our Constitutional right and of the Federal duty would be complete?

"The doctrine of Congressional protection for slavery in the territories," he continued, "goes back to the foundation of the Government. It is traceable down through all the early controversies, and they arose at least as early as 1790. It is found in the messages of Mr. Jefferson and Mr. Madison, and in the legislation of Congress; and also in the messages of the earlier Adams. . . . If the division in the Democratic party is to arise now, because of this doctrine, it is not from the change by those who assert it, but of those who deny it."

On May 16th the Republican national convention met with hope, but also with apprehension. They knew that the abolitionists would make demands which, if granted, would endanger political success. "On the great question," Lowell wrote in an essay interpretative of the condition which faced them, "Mr. Bell has no opinion at all, Mr. Douglas says it is of no consequence which opinion prevails, and Mr. Breckinridge tells us vaguely that 'all sections have an equal right in the common territories.' " Upon what the leader to be chosen would say would depend the verdict of November.

In American politics the number of candidates seeking a party nomination is considered an index of its chances in the election to follow. In this instance, candidates were many, and strong. Seward was prime favourite, even his bitter enemy, Horace Greeley, regarding his nomination as almost certain. Chase bore a national reputation scarcely second to that of Seward. Greeley's powerful influence, despite his vision of failure, was squarely behind Edward Bates, of Missouri, and Pennsylvania's delegation, with a wide circle of allies, came to nominate Simon Cameron. With such a field from which to choose, the hopes of the Illinois delegation, which paraded the streets with "fence rails cut by Abraham Lincoln," seemed almost presumptuous. The idea of nominating at such an hour a man who had never administered anything larger than a country post-office appealed to many Republicans as merely absurd.

On the first day, the relative strength of the factions was shown by the election of David Wilmot, author of the Wilmot Proviso, as temporary chairman: and that of Webster's friend, George Ashmun of Massachusetts, as permanent chairman. An even stronger indication was manifested the second day when a draft platform was reported. The abolitionist wing, dissatisfied with its cautious handling of the slavery question, moved to incorporate the famous words of the Declaration of Independence: "All men are created equal." If now incorporated in the Republican platform, it would be interpreted as committing the party to abolitionism, which many of the delegates, and millions of their constituents, then thought of much as many conservatives of today think of bolshevism. Therefore the cautious rallied and the clause was rejected.

At this, George William Curtis offered a similar amendment, asking significantly whether the convention was "prepared to go on record before the country as voting down the words of the Declaration of Independence." This was an ultimatum from a faction already committed to the proposition of disunion rather than permanent union with slaveholders, and it was evident that a second rejection might mean a secession not less dramatic than that which had wrecked the Democratic party. The cautious element, therefore, wisely yielded and the clause was inserted in the second plank, from the words of the Declaration "that all men are created equal," to the end of the phrase, "deriving their just powers from the consent of the governed." A failure to use the above phrase would have been, to quote again James Russell Lowell, "a defiance of the public sentiment of the civilized world." But to most of the convention the words meant no attack on slavery. The platform said "all men are created equal," but meant, as the authors of the Declaration of Independence had themselves meant, "some men."

The remainder of the platform was pressed by its sponsors with determination. The repudiation of John Brown, demanded by political expediency, was balanced by the denial of the authority of Congress, of a territorial legislature, or of any individual to give legal existence to slavery in the territories. The avoidance of the dangerous questions: the Fugitive Slave Laws, Personal Liberty Laws, abolition of slavery in the District of Columbia, and the Dred Scott decision, aroused in the abolitionists no new threats of revolt, and thus at last the difficult task of agreement upon a platform by men with little area of agreement was complete.

In the nomination which followed, the number of votes was 465, of which, 233, a bare majority, were necessary for a choice. On the first ballot Seward polled 173½ to Lincoln's 102, and thereafter, until the dramatic climax, the latter's friends, like those of all other candidates, played politics for victory. Vainly did Lincoln, from his home in Illinois, instruct his managers to "make no contracts that will bind me." His managers wanted the nomination more than Lincoln wanted it, and they secured the Indiana delegates by a promise of a Cabinet post for Caleb Smith, and the Pennsylvania delegates by promising that Lincoln would make Simon Cameron Secretary of War.

On the third ballot, Lincoln's column showed 231½ and Seward's 180. Then came the landslide, the possibility of which gives such thrilling interest to the monotonous process of recording the votes in a national convention. Lincoln was declared the unanimous choice: and a telegram was sent to him at Springfield.

As the telegraph messenger approached Lincoln, who was engaged in a game of baseball on the public green, he waved the envelope, crying, "The Convention has made a nomination, and Abraham Lincoln—!" Lincoln took the telegram, announced its import, and remarked: "I guess I'll tell a little woman down the street the news."

Although entirely in sympathy with his party's determination to keep slavery out of the territories, Lincoln's views concerning the legal right of the states to maintain it within their own areas differed little from those of Davis. Bitter as was his hatred of the institution, he felt that the Fugitive Slave Law must be supported, and the Federal Government must not seek to interfere with slave property within the slave states. Lowell declared, indeed, that "the chief complaint made against Mr. Lincoln by his opponents is that he is too Constitutional." Yet, his nomination alarmed the South like a fire-bell in the night. This was due to the abolitionist victories in the Republican national convention, after which, reported William Tecumseh Sherman, then head of the Louisiana State Military College, "all the reasoning and truth in the world would not convince a Southern man that the Republicans are not abolitionists."

In this Davis was a thoroughly Southern man. He was convinced that Lincoln's election would mean a consolidated government, and the latter's oft-repeated vow to respect the rights of slavery in the states where it existed and his platform declaration, that "the lawless invasion by armed force of the soil of any state, or territory, no matter under what pretext, is . . . among the gravest of crimes," reassured him not at all. He believed that Lincoln would prove but a convenient figurehead behind whom, and through whom, the abolitionists would destroy the essential features of the Constitution, and destroy slavery, thus making easy the task of destroying the other reserved rights of the states which the Constitution guaranteed.

It is but fair to add that the abolitionists, the immediate emancipators, were not the only Americans who looked forward to a day when slavery would cease. The South had many patient emancipationists, if we may so call them, men who while doubting the wisdom of immediate abolition, yet hoped for the freedom which would follow development. Robert E. Lee was one of these. Henderson, in his life of "Stonewall" Jackson, thus quotes him: "In this enlightened age there are few, I believe, but will acknowledge that slavery as an institution is a moral and political evil. It is useless to expatiate on its disadvantages. I think it a greater evil to the white than to the coloured race, and while my feelings are strongly interested in the latter, my sympathies are more deeply engaged for the former. The blacks are immeasurably better off here than in Africa—morally, socially and physically. The painful discipline they are undergoing is necessary for their instruction as a race, and, I hope, will prepare them for better things. How long their subjection may be necessary is known and ordered by a merciful Providence. Their emancipation will sooner result from the mild and melting influence of Christianity than from the storms and contests of fiery controversy. This influence, though slow, is sure."

Lincoln, in his debates with Douglas, in 1858, had shown that he was nearer to these patient emancipationists than to the abolitionist wing of his own party. By limiting slavery to the territory which it already occupied, he had explained, we will place it in a position where the public mind may rest in the assurance that it is on the way to ultimate extinction. He admitted that this ultimate extinction would be long delayed, but that "in an hundred years it would be accomplished."

Ardent defender of slavery as he was, Davis too must be enrolled in the list of patient emancipationists. Over and over again he elaborated the idea that slavery was slowly giving to the negro race religious and economic ideals far higher than they had ever attained elsewhere, or were likely to attain in America if suddenly set free in a world in which they were not fitted to compete.

The obvious fact that the division of the Democrats would mean Lincoln's election, did not cause Davis to relax his efforts to pass his resolutions through the Senate, and on May 24th and 25th he succeeded. The vote was divided on party lines, but not sectionally, the Democrats, Northern and Southern alike, in general sustained the resolutions, while the Republicans either opposed them or abstained from voting. Senator Douglas, who had been Davis' chief opponent in the debate, was absent when the vote was taken. Had he foreseen the effect which these resolutions were to have in the near future upon his long cherished presidential aspirations, it is doubtful whether the malady from which he suffered could have kept him from his place.

Though conscious that he could not expect the assent of the House of Representatives, Davis hoped that the support given by the Senate would discourage Douglas' followers, and result in a nomination which the southern Democrats could follow. He wrote to Pierce five days before the reconvening of the Democratic national convention at Baltimore:

"We all deplore the want of unanimity as to the candidate among our Southern friends and I do not see any satisfactory solution of the difficulty. The darkest hour precedes the dawn and it may be that light will break upon us when most needed and least expected.

"If your hope should be realized as to the action of the N. E. and N. Y. delegation in relation to the delegates to be admitted from the South, it will have a good effect, if they should otherwise decide in favour of the previous delegates the Democratic party will become historic.

"Our people will support any sound man, but will not vote for a 'squatter sovereignty' candidate any more than for a 'free soiler.'

"If northern men insist upon nominating Douglas we must be beaten and with such alienation as leaves nothing to hope for in the future, of nationality in our organization.

"I have urged my friends to make an honest effort to save our party from disintegration as the last hope of averting ruin from the country. They would gladly unite upon you, or Dallas and would readily be brought to any one of like character and record. I urged upon Mr. Minot before he went to Charleston the evil effect of permitting N. H. to be mustered in under the banner of Douglas, but it was of no avail. Matters are now more complicated and men are more unreasonable. Some are unwilling to go into the Convention at Baltimore and are disposed to rush blindly on dangers which they feel are at hand but do not appreciate, others see in the crisis only the vulgar struggle of the ins and the outs, and have no fear of a catastrophe, whilst a few are willing to abandon the government to get rid of men who are unfaithful to it.

"I have never seen the country in so great danger and those who might protect it seem to be unconscious of the necessity. If one little, grey, drinking, electioneering, Demagogue can destroy our hopes, it must be that we have been doomed to destruction."

The seceding delegates did join the convention at Baltimore, however, but as some of their places were by then occupied by other delegates sent by their states, the confusion and bitterness were greatly increased, and on the fifth day there occurred a second secession. Chairman Cushing retired and was followed by some or all of the delegates from Virginia, North Carolina, Tennessee, Delaware, Maryland, Kentucky and California. These, with the delegates who had seceded at Charleston, organized in Institute Hall a Southern Democratic party. To give a national flavour to their ticket, they combined a Presidential candidate, John C. Breckinridge, of Kentucky, with a Vice-Presidential candidate from Oregon, Joseph Lane; and they based their platform upon Congressional protection of slavery in the territories. The remains of the Charleston-Baltimore Democratic national convention, thus freed from its anti-Douglas delegates, nominated Douglas of Illinois for President and Herschel V. Johnson of Georgia for Vice-President.

On July 1, 1860, Stephens wrote: "The Charleston rupture was bad enough, but that at Baltimore was much worse. What the friends of Mr. Douglas meant by pressing his nomination in the face of the secession of Tennessee, Kentucky, and Virginia, to say nothing of other states, I can not imagine. As I view the field, he has no probable chance of election. . . . The only use or public benefit his running can be . . . is for him to carry enough Northern electoral votes to defeat Mr. Lincoln . . . and throw the election into the House, where his party rival, Mr. Breckinridge, may make him a stepping-stone in his elevation to power and place. Had Douglas been nominated at Charleston, he would have carried the South against a Richmond nomination. But at present it is impossible. The Baltimore convention, instead of stopping the break in the levee, only made it deeper and wider." In this, Stephens was a better political prophet than Davis: but he lacked the latter's fighting qualities, and weakly added: "In this state of things . . . I am satisfied that the best course I can take is, to leave the whole matter with those who have undertaken the management of this crisis."

Lowell thus interpreted the situation: "Although there are four candidates, there are really, as everybody knows, but two parties, and a single question that divides them . . . the interpretation to be put upon certain clauses of the Constitution. All . . . parties equally assert their loyalty to that instrument. Indeed, it is quite the fashion. The removers of all the ancient landmarks of our policy, the violators of thrice-pledged faith, the planners of new treachery to establish compromise, all take refuge in the Constitution,

> 'Like thieves that in a hemp-plot lie,
> Secure against the hue and cry.'

. . . What do they mean by the Constitution? Mr. Breckinridge means the superiority of a certain exceptional species of property over all others; nay, over man himself. Mr. Douglas, with a different formula for expressing it, means practically the same thing. Both of them mean that labour has no rights which capital is bound to respect—that there is no higher law than human interest and cupidity. . . ."

There were indeed "only two parties," but the subject was by no means so simple as Lowell sought to make it appear. All American history must be written into it, if we are to understand it. Slavery was certainly an important element, and one that helped to emphasize the importance of the others, but the basis of this party division, as of all others, since Jefferson faced Hamilton in Washington's Cabinet, was not slavery, but a conflict of decentralization against consolidation; and upon that issue Davis knew that he could count upon a united South.

In this connexion it is interesting to quote the words of Colonel Henderson, the brilliant commentator of later years: "When, in process of time the history of secession comes to be viewed with the same freedom from prejudice as the history of the Seventeenth and Eighteenth Centuries, it will be clear that the fourth great revolution of the English-speaking race differs in no essential characteristic from those which preceded it. . . . In each case a great principle was at stake: in 1642 the liberty of the subject; in 1688 the integrity of the Protestant faith; in 1775 taxation only with consent of the taxed; in 1861 the sovereignty of the individual states."

As the campaign progressed, it became ever more apparent that no one of Lincoln's opponents, Douglas, Breckinridge or Bell, could defeat the united Republican organization, and Davis, therefore, sought to induce them to unite their forces for the defeat of Lincoln. He found Breckinridge and Bell ready to make the personal sacrifice in favour of some union candidate; but Douglas declined, declaring that his followers, if unable to follow him, would go to the support of Lincoln. Accordingly, on October 5th, Governor Gist, of South Carolina, sent a confidential letter to the governors of all the cotton states, Governor Sam Houston of Texas excepted, suggesting concerted action in the event of Lincoln's election. "If a single state secedes," it said, "we will follow her. If no other state takes the lead, South Carolina will secede (in my opinion) alone, if she has any assurance that she will soon be followed by another or other states. . . ."

Two days later, in a letter to L. P. Conner and others, dated at "Brierfield," October 7, 1860, Davis wrote: "Confronted by a common foe, the South should, by the instinct of self-preservation, be united. Differences on minor questions might, it would seem, be forgotten in the face of an issue so momentous as is now presented. To rally the men of the North, who would preserve the Government as our Fathers found it, we—for whose rights under the Constitution and the laws they are contending—should offer no doubtful or divided front. . . . Breckinridge is the best representative of the interests and avowed policy of the South, as well as the best hope of the preservation of our Constitutional Union.

"Had the doctrine of states' rights . . . been the accepted creed of the whole country, no sectional strife could have arisen because of differences in the domestic institutions of the states, no obstacle could have been presented to the fulfilment of the great purpose of the Union, the concentration of the power of all for the security and safety of each against danger, whether foreign or domestic. A return to the original spirit and purpose of the Government is the necessity of the time; and it needs no argument to show that this is most clearly indicated by the most unequivocal antagonism to the party which seeks to seize upon the government as a means to make war upon the domestic tranquillity, welfare and sovereignty of the slaveholding states of the Union. The recent declarations of the candidate and leaders of the 'Black Republican' party are familiar to you and need not be recited; they must suffice to convince many who have formerly doubted the purpose to attack the institution of slavery in the states. The undying opposition to slavery in the United States means war upon it where it is, not where it is not; and the time is at hand when the great battle is to be fought between the defenders of the constitutional government and the votaries of mob rule, fanaticism and anarchy. . . ."

As election day approached, Lincoln's followers, fearful lest his enemies, by branding him as an abolitionist, might weaken his chances even at the North, urged him to deny again the charge. On October 23rd he answered: "I have already done this many, many times; and it is in print, and open to all who will read. Those who will not read or heed what I have already publicly said would not read or heed a repetition of it. 'If they hear not Moses and the prophets, neither will they be persuaded though one rose from the dead.'" And to George D. Prentice, the brilliant editor of the *Louisville Courier Journal*, he wrote in confidence, six days later, "I have not decided that I will not do substantially what you suggest. If I do finally abstain, it will be because of apprehension that it would do harm. For the good men of the South—and I regard the majority of them as such—I have no objection to repeat seventy and seven times. But I have bad men to deal with, both North and South; men who are eager for something new upon which to base new misrepresentations; men who would like to frighten me, or at least to fix upon me the character of timidity and cowardice. They would seize upon almost any letter I could write as being an 'awful coming down.'"

On November 6th came the news that the majority of electors chosen by the states were pledged to Lincoln and Hamlin; and at once the watchers on the streets of Charleston and other South Carolina towns raised cheers for the Southern Confederacy.

Unofficial news of Lincoln's victory reached Davis at "Brierfield," and with it a letter from R. B. Rhett, Jr., of South Carolina, asking his opinion about an immediate and separate secession by South Carolina, to which Davis replied on November 10: ". . . Reports leave little doubt that . . . electors have been chosen securing the election of Lincoln. . . . My home is so isolated that I have no intercourse with those who might have aided me in forming an opinion as to the effect produced on the mind of our people by the result of the recent election, and the impressions which I communicate are founded upon antecedent expressions. . . .

"I. I doubt not that the Governor of Mississippi has convoked the legislature . . . to decide upon the course which the state should adopt in the present emergency. Whether the legislature will direct the call of a convention of the state, or appoint delegates to a convention of such Southern states as may be willing to consult together for the adoption of a Southern plan of action, is doubtful.

"II. If a convention of the states were assembled, the proposition to secede from the Union, independently of support from neighbouring states, would probably fail.

"III. If South Carolina should first secede, and she alone should take such action, the position of Mississippi would not probably be changed by that fact. A powerful obstacle to the separate action of Mississippi is the want of a port; from which follows the consequence that her trade being still conducted through the ports of the Union, her revenue would be diverted from her own support to that of a foreign government; and being geographically unconnected with South Carolina, an alliance with her would not vary that state of the case.

"IV. The propriety of separate secession by South Carolina depends so much upon collateral questions that I find it difficult to respond to your last enquiry . . . Georgia is necessary to connect you with Alabama, and thus to make effectual the co-operation of Mississippi. If Georgia would be lost by immediate action, but could be gained by delay, it seems clear to me that you should wait. If the secession of South Carolina should be followed by an attempt to coerce her back into the Union, that act of usurpation, folly, and wickedness would enlist every true Southern man for her defence. If it were attempted to blockade her ports and destroy her trade, a like result would be produced, and the commercial world would probably be added to her allies. It is probable that neither of those measures would be adopted by any administration, but that Federal ships would be sent to collect the duties on imports outside of the bar; that the commercial nations would feel little interest in that; and the Southern states would have little power to counteract it.

"The planting states have a common interest of such magnitude, that their union, sooner or later, for the protection of that interest, is certain. United they will have ample power for their own protection, and their exports will make for them allies of all commercial and manufacturing powers.

"The new states have a heterogeneous population, and will be slower and less unanimous than those in which there is less of the Northern element in the body politic, but interest controls the policy of states, and finally all the planting communities must reach the same conclusion.

"My opinion is, therefore, as it has been . . . to bring those states into co-operation before asking for a popular decision upon a new policy. . . . If South Carolina should resolve to secede before that co-operation can be obtained, to go out leaving Georgia, and Alabama, and Louisiana in the Union, and without any reason to suppose they will follow her, there appears to me to be no advantage in waiting until the government has passed into hostile hands, and men have become familiarized to that injurious and offensive perversion of the general government from the ends for which it was established. I have written with the freedom and carelessness of private correspondence, and regret that I could not give more precise information."

CHAPTER XI

SECESSION OF SOUTH CAROLINA

ON NOVEMBER 10, 1860, South Carolina's legislature unanimously adopted a call for a "Sovereignty Convention" of the state, to meet a week later: and on November 10th and 13th, respectively, James Chestnut and James H. Hammond, her two United States Senators, resigned their seats, their action being looked upon in the South much as nations regard demands for passports, when foreign ambassadors retire in hours of crisis from the capitals of nations to which they have been accredited. Their resignation was approved by Davis upon grounds which he had formulated two years earlier. "If I should ever, whilst a Senator, deem it my duty to assume an attitude of hostility to the Union, I should . . . feel bound to resign the office, and return to my constituency to inform them of the fact. It was this view of the obligations of my position, which caused me, on various occasions, to repel, with such indignation, the accusation of being a disunionist, while holding the office of Senator of the United States."

At this critical moment Governor Pettus called a conference of the Senators and Representatives of Mississippi, to consider whether the state should "pass an ordinance of secession . . . or . . . endeavour to hold South Carolina in check, and delay action herself, until other states can get ready through their conventions to unite with them . . . and secede in a body."

Upon the one side it was argued "that South Carolina could not be induced to delay action a moment beyond the meeting of her convention, and that . . . to delay action would be to have her crushed by the Federal Government."

There were many views expressed, but, according to the account of one of the members, "Mr. Davis . . . opposed immediate and separate state action, declaring himself opposed to secession as long as the hope of a peaceable remedy remained. He did not believe we ought to precipitate the issue, as he felt certain from his knowledge of the people, North and South, that, once there was a clash of arms, the contest would be one of the most sanguinary the world had ever witnessed," a statement which contrasts strangely with General Grant's later assertion that Davis had declared his readiness "to drink all the blood spilled south of Mason and Dixon's line, if there should be a war." He, however, announced at the end of the discussion, that he would stand by any decision which the majority might make, in order "that no delay should be interposed to separate state action."

Before the end of the conference a telegram from two members of Buchanan's Cabinet was handed to Davis requesting his immediate return to Washington. He reported its contents to the conference, which expressed the opinion that he should start at once. It appeared that most of the members were anxious to be rid of him, believing, as Mr. Singleton says, that "he was entirely opposed to secession, and was seeking to delay action upon the part of Mississippi, in the hope that it might be averted." His recall to Washington proved to be due to Buchanan's desire to consult him upon a message he was preparing. Clearly he was still upon friendly terms with the Democratic President, even if less influential than he had been under President Pierce.

Meanwhile, the press of the Southern and Border states set their best writers to prove by an interpretation of election statistics that Lincoln, when the electoral colleges should vote, would become only a minority President, a thesis easy to establish. Pamphleteers flooded the market with elaborate and often fantastic argument along the same line. As he was still being represented as hostile to the South and a menace to her "peculiar institution," his friends renewed their demand that he make a public statement to the contrary. But to each he returned a reasoned reply: For the present he thought it best to stand upon utterances already published, in which he had repeatedly declared friendship for the people of the South and acceptance of the fact that slavery within the states was beyond the powers of a President-elect, a President, or a national Congress. It was difficult for him to understand why he should be regarded as so serious a menace to the Southern states whose institutions he did not plan to attack or to overthrow.

On December 11th, however, he restated his views in confidence to William Kellogg, who had asked advice: "Entertain no proposition for a compromise in regard to the extension of slavery," he said. "The instant you do they have us under again; all our labour is lost, and sooner or later must be done over. Douglas is sure to be again trying to bring in his popular sovereignty. Have none of it. The tug has to come, and better now than later. You know I think the fugitive-slave clause of the Constitution ought to be enforced—to put it in its mildest form, ought not to be resisted." In striking contrast is Davis' opinion that the return of fugitive slaves was "not a proper subject for legislation by the Federal Government." Both Lincoln and Davis were legalists; both admitted the right of the states to have slave property protected: but Lincoln assigned the duty to the Federal Government, while Davis assigned it to the states.

Lincoln was a strange combination of fancy and common sense. His ideals were those of a practical leader, who, as Lowell once said, aimed at the best, but was content to take the next best, if "lucky enough to get even that." There can be no doubt of his detestation of slavery, which appears in his spoken and written utterances of every period, but he was willing to take what he conceived to be the only thing legally obtainable, the restriction of slavery to areas where it already enjoyed the protection of laws, made by the joint votes of North and South. If his imagination pictured a future in which he could carry out the desire, long ago expressed, as he turned away from a slave auction, "to hit slavery hard," he as yet gave no intimation of it, and his readiness to enforce the Fugitive Slave law shows that he was not yet freed from Whig influence in which he had been reared, although he must have realized that the Whig willingness to protect slavery by Federal laws justified the charge later formulated by Gerrit Smith, in the words: "Scarcely less responsible than the South for the generation and growth of this infernal spirit [the spirit that denied the rights of man], the North has sought as earnestly as the South to serve herself of slavery. She as well as the South has ever maintained that the Nation is bound by her organic law to uphold slavery. Politically, ecclesiastically, commercially, socially, she has upheld slavery."

This indictment was true. Even James G. Blaine later recorded that up to this period "every demand which the South had made . . . had been conceded," and every law for the protection of slave property had thereby become not a sectional but a national sin. And it is well to note that while the South had voted for laws to protect an institution which it accepted as God's will, the North had of late voted for them, while professing to believe slavery morally unjustifiable. The abolitionists, alone, refused to vote for the protection of an institution which they regarded as pernicious, although the Constitution sanctioned it.

On December 14, 1860, members of the Senate and House from the states of Alabama, Georgia, Florida, Arkansas, Mississippi, North Carolina, Louisiana, Texas and South Carolina joined in an address entitled to "Our Constituents," the purpose of which was to influence the several state conventions, then soon to assemble, in favour of immediate "separate state secession." The address when written by Senator Wigfall and James L. Pugh, was sent to Davis, who made some verbal alterations and put it into its final form. It was then dispatched to Southern voters, urging them to prepare for secession. This incident seems at first glance to place Davis unmistakably in the ranks of those who wished to bring about a dissolution of the Union. But the same logic would fasten the charge upon Horace Greeley who, three days later, published in the *New York Tribune* an article which declared: "If the cotton states shall become satisfied that they can do better out of the Union than in it, we insist on letting them go in peace. . . . We must ever resist the right of any state to remain in the Union, and nullify or defy the laws thereof. To withdraw from the Union is quite another matter; and whenever any considerable section of our Union shall deliberately resolve to go out, we shall resist all coercive measures designed to keep it in. We hope never to live in a Republic whereof one section is pinned to another by bayonets," and added the argument so often used by Davis: If the Declaration of Independence "justifies the secession of three millions of Colonists in 1776, we do not see why it would not justify the secession of five millions of Southerners from the Federal Union in 1861."

December 20th provided justification for Davis' prophecy that South Carolina would not delay action long enough to effect a previous union of the cotton states. On that day her sovereignty convention passed an ordinance which declared: "that the Union now subsisting between South Carolina and other states under the name of 'The United States of America' is hereby dissolved." With meticulous care it observed the maxim of Noyes, "Unum quoque dissolutur eo modo colligatur—everything is dissolved by the same means by which it was constituted." After a careful study of the process by which South Carolina had ratified the Federal Constitution, they unratified it by reversing that process. Unanimity was complete, the 169 delegates voting "yea," with no dissenting voice.

The signing of the ordinance was made a public function, and before the hour appointed for the ceremony, Institute Hall was crowded to capacity. When the delegates, attended by the officials of the commonwealth, had taken their places, a white-haired clergyman prayed for the blessing of God upon the solemn act now to be consummated. The president of the convention then read the ordinance of secession. At the word, "dissolved," cheers arose from the audience, and were echoed by the throngs outside. The members of the convention then came forward, one by one, and affixed their signatures to the document. At the end of two hours the signing was complete and the president concluded the ceremony with the words:

"I proclaim the State of South Carolina an independent commonwealth."

It was a misfortune for the Southern cause, that the state which thus took the lead in secession should have been the one where the great slaveholding aristocracy held most complete control of politics—for the documents which they issued went far to support the later interpretation of the war as a crusade against slavery. Davis still laboured to convince the public that the South's aim was what the Fathers' aim had been in the Revolution, to defend the Constitution and the right of sovereign states to enjoy the kind of government desired by their inhabitants, but the leaders of South Carolina so definitely indicated the protection of slave property as their chief motive that he ever thereafter fought a losing battle. The abolitionists were quick to seize the advantage given them by South Carolina; and Charles Eliot Norton declared: "When the history of American slavery is written, its open decline and fall will be dated from the day in which the South Carolina declaration of independence was adopted."

The situation created by South Carolina's secession demanded of the Federal Government definite plans in reply, but definite plans were out of the question. President Buchanan's views made action almost impossible; and Lincoln, by the strange provision of the American system, was doomed to remain a private citizen until March 4, 1861. In vain did General Winfield Scott urge the prompt garrisoning of the Federal forts in the cotton states, as

Attorney-General Black had long urged. In vain did Anderson
ask for reinforcements and supplies. Buchanan would do nothing
because in his opinion there was nothing which he could do.
While holding that a state has no right to secede, he also held
that the Federal Government had not been granted power to prevent secession. This meant, as Blaine caustically pointed out in
later days, "that the power to destroy was in the state. The power
to preserve was not in the nation"; or, to quote the more sarcastic
interpretation of Seward: "it is the duty of the President to execute the laws—unless somebody opposes him; but that no state
has a right to go out of the Union—unless it wants to."

Davis held that it was within Buchanan's power to prevent
other Southern states from supporting South Carolina, if he only
had the courage to act. "Mr. Buchanan," he later said, "was an
able man, but a very timid one. If he had had the nerve to deal
with the situation, as its gravity demanded, I doubt exceedingly
whether any other State would have followed South Carolina
into secession. Had he withdrawn the troops from Sumter, it
would have been such a conspicuous act of conciliation that the
other States would not, I believe, have called conventions to consider the question of secession, or if they had, the ordinances
would not have been passed. I was not one of those who believed
that there could ever be a peaceful separation of the States, but
could not convince our people of it. I had years before become
convinced by my association with public men, and especially with
Mr. Webster, that the North would never consent to it. I knew
that secession meant war, and, therefore, did my utmost to prevent it."

South Carolina's secession furnished also a concrete issue calculated to rouse "the drumming guns that know no doubts," as the
ultimate ownership of her forts now became a critical question.
In his message of December 3rd, Buchanan had declared that the
land on which these forts stood had "been purchased for a fair
equivalent 'by the consent of the legislature of the state, for the

creation of forts, magazines, arsenals etc.' and over these the authority 'to exercise exclusive legislation' had been granted, by the Constitution, to Congress."

Davis held a very different view: "The ultimate ownership of the soil, or eminent domain," he wrote, "remains with the people of the State in which it lies, by virtue of their sovereignty." Moreover, the United States had been ceded the forts and fortifications in Charleston harbour, in 1805, upon the condition: "that if the United States shall not, within three years from the passing of this act, . . . repair the fortifications . . . and keep a garrison or garrisons therein; in such case this grant or cession shall be void and of no effect." This condition had not been fulfilled, and, early in December, 1860, Lewis Cass, Buchanan's Secretary of State, after vainly urging its fulfilment, had resigned in protest, leaving two of these forts unoccupied, and the third, Fort Moultrie, garrisoned by only 100 men. Clearly in Davis' view, the other two forts being still ungarrisoned, had reverted to South Carolina, under the terms of the deed of cession.

It should have been evident to Buchanan that out of such a difference of opinion, a crisis might arise at any moment. Instead, however, of starting a proper investigation of the justice of these claims, he took no action. Without his authorization, however, Cass had ordered Major Anderson to defend his possession of Fort Moultrie so long as he was reasonably confident of his ability to hold it, but "not, without evident and imminent necessity, to take up any position which could be construed into the assumption of a hostile attitude," and "to avoid every act which would needlessly tend to provoke aggression."

Matters stood thus when South Carolina sent to the President a copy of her ordinance, sealed with the state's great seal. With the assumption that the Federal Government would not attempt to keep her in the Union by force, but would treat with her as a foreign state, she sent also a commission authorized to seek an agreement for a proper division of the national debt, and for an equable division of public property; and by "equable" she meant that the forts in South Carolina waters should be acknowledged to be South Carolina property. This procedure, being in line with his view of the ownership of the forts, Davis considered eminently proper, in the interest of peace, and in strict accordance with the theory long held by both sections of the nation.

That both sections had at times held it the right of a state to secede from the Union is beyond question. Mr. Justice Chase declared as early as 1796, "I consider this [the Declaration of Independence] a declaration, not that the United States jointly, in a collective capacity, were independent states, &C., but that each of them was a sovereign and independent state, that is, that each of them had a right to govern itself by its own authority and its own laws, without any control from any other power." Josiah Quincy said in Congress, fifteen years later, "I am compelled to declare it as my deliberate opinion that if this bill passes, the bonds of this Union are virtually dissolved; that the states which compose it are free from their moral obligations, and that, as it will be the right of all, so it will be the duty of some, to prepare definitely for a separation, amicably, if they can, violently if they must." The Hartford convention of December, 1814, adopted, unanimously, a report that: "In case of deliberate, dangerous, and palpable infractions of the Constitution, affecting the sovereignty of a state, and the liberties of the people, it is not only the right, but the duty of such a state to interpose its authority for their protection, in the manner best calculated to secure that end. When emergencies occur, which are either beyond the reach of judicial tribunals, or too pressing to admit of the delay incident to their forms, states which have no common umpire, must be their own judges and execute their own decisions." And even Andrew Jackson had approved the publication of an article by his able Secretary of State, Edward Livingston, placing him squarely behind the doctrine that a state may leave the Union, but that so long as she remains in the Union, she must obey Federal laws. This distinction

Jefferson Davis accepted as the very bedrock of his political philosophy, and he never abandoned it.

The French philosopher, Pascal, declared: "We must put together justice and force; and therefore so dispose things that whatever is just is mighty, and whatever is mighty is just." Or as Woodrow Wilson expressed it to the plenary session engaged in drafting the Covenant of the League of Nations, "armed force is the background in this program, but it is in the background, and if the moral force of the world will not suffice, the physical force of the world shall."

While the question of the legal ownership of the South Carolina forts was still in dispute, the Federal Government turned to the question of the wisdom of using force to keep possession of them. To resort to force was to court resistance by force, and to raise the question of the right to coerce a state. Davis strongly advocated the removal of all garrisons from them, and on the day of South Carolina's secession, he said in the Senate:

"If there be danger, permit me here to say it is because there are troops in it, not because the garrison is too weak. Who hears of any danger of the seizure of forts where there is no garrison? There stand Forts Pulaski and Jackson, at the mouth of the Savannah River. Who hears of any apprehension lest Georgia should seize them? There are Castle Pinckney and Fort Sumter, in Charleston harbour. Who hears of any danger of seizure there? The whole danger . . . arises from the presence of United States troops. Is the remedy, then, to increase the garrison? It is impracticable to do it, if that were the remedy; and if it were practicable, I hold it would only increase the danger. It would only be multiplying the chances of collision."

On that same day, the Senate decided to appoint a committee of thirteen, to consider and report upon the agitated condition of the country, and Davis was asked to serve as a member. After some reluctance, he accepted in the words:

"If, in the opinion of others, it be possible for me to do anything for the public good, the last moment while I stand here is at the command of the Senate. If I could see any means by which I could avert the catastrophe of a struggle between the sections of the Union, my past life, I hope, gives evidence of the readiness with which I would make the effort. If there be any sacrifice which I could offer on the altar of my country to heal all the evils, present or prospective, no man has the right to doubt my readiness to make it."

The committee consisted, Davis later wrote, of "States-rights men of the South . . . Radicals of the North and Northern Democrats, with one member who did not acknowledge himself as belonging to any one of the three, Mr. Crittenden, an old-time Whig and the original mover of the compromise resolutions." They agreed that unless some measure could be devised which would command the support of a majority of each of these three divisions, it would be useless to present any report. "After many days of anxious discussion," writes Davis in his *Autobiography*, during which the chairman, Mr. Crittenden, and the two Democratic groups frequently agreed, it was evident that "they could never get a majority of the Northern Radicals to unite with them in any substantive proposition." Douglas "defiantly challenged the Northern Radicals to tell what they wanted. As they refused everything, he claimed that they ought to be willing to tell what they proposed." But no way could be found to unite the three groups, although, as Douglas later reported to the Senate, Davis "was ready at all times to compromise on the Crittenden proposition. I will go farther and say that Mr. Toombs was also ready to do so. . . . If the Crittenden proposition could have passed early in the session, it would have saved all the states except South Carolina."

The committee of thirteen was followed by a committee of thirty-three, one from each state; but even had there been a chance of conciliation by compromise when it began its conferences, the chance was greatly reduced before its adjournment by sudden and startling developments in Charleston harbour.

It was commonly reported in Southern circles at the time, though stoutly denied by Davis, that President Buchanan had promised not to send reinforcements to the Charleston forts, nor to alter their military status until questions arising out of South Carolina's secession should be discussed with her representatives. Buchanan's denial of such a pledge was even more positive, and more frequent than Davis'; but he added, later: "I acted in the same manner I would have done had I entered into a positive and formal agreement. . . . I have never sent any reinforcements to the forts . . . and I have certainly never authorized any change to be made 'in their relative military status.' " Clearly, he had no intention of seeking to solve this enigma, which the popular voice had already called another to solve.

Up to this point Lincoln had resisted all appeals for a restatement of his attitude, to allay the fears of the South. But South Carolina's ordinance of secession, and the two addresses issued by the convention in explanation of its adoption, had pilloried him as in effect committed to the destruction of slavery in the Southern states: and he at last consented to utter the reassuring words which friend and foe alike had failed to draw from him during the campaign and immediately after his election. On December 22nd, in response to Stephens' warning that "force may perpetuate *a* Union, . . . but such a Union would . . . be nothing short of a consolidated despotism," Lincoln replied: "Do the people of the South really entertain fears that a Republican administration would, directly or indirectly, interfere with the slaves, or with them about the slaves? If they do, I wish to assure you, as once a friend, and still, I hope, not an enemy, that there is no cause for such fears. The South would be in no more danger in this respect than it was in the days of Washington. I suppose, however, this does not meet the case. You think slavery is right and ought to be extended, while we think it is wrong and ought to be restricted.

That, I suppose, is the rub. It certainly is the only substantial difference between us."

Davis, however, believed that there was another substantial difference, being convinced that Lincoln's aim was to convert a Federal Republic of sovereign states into a consolidated nation with the right to dominate the states, the old idea which had precipitated the American Revolution. He feared the Federal Government only in what he considered its usurpations, the chief of which Stephens described as "that deformed and hideous monster which rises from the decomposing elements of dead states, the world over, and which is well known by the friends of constitutional liberty, everywhere, as the demon of centralization, absolutism and despotism!"

It is only just to remind the reader, at this point, of the fate which has overtaken the many nations which have recently yielded to this same "demon of centralization, absolutism and despotism."

Had Davis and Stephens lived to witness these transformations, and could they have seen the League of Nations and the British Commonwealth of Nations, built upon an acknowledgment of the right of sovereign states to secede, and upon a denial of the right of coercion to prevent secession, they would have been strengthened in the belief which Stephens formulated: "The federative principles are the world's best hope, in the great future, for the regeneration, the renaissance, of the nations of the earth." Thus the fear that Lincoln contemplated the use of power, illegally seized, to interfere with slavery, caused Davis to view with less and less unwillingness the idea that, to quote Mr. Justice Campbell, it might soon be necessary to "abandon the Union and save the Constitution."

The abolitionists, on the other hand, had long since announced their willingness to destroy the Constitution if necessary, in order to destroy slavery; and circumstances were rapidly preparing for Lincoln a situation in which he must make the choice. Often he had declared that the Constitution gave the Federal Government no power over slavery in the states. Yet to his mind the Union was "the last best hope of man." To preserve it, he felt at liberty to destroy slavery, to let it live, or to destroy part of the institution and preserve the other part; in short, "to abandon the Constitution to save the Union."

These discordant views, representative of sections rather than of men, were held with equal honesty, equal devotion. To the one group the preservation of the Constitution as written was the paramount duty: to the other, the preservation of the Union. And between opposite paramount duties there can be no moral compromise. Each might admit the honesty, even the patriotism of the other, but neither could, without moral lapse, adopt the point of view of the other. "I never blamed a Northern man," said Mr. Justice Campbell, "for supporting *his* country . . . and, before the bar of justice and fairness, I demand the same recognition for myself and my countrymen in supporting ours." And Gerrit Smith later matched this sentiment with the words: "I do . . . blame the Davises and Lees, and Breckinridges for choosing Patrick Henry, Jefferson, Madison, and Calhoun, instead of Washington, Hamilton, Jay, and Webster for their teachers at this point. Nevertheless, I am reasonable enough to pity as well as blame them. . . . In their circumstances, you and I would, in all probability, have been tempted to do as they did. In all probability, we would have, under the teachings and influences which they came under."

Had not this attempt of Davis and his associates to save the Constitution involved also the saving of the institution of slavery, it would have been comparatively easy to reconcile the positions of the North and South. But with the preservation of that institution involved, Seward's view of a "higher law" stirred apprehensions which even Lincoln's denial of the purpose or right to interfere with slavery could not allay; and these apprehensions were greatly increased on December 26th, when Anderson unexpectedly moved his troops from the exposed position at Fort Moultrie to the comparative security of Fort Sumter. As soon as the report was verified, Davis, accompanied by Trescot and Hunter, went to the White House. "Have you received any intelligence from Charleston in the last few hours?" Davis asked Buchanan, and upon receiving a negative reply, continued, "Then I have a great calamity to announce to you." When Buchanan had heard the news, "My God!" he exclaimed, "are calamities never to come singly? I call God to witness, you, gentlemen, better than anybody, know that this is not only without, but against, my orders. It is against my policy." But despite this denial, all their urging, followed next day by a demand of the South Carolina commissioners that Anderson be sent back to Moultrie, could not induce him publicly to disavow the act.

It was evident that this incident, clearly indicative of a determination to hold the crucial position at Charleston, would cause the South to suspect Lincoln's oft-repeated declarations of peaceful intent: and, late in December, being again appealed to, he wrote a letter which contained the following words: "The maintenance inviolate of the rights of the states, and especially the right of each state to order and control its own domestic institutions according to its own judgment exclusively, is essential to that balance of powers on which the perfection and endurance of our political fabric depend," and he repeated from his platform: "I denounce the lawless invasion by armed force of the soil of any state or territory, no matter under what pretext, as the gravest of crimes." This statement he declared himself willing to have published "upon the condition that six of the twelve United States Senators from the states of Georgia, Alabama, Mississippi, Louisiana, Florida, and Texas shall sign their names to the following declaration:

"We recommend to the people of the states we represent respectfully to suspend all action for dismemberment of the Union, at least until some act deemed to be violative of our rights shall be done by the incoming administration."

It was now, however, too late for such general assurances to satisfy the South. On December 28th, the very day on which Lincoln posted the letter, South Carolina's commissioners sent to President Buchanan a protest against Anderson's having changed his position, "thus altering to an important extent, the condition of affairs under which we came. Until these circumstances are explained . . . we are forced to suspend all discussion. . . . We would urge upon you the immediate withdrawal of the troops from the harbour of Charleston. Under present circumstances, they are a standing menace, which renders negotiation impossible, and . . . threatens speedily to bring to a bloody issue questions which ought to be settled with temperance and judgment." In his reply, Buchanan declared it no business of the Executive "to decide what shall be the relations between the Federal Government and South Carolina," and that any acknowledgment of the independence of that State would mean assumption of power competent to recognize "the dissolution of the Confederacy among our thirty-three sovereign states." The most he could promise was "to submit to Congress the whole question, in all its bearings." He admitted that "Major Anderson acted upon his own responsibility and without authority, unless, indeed, he had 'tangible evidence of a design to proceed to a hostile act' on the part of the authorities of South Carolina, which has not yet been alleged." But he would not disavow him.

Floyd, Buchanan's Secretary of War, now declared that Anderson's act was a violation of a pledge which the Government had given, and that his garrison should be at once removed from Charleston harbour. This Buchanan refused to sanction, and Floyd resigned, on December 29th, to be instantly accused of having employed his official position to prepare his section for war against the Union which he served. That this accusation was but an example of war hysteria appears from the later calm declaration of General Gorgas, sent to Davis when he was gathering material for his *Rise and Fall of the Confederate Government*: "The transactions which gave rise to the accusation were in the ordinary course of an economic administration of the War Department."

The final note from the South Carolina commissioners, dated January 1, 1861, was in places so insulting that the President refused to receive it. It charged him with hypocrisy, double dealing and even treachery. "You have," it said, "resolved to hold by force what you have obtained through our misguided confidence, and by refusing to disavow the action of Major Anderson have converted his violation of orders into a legitimate act of your executive authority. . . . By your course you have probably rendered civil war inevitable. Be it so. . . . We propose returning to Charleston on tomorrow afternoon."

This announcement was quickly followed by the seizure of the two ungarrisoned forts, Moultrie and Castle Pinckney, and the garrisoning of them with South Carolina troops. The Charleston customs-house and post-office were also seized, the Federal officials forced to resign, and soon the palmetto flag of South Carolina waved above them all.

CHAPTER XII

FAREWELL TO THE SENATE

WITH South Carolina's secession and the seizure of Forts Moultrie and Castle Pinckney, the question of the power of the Federal Government to preserve the Union by force became ever more acute, and Davis grew ever more confident that, whatever Buchanan might do or not do, Lincoln would resort to coercion as soon as the reins of government were in his hands. Governor Pettus of Mississippi, holding similar views and faced with the necessity of replying to South Carolina's invitation to join her in forming a Southern Confederacy, to resist force with force, sought Davis' advice, and that of Mississippi's other representatives in Congress: The chief point in the Governor's inquiry was: "Shall Mississippi, as soon as her convention can meet, pass an ordinance of secession, thus placing herself by the side of South Carolina, regardless of the actions of other states: or shall she endeavour to hold South Carolina in check . . . until other states can get ready . . . to unite with them, and then, on a given day and at a given hour, by concert of action, . . . secede in a body?" Davis replied as follows:

Washington, *January 4, 1861.*

My dear Sir:

In my frequent, brief, and hasty notes, I have not replied to your enquiry as to my present opinion in relation to the time when the ordinance of secession of Mississippi should take effect. This being a day set apart for "humiliation and prayer" I will

242

assign a part of it to the duty of stating my views on this point. . . .

On the 8th, the attempt will be made to pass a force bill through the House of Representatives and it will probably succeed. The Senate as it now stands can defeat it. A loan bill of huge proportions will be requisite to enable Mr. Lincoln to carry out his policy of coercion. It is important to defeat that measure of finance. Mr. Buchanan will no doubt, seek to fill all vacancies occurring in the seceding states by the appointment of Northern men. It will be better to reject them than to require our people to expel them; to do this will require all the Southern Senators to be present.

Post-offices and post-route contractors are necessary to the commercial, political, and social relations of our people. To substitute new arrangements for those now existing will require time. Commercial machinery will be required alike for exports and imports. Even if we should adopt free trade, we must have the ability to clear vessels carrying cargoes to foreign ports. But it is needless to . . . enumerate all the points for which provision must be made, to avoid the imposition of onerous embarrassments on our people at the period of transition from the old to the new governmental relations.

We should not halt, least of all hesitate; the moral power of steady progress must not be impaired; but let us advance with calm deliberation, and due regard to the necessities of the case. If when Lincoln comes to his office he finds no new powers granted for the collection of revenue, no additional force provided for, no funds beyond the accruing revenue, no extraordinary appropriations, he will have little power until the meeting of another Congress. He cannot convoke the Congress before next fall, unless he chooses to assemble it in despite of the fact that several of the border slave states have not held an election. To disregard that fact will drive them forthwith into alliance with us; to wait for them gives us the time for preparation which we now most need.

It has therefore seemed to me that it would be well in enacting an ordinance of secession to provide for a temporary continuance of the federal officers and representatives of the State so far as the same may be necessary. It will hardly be possible to inaugurate a government for the new Confederacy before the 4th of March, but it should not be postponed to a later date. When on a former occasion I selected that date, it was for the twofold consideration, that less than the intervening time would hardly suffice, and that that date would present in palpable form the fact of our resistance to Black-Republican domination. With this rapid statement of my opinion I leave the case to those to whom its decision belongs, confident that they will judge wisely, and satisfied to abide by and sustain their decision.

President Buchanan has forfeited any claim which he may have had on our forbearance and support. I regard his treatment of South Carolina as perfidious, and place no reliance upon him for the protection of our rights or abstinence from hostilities to us. In this, however, do not understand me as alleging a wicked purpose; his evil deeds rather spring from irresolution and an increasing dread of northern excitement. He is said to fear that his house at "Wheatland" may be burned, and it is reported that he apprehends impeachment when the withdrawal of Southern Senators shall give the Black Republicans the requisite majority in the Senate to convict him.

Please let me hear from you as often and as fully as your convenience will permit, and believe me ever truly your friend,

JEFFERSON DAVIS.

On January 5, 1861, Davis joined the United States Senators from Georgia, Florida, Alabama, Mississippi, Louisiana, Texas, and Arkansas in passing the following resolutions:

"That in our opinion, each State should, as soon as may be, secede from the Union.

"That the provision should be made for a convention to organize a Confederacy of the seceding states: the convention to meet not later than the 15th of February in the city of Montgomery, in the state of Alabama.

"That, in view of the hostile legislation that is threatened against the seceding states, and which may be consummated before the 4th of March, we ask instructions whether the delegations are to remain in Congress until that date, for the purpose of defeating such legislation.

"That a committee be and are hereby appointed, consisting of Messrs. Davis, Slidell, and Mallory, to carry out the objects of this meeting."

This action was taken openly, full details were furnished to the press, and Senator Toombs, who had taken part in the procedure, appeared in the Senate, on January 7th, and announced the plan, in a speech which Stephens later compared to Pericles' Oration to the Athenian Council, just before the outbreak of the Peloponnesian War. Such praise was certainly excessive; but it cannot be denied that Toombs made a deep impression upon his fellow Senators. While declaring his opinion, that the Fathers had given the nation a faulty Constitution, he admitted that "a very large portion of the people of Georgia . . . prefer to remain in this Union with their Constitutional rights—I would say ninety per cent of them—believing it to be a good government. . . . Restore us these rights as we had them, as your court adjudges them to be, . . . and it will restore fraternity and peace. . . . Refuse that, and you present us war."

Such developments deepened the perplexity of Buchanan, bound as he was by political theories which seemed to him to make effective action impossible. Davis later wrote of him, that he "would as soon have thought of aiding in the establishment of a monarchy among us as of accepting the doctrine of coercing the states into submission to the will of the majority. . . . He yielded a ready assent to the proposition that the cession of a site for a fort, for purposes of public defence, lapses whenever that fort should be employed by the grantee against the state by which the concession was made." "His abiding hope was to avert a collision, or at least to postpone it, to a period beyond the close of his official term."

On January 9th Davis rose in the Senate to discuss the President's last message, which he felt constrained to attack as it presented the Carolina commissioners' letters of December 28 and 30, 1860, but omitted their communication of January 1, 1861, a fact which he hotly resented. In his opinion, the legislative branch was entitled to the whole truth, and he proposed that the missing letter should be put into the record. Fierce opposition at once arose, and bitter words. King of New York likened the South Carolina commissioners to Benedict Arnold and Aaron Burr, calling them "messengers of treason"; but such opposition only deepened Davis' determination, and he pressed his point until a vote was taken and the clerk was ordered, by 36 to 13, to read the letter. When the reading was over, Davis demanded, "Now read the endorsement," and the clerk read as follows: "Executive Mansion, 3½ o'clock, Wednesday. This paper, just presented to the President, is of such a character that he declines to receive it."

"Why . . . did this paper (harsh, I admit, in some of its terms) not change the purpose of the President?" Davis asked his fellow-Senators. "Why did he not then call upon them for the means by which peace may be restored to South Carolina? Thus he might have turned the threatening brow of civil war away. Then we should not have stood as we do today, waiting hourly for what the telegraph may bring, to decide whether we have peace or war in our land."

But although Davis did not know it, war was making at this very hour in South Carolina waters. Buchanan, impelled by what motive it is hard to say, but probably by the insistence of certain new members of his Cabinet, had decided to reinforce Anderson at Fort Sumter. Selecting a small unarmed merchant vessel, the

Star of the West, he placed 250 men aboard her and on January 5th started her towards Charleston Harbour. She arrived on January 9th to find that South Carolina had none of Buchanan's scruples against employing force. The guns of the batteries opened upon her, and she without a gun with which to reply. "She continued her course, however," said the *New York Herald* in its report of the incident, "until opposite Morris Island, three-quarters of a mile from the battery, when a ball was fired athwart her bows. The *Star of the West* displayed the Stars and Stripes. As soon as the flag was unfurled the fortification fired a succession of heavy shot. The vessel continued her course, with increased speed, until two shots taking effect upon her, she concluded to retire. Fort Moultrie fired a few shots after her, but she was out of range. The damage done the *Star of the West* is trifling."

The damage done to the cause of peace, however, was far from trifling. The incident proved a justification of Davis' warning, uttered that very day, that Fort Sumter, open and unguarded, would be safe, but that any effort to defend it would probably precipitate civil war. It was also an example of the uncertain touch of the Federal Government at an hour when certainty was much needed; for before the *Star of the West* had been many hours at sea orders had been issued commanding her not to sail, as news had come from Major Anderson that "the harbour of Charleston was defended by heavy batteries," a fact which she had now discovered for herself.

This feeble attempt to relieve Fort Sumter was followed by equally feeble negotiations with nine Senators from the cotton states, headed by Jefferson Davis, which resulted in the impression's being left with some of them that Buchanan pledged himself to make no further attempt to reinforce the forts in Charleston harbour, in return for their guarantee that no attempt would be made to capture Sumter during his term of office.

On that same January 9, 1861, Mississippi passed an ordinance of secession: and Davis at once sent the following dispatch to the Governor:

Washington, D. C., *January 9, 1861.*

GOVERNOR J. J. PETTUS.

Jackson, Miss.

Wrote you on 7th inst. stating objections. Judge what Mississippi requires of me and place me accordingly.

JEFFERSON DAVIS.

After hours of anxious thought, however, he decided that, although he must retire from the Senate, he would await official notice of Mississippi's secession, and intent, as he later wrote "to avert the impending calamity" of war, and drove at once to the White House to make a last appeal to Buchanan. Again he urged the removal of the garrison from Fort Sumter, a garrison too small to repel, but large enough to challenge, attack. But he urged in vain. In firing upon the American flag, South Carolina had ventured upon an act of war, and, despite Davis' arguments, Buchanan so notified Governor Pickens. Pickens replied that he considered the action "perfectly justified." And so ended that crowded 9th of January, 1861, so far as official business was concerned, and Davis returned to his home to prepare for the next day's meeting of the Senate.

When the Senate convened, and the floor was his, he declared: "I intended to adduce some evidence which I thought conclusive in favour of the opinions which I entertain; but events have borne me past the point where it would be useful for me to argue . . . the question of rights. Today, therefore, it is my purpose to deal with events." "Had the garrison at Charleston . . . been called away thirty days, nay, ten days ago, peace would have spread its pinions over this land, and calm negotiations would have been the order of the day." But, "Feeble hands now hold the reins of state . . . drivellers are taken in as counsellors . . . and the policy

of this great Government is changed with every changing rumour
. . . with every new phase of causeless fear.

"Had an ordinance sergeant there represented the Federal Government; had there been no troops, no physical power to protect
it, I would have pledged my life upon the issue that no question
would have been made as to its seizure." Even "Fort McHenry,
memorable in our history as the place where under bombardment,
the Star-spangled Banner floated through the darkness of the
night (the place consecrated by our national song), . . . has been
garrisoned by a detachment of marines, . . . sent under cover of
the night. . . . What then is our policy? Are we to drift into
war? Are we to stand idly by and allow war to be precipitated
upon the country? Allow an officer of the army to make war?
Allow an unconfirmed head of a department to make war? Allow
a general . . . a President to make war? No. Our fathers gave to
Congress the power to declare war, and even to Congress they
gave no power to make war upon a state of the Union. . . . It
was well said by the Senator from New York [Mr. Seward] . . .
in a speech wherein I found but little to commend, that this
Union could not be maintained by force, and that a Union of
force was a despotism. . . . Against it, so long as I live, with
heart and hand, I will rebel.

"The want of a policy, the obstinate adherence to unimportant
things, have brought us to a condition where I close my eyes, because I cannot see anything that encourages me to hope. . . .
God who knows the hearts of men will judge between you and
us, at whose door lies the responsibility."

"To argue that a man who follows . . . his state, resuming her
sovereign jurisdiction and power, is disloyal to his allegiance to
the United States, which allegiance he only owes through his
state, is such a confusion of ideas as does not belong to an ordinary
comprehension of our Government. It is treason to the principle
of community independence. It is to recur to that doctrine of

passive obedience which, in England, cost one monarch his head and drove another into exile; a doctrine which, since the revolution of 1688, has obtained nowhere where men speak the English tongue; and yet all this it is needful to admit before we accept this doctrine of coercion."

"The time is near at hand when the places which have known us as colleagues labouring together, can know us in that relation no more for ever. I have striven unsuccessfully to avert the catastrophe which now impends over the country. For the few days which I may remain I am willing to labour in order that that catastrophe shall be as little as possible destructive to public peace and prosperity. If you desire at this last moment to avert civil war, so be it; it is better so. If you will but allow us to separate from you peaceably, since we cannot live peaceably together, to leave with the rights we had before we were united, since we cannot enjoy them in the Union, then there are many relations which may still subsist between us, drawn from the associations of our struggles from the Revolutionary era to the present day, which may be beneficial to you as well as to us. If you will not have it thus; if in the pride of power, if in contempt of reason and reliance upon force, you say we shall not go, but shall remain as subjects to you, then, Gentlemen of the North, a war is to be inaugurated the like of which men have not seen."

The day of the delivery of this his last extended speech in the Senate, was made memorable by the secession of Florida; and Alabama followed on January 11th. James Russell Lowell, in commenting upon these important events, lightly declared: "We shall need something like a Fugitive State law for runaway Republics, and must get a provision inserted in our treaties with foreign powers, that they shall help us catch any delinquent who may take refuge with them, as South Carolina has been trying to do with England and France."

On January 11th, Governor Pickens requested Anderson to give over Fort Sumter, and received the reply that he had no authority for such surrender, but that he advised the Governor to make his demand of the President of the United States. Accordingly, on the same day, the Honourable I. W. Hayne, Attorney-General of South Carolina, was sent with a letter to President Buchanan, and was instructed to demand "the delivery of Fort Sumter . . . to the constituted authorities of the State of South Carolina," and to "require a positive and distinct answer." Should the President claim the right to introduce troops within the limits of South Carolina, or occupy Fort Sumter, he should be told that such an attempt would be regarded as an act of war. Any claims which the United States might assert against South Carolina were to be dealt with by a promise of adjustment "upon the principles of equity and justice always recognized by independent nations."

Before Hayne was able to seek an interview with the President —and custom would seem to have demanded that it be with the Secretary of State—he received a letter from the Senators of the seceding states, and those which planned to secede before February 1st, declaring their unanimous desire to avoid war, and asking him to seek an arrangement with the President to ensure peace until February 15th, "by which time your and our states may, in convention, devise a wise, just, and peaceable solution of existing difficulties. . . . In the meantime, we think your state should suffer Major Anderson to obtain the necessary supplies of food, fuel, and water, and enjoy free communication, by post or special messenger, with the President; upon the understanding that the President will not send him reinforcements during the same period." Hayne promised to comply with these suggestions so far as they fell within his special powers, "Provided you can get assurances with which you are entirely satisfied that no reinforcements will be sent to Fort Sumter in the interval and that public peace shall not be disturbed by any act of hostility."

In seeking to decide upon the next step, Governor Pickens invited Senator Davis to confer with him. Davis answered by telegram, and later by the following letter:

Washington, D. C.
January 13, 1861.

GOVERNOR F. W. PICKENS:

My dear Sir:

... [Your] request for a conference on questions of defence ... found me under a proposition from the Governor of Mississippi, to send me as a commissioner to Virginia, and another to employ me in the organization of the state militia. But, more than all, I was endeavouring to secure the defeat of the nomination of a *foreign collector* for the port of Charleston, and at the time it was deemed possible that in the Senate we could arrest all hostile legislation such as might be designed either for the immediate or future coercion of the South. It now appears that we shall lack one or two votes to effect the legislative object just mentioned, and it was decided last evening, in a conference which I was not able to attend, that the Senators of the seceded states should promptly withdraw upon the telegraphic information already received. . . . I cannot place any confidence in the adherence of the administration to a fixed line of policy. The general tendency is to hostile measures, and against these it is needful for you to prepare. I take it for granted that the time allowed to the garrison of Fort Sumter has been diligently employed by yourselves, so that before you could be driven out of your earthworks you will be able to capture the fort which commands them.

I have not sufficiently learned your policy in relation to the garrison at Fort Sumter, to understand whether the expectation is to compel them to capitulate for want of supplies, or whether it is only to prevent the transmission of reports and the receipt of orders. To shut them up with a view to starve them into submission would create a sympathetic action much greater than any which could be obtained on the present issue. I doubt very much the loyalty of the garrison, and it has occurred to me that, if they could receive no reinforcements—and I suppose you sufficiently command the entrance to the harbour to prevent it—there could be no danger of the freest intercourse between the garrison and the city. . . . We are probably soon to be involved in that fiercest human strife, a civil war. The temper of the Black-Republicans is not to give us our rights in the Union, or allow us to go peaceably out of it. If we had no other cause, this would be enough to justify secession, at whatever hazard. . . .

Very sincerely yours,

JEFFERSON DAVIS.

GOVERNOR F. W. PICKENS.

This letter shows that Davis was fully convinced of the need of Southern preparation to resist a coercive policy, should it come, but falls far short of Grant's oft-repeated statement that he was the leader of the secessionists.

On January 19th, the seceding Senators sent to President Buchanan copies of the correspondence between themselves and Mr. Hayne, and asked for his consideration of the subject.

In reply they received a letter from Joseph Holt, Secretary of War *ad interim*, on behalf of the President, which stated that the President "has no authority to enter into such an agreement or understanding," and declared that, in Holt's opinion "the happiest result which can be attained is, that both he [Major Anderson] and the authorities of South Carolina shall remain on their present amicable footing, neither party being bound by any obligations whatever, except the high Christian and moral duty to keep the peace."

Meanwhile, on January 19th, Georgia had passed an ordinance of secession, against the urgent advice of her ablest citizen, Alexander H. Stephens, and the day following, Davis received from the Governor of Mississippi the official announcement that his state too no longer belonged to the United States of America.

Therefore, he at once made ready to resign his seat in the Senate. On January 20th, he wrote to Pierce:

Washington, D. C.
January 20, 1861.

MY DEAR FRIEND:

I have often and sadly turned my thoughts to you during the troublous times through which we have been passing, and now I come to the hard task of announcing to you that the hour is at hand which closes my connexion with the United States, for the independence and union of which my father bled, and in the service of which I have sought to emulate the example he set for my guidance.

Mississippi, not as a matter of choice but of necessity, has resolved to enter on the trial of secession. Those who have driven her to this alternative threaten to deprive her of the right to require that her Government shall rest on the consent of the governed, to substitute foreign force for domestic support, to reduce a State to the condition from which the colony rose. In the attempt to avoid the issue which has been joined by the country, the present administration has complicated and precipitated the question. Even now, if the duty to preserve the public property was rationally regarded, the probable collision at Charleston would be avoided. Security far better than any which the Federal troops can give might be obtained in consideration of the little garrison at Fort Sumter. If the disavowal of any purpose to coerce South Carolina be sincere, the possession of a work to command the harbour is worse than useless.

When Lincoln comes in he will have but to continue in the path of his predecessor to inaugurate a civil war and leave a *soi disant* Democratic administration responsible for the fact. General Cushing was here last week and when we parted it seemed like taking leave of a brother.

I leave immediately for Mississippi and know not what may

devolve upon me, after my return. Civil war has only horror for me, but whatever circumstances demand shall be met as a duty, and I trust be so discharged that you will not be ashamed of our former connexion or cease to be my friend. . . . May God bless you is ever the prayer of your friend.

JEFFERSON DAVIS.

On the same day, Davis wrote to Governor Pickens, urging him against precipitate action:

Washington, *20th January, 1861.*

Governor F. W. Pickens.

Dear Sir:

. . . You will not be surprised when I say that my quiet hours are mostly spent in thoughts of Charleston Harbour, and may therefore pardon the frequency of my letters.

Colonel Hayne has doubtless informed you of the condition in which he found matters here. The opinion of your friends . . . is adverse to the precipitation of a demand for the evacuation of Fort Sumter. The little garrison in its present position presses on nothing but a point of pride, and to you I need not say that war is made up of real elements. . . . I hope we shall soon have a Southern Confederacy that shall be ready to do all which interest or even pride demands, and in the fulness of a redemption of every obligation. . . . The occurrence of the *Star of the West* puts you in the best condition for delay, so long as the Government permits the matter to stand still so far as the presence of the garrison is concerned, and if things continue as they are for a month, we shall be in a condition to speak with a voice which all must hear and heed. . . . Permit me to assure you that my heart will be with you, and my thoughts of you.

Very respectfully and truly,
Yours,
JEFFERSON DAVIS.

No secret had been made of the fact that on January 21st, Jefferson Davis would deliver his farewell address to the Senate, and by seven o'clock in the morning admission was being eagerly sought by men and women. When the hour of session came, it was with difficulty that Davis himself could gain entrance, so dense was the crowd. Every Senator was in his seat, and the members of the House stood in every available space, while the galleries were packed to the doors.

As Davis rose to speak he showed signs of deep emotion. "Had he been bending over his father, slain by his countrymen," wrote Mrs. Davis, "he could not have been more inconsolable." His first words came tremblingly, uncertainly forth, as the audience waited in perfect silence:

"I rise, Mr. President, for the purpose of announcing to the Senate that I have satisfactory evidence that the State of Mississippi, by a solemn ordinance of her people in convention assembled, has declared her separation from the United States. Under these circumstances, my functions here are terminated. It seems to me proper, however, to appear in the Senate to announce that fact to my associates, and I will say but little more. The occasion does not invite . . . argument; and my physical condition would not permit [argument] . . . if it were otherwise. . . ." As he proceeded, the full, flutelike tones which ordinarily characterized his speech returned, and he spoke with force, but with no bitterness, or defiance. One reads his brief valedictory with a sense of wonder that it could have been so quiet, so free from the taint of anger or resentment.

"It is known to Senators who have served with me here," he continued, "that I have for many years advocated as an essential attribute of state sovereignty, the right of a state to secede from the Union. Therefore, if I had not believed there was justifiable cause . . . I should still, under my theory of government . . . have been bound by her action. I may, however, be permitted to say that I do think she has justifiable cause, and that I approve of her act. I conferred with her people before that act was taken, counselled them that if the state of things which they apprehended should exist when the convention met, they should take the action which they have now adopted."

Equally frank, but far less convincing, was his refutation of the claim that the Declaration of Independence meant equality of the races, and that the words, "created equal," were only an assertion "that no man was born—to use the language of Mr. Jefferson—booted and spurred to ride over the rest of mankind; that men were created equal—meaning the men of the political community; that there was no divine right to rule; that no man inherited the right to govern; that there were no classes by which power and place descended to families, but that all stations were equally within the grasp of each member of the body politic. These were the great principles they announced. . . . They have no reference to the slave; else, how happened it that among the items of arraignment made against George III was that he endeavoured to do what the North has been endeavouring of late to do—to stir up insurrection among our slaves? Had the Declaration announced that the negroes were free and equal, how was the king to be arraigned for stirring up insurrection among them?"

In his closing sentences, Davis assured his colleagues that he bore away with him neither hostility nor bitterness. "In the presence of my God," he said, "I wish you well; and such, I am sure, is the feeling of the people whom I represent toward those whom you represent. It only remains for me to bid you a final farewell." He looked round upon the Senate and passed out into what might well have been thought to be comparative obscurity.

So far as mortal eye could see, Jefferson Davis had given up more, with the prospect of gaining less, than any other Confederate. He had opposed the secession of his own state, and could hardly hope to be chosen leader of the movement which had triumphed over his opposition. The Union which he was leaving had heaped honours upon him, and more honours would have been his had he remained. In resigning he followed not his star but his conscience.

CHAPTER XIII

DRAFTED INTO A PRESIDENCY

THE night following his farewell to the Senate, Davis slept not at all, and was heard whispering the words: "May God have us in His holy keeping, and grant that before it is too late peaceful councils may prevail." During the next week, which he spent in Washington, he sent letters and telegrams to leaders in every Southern state, in an endeavour to prevent hasty and violent action. "The only time he seemed cheerful," wrote Mrs. Davis, "was when he spoke of his hope that the moderation of the President and his advisers, would restrain the ardour of the anti-slavery men." Sumner later declared, "Had the President . . . interfered promptly and loyally, it cannot be doubted that this whole intolerable crime might have been trampled out for ever." "The pretension of States' Rights made the apology for imbecility." Davis' view was that "violence, on the one side, and extreme measures on the other, now, will dissolve the Union; but if they will give me time, all is not lost"—a sufficient answer to the later propaganda which made him an arch-conspirator, seeking with mad ambition to tear down the structure which he had sworn to defend.

From time to time rumours reached him of a plan for his arrest: but these troubled him little, for he knew that the Federal courts would not consider either criminal or treasonable his former open support of the right of secession, and of South Carolina's claim to ownership of the forts within her territory.

His chief anxiety was for news of the plans for the meeting of the seceded states at Montgomery, and for information from

Charleston, where the menace of war was greatest. Governor Pickens had written to him, on January 23rd: "The truth is that I have not been prepared to take Sumter. It is a very strong fortress and in the most commanding position. I found everything in utter confusion when I came into office, and really no military supplies. Everything was on a small military scale. The movement of Anderson from Moultrie . . . plunged me into the highest and most scientific branches of modern warfare, and also the most expensive. I found great difficulty in repairing and altering Moultrie. . . .

"Of course I would desire to do nothing to prejudice our cause with our sister states of the South. . . . If the meeting of the convention at Montgomery can give us our rights and our possessions without blood, I shall rejoice, but if not, blood must follow. They will throw the fleet of the United States navy and large vessels into Pensacola and hold Fort Pickens. . . . As soon as the states meet at Montgomery they should elect a commander-in-chief and assess the states their quota in army and men and money. . . . Allow me to say that I think you are the proper man to be selected at this juncture, and I hope it will be unanimously. . . . We must have all the organization and form of government in full operation before the 4th of March [Lincoln's inauguration day], and if anything can save the peace of this country it will be this. As to who may be selected to fill the highest civil offices, it is not of so much consequence at present, only that they should be . . . gentlemen of exemplary honesty and firmness of character. . . . We must start our government free from the vulgar influences that have debauched and demoralized the Government at Washington. . . . I rejoice that South Carolina has proposed the Constitution of the United States as a basis of a new Government for the Southern States. . . ."

Three days later, Louisiana passed an ordinance of secession, and thus, when Davis left Washington, six "independent" states were preparing for the projected congress at Montgomery. At

JEFFERSON DAVIS IN MAJOR-GENERAL'S UNIFORM

From a photograph now in the possession of Dr. Dold, of Charlottesville, Va.
The uniform was especially designed for him when he was made
Major-General of the Mississippi State Militia.

least one governor was eager for his election as its chief military leader, but there is no indication that he was being considered for, or desired, the Presidency. Nor had he, so far as appears from the documents, thought of the fact that as the Federal Constitution had made the President commander-in-chief of the army and navy, with the evident purpose of enabling Washington to continue his military leadership in case of war, so, by a similar provision, might the Montgomery convention make him, Davis, both civil and military head of the new Confederation.

It is clear that Davis thought of the coming convention as intended not to destroy the Constitution, but, as Stephens later said, "to save the principles of the Constitution" in its original conception. It is also clear that its purely political aspects interested him less than the problem of preparing the South for effective defence in the event of an attempt to force the seceded states back into a Union, bent, as he considered, upon disregarding the provisions of its own Constitution. Mississippi, remembering his career in the Mexican War, had commissioned him major-general, placing him in command of her local forces, which amounted to some 10,000 men, and in this capacity, he now turned his mind to problems of organization, drill, and equipment; in preparation for what he believed would be a long and severe struggle.

The papers of the Military Board of Mississippi show him at Jackson on January 29th, arranging for armies and equipment. He found, as he had expected, that there were few serviceable weapons available, and no establishment for their manufacture or repair. But he found, and was doubtless surprised to find, the board carefully arranging that "the Major-General's coat shall have two rows of buttons, seven in each row, placed at equal distances"; that his collar shall stand up and be made of black velvet; that he shall wear "a broad-brimmed black felt hat to be looped up on three sides when on parade, and to be ornamented with cord, tassel, and plume."

These facts he accepted as indicating that his state was not planning war, with which conclusion Samuel G. French, Mississippi's Chief of Ordnance, was in hearty accord. When "I was appointed Chief of Ordnance and Artillery of the State of Mississippi," he wrote, " . . . few persons . . . believed there would be war and those that thought otherwise had no conception of the magnitude and proportions that it eventually assumed. . . . The only arms fit for service were the muskets, and they were old-fashioned flintlocks. . . . Of powder we had none. . . . I could not find a man in the state who knew how to make leather collars for the artillery horses, so dependent on the North were our people for supplies of every kind. We had no means of making lead balls for the small arms by compression. Through a house in Philadelphia I was offered a modern machine just completed for the Governor-General of Cuba, with dies for all calibres of arms. I could not get the governor's permission to purchase it. . . . The governor was in favour of shotguns and ambushing every Yankee that dared to set foot on the sacred soil of Mississippi. We called a council of his generals and I was instructed to prepare an order so that the generals in their respective departments could send agents throughout the state and purchase shotguns. After a time the guns began to arrive. If the god of war ever smiles, then Mars smiled when he beheld them. Had Falstaff's company been armed with them, Sir John would have sworn worse than Uncle Toby did. In that assortment were some remarkable weapons . . . an old musket barrel strapped to a piece of cypress rail, crooked at one end . . . the contribution of a negro slave to the cause."

As Davis inspected this equipment he doubtless wondered at the incapacity of man to learn the lessons of war; for he had himself equipped the First Regiment of Mississippi Volunteers, in 1845, with modern rifles before leading them to Mexico, where they had learned in practice the superiority which General Winfield Scott had refused to admit.

News soon reached him that on February 4th the delegates of

South Carolina, Georgia, Florida, Alabama, Mississippi, and Louisiana had opened the convention, and that those from a seventh seceded state, Texas, were on their way. They were confident that Arkansas, North Carolina, Virginia, and Tennessee would soon secede and unite with them, and the more sanguine believed that the border states, Missouri, Kentucky and Maryland, would follow.

The average ability of those delegates Alexander H. Stephens declared higher than that of "any of the sixteen Congresses I have been in at Washington." Nor was the Convention radical; a majority of its members had been opposed to secession. Indeed, its most striking characteristic was admiration for the Federal Constitution, as was shown by its adopting, on February 8th, a Provisional Constitution, modelled on the principles of the government of the United States. Where there were variations, it was to make definite certain ideas which, its members believed, had been made implicit, but vague, by the Fathers.

After careful study of the document Davis declared it, "A model of wise, temperate, and liberal statesmanship." He was particularly pleased with the section intended to clarify the words of the Federal Constitution, "We, the people," which the Montgomery convention interpreted as "each state acting in its sovereign and independent character." The section that avowed the principle of free trade in its entirety was hailed by him as the embodiment of his own carefully formed convictions. He also expressed his satisfaction with the answer to the accusation that the South aimed to restore the African slave trade. "Section seven, article one," he wrote, "provides that the importation of African negroes from any foreign country other than the slaveholding states of the United States is hereby forbidden, and Congress is requested to pass such laws as shall effectively prevent the same." For although he constantly defended the traffic on the ground of the opportunity it secured to the negro for civilizing and Christianizing contacts, he did not desire to see the South flooded with new importations from Africa.

During the convention, a committee, headed by R. Barnwell Rhett, of South Carolina, with two delegates from each state, was chosen to prepare a permanent Constitution, and it worked on similar lines. Cobb and Toombs, the Georgia members, classed at the North among the "fire-eaters," displayed a like desire to follow as their model the Federal Constitution, in conformity with the wishes of the Georgia convention. Cobb, whose enthusiasm for secession Stephens likened to Peter the Hermit's flame for the rescue of the Holy Sepulchre, struggled in vain to persuade the committee to call the new government "the Republic of Washington." He failed also in his effort to prohibit the carrying of mails on the Sabbath day, but he succeeded in incorporating a definite prohibition of the African slave trade.

Like the Provisional Constitution, this Permanent Constitution, as Davis later wrote, differed "from that of our Fathers only in so far as it is explanatory of their well-known intent," and Stephens declared that the leading object of both was to "uphold and perpetuate the fundamental principles of the Constitution of the United States."

This Permanent Constitution, to go into effect a year later, was adopted on March 11, 1861, by the unanimous consent of the seven Confederate states, the Texas delegates having now arrived and taken their seats.

In commenting upon "the calm and constitutional manner in which the Southern people had proceeded, in forming their Government," the British *Quarterly Review* later declared it "strange that ministerial responsibility should not have been ordained, for this seems to us an absolutely essential feature in a Constitutional Government." Indeed, had Stephens succeeded in his effort to require the Confederate President to appoint his Cabinet from men elected to Congress, the result would have meant in time a Confederate Government with a responsible

Ministry, in which event, the comparative merits of Cabinet Government and Presidential Government would have been tested in the coming conflict.

Meanwhile, the Provisional Government had been put into operation by the administration, to the members of the convention of the oath to support the Provisional Constitution, a course which Davis had expected; but the next decision surprised him. Before starting to his plantation to look after his private interests, in the interim of his military duties, he had taken "what appeared to me adequate precautions" against the possibility of being chosen Provisional President of the Confederacy. West Point and the army had made him familiar with the difference between manœuvres and strategy: the one, operations in the enemy's sight, the other, behind his back. In Washington he had found that executive work depends largely on the latter, and he had no love for it. "I had been so near the office [of President], for four years while in the Cabinet of Mr. Pierce," he explained later, "that I saw it from behind the scenes, and it was to me an office in no wise desirable. I thought myself better adapted to command in the field."

His admirers in the convention, however, had no such idea, agreeing, as they did, with the opinion of Seward, expressed to Russell, the *Times* correspondent: that Davis was the only man in the South with brains enough to carry the revolution through. Mrs. Chestnut, in *A Diary from Dixie*, writes: "Everybody wants Jefferson Davis to be General-in-Chief, or President," and adds, inconsistently: "Keitt and Boyce and a party prefer Howell Cobb, and the fire-eaters *per se* want Barnwell Rhett," who has, she added, "howled nullification and secession so long that when he found his ideas taken up by the Confederate world, he felt that he had a vested right to leadership." But neither Cobb nor Rhett had a chance of election. Cobb's downright methods had made him many enemies, and Rhett was too radical for such a convention.

Toombs, however, was considered, and Stephens declared that he would have been nominated but for a misunderstanding of the desires of the Georgia delegation. "A majority of the states," he wrote, "were looking to Georgia for the President," and ". . . Mr. Toombs was the man whom they [the Georgia delegation] . . . unanimously agreed to present." After this decision had been reached, however, news came that two or three other states, in their caucuses, had decided to vote for Davis. To avoid a contest, Stephens adds, "Mr. Toombs asked that his name be not presented." What would have resulted, had the Georgia delegation presented Toombs' name, is speculation. What is certain is that, when the convention met, Davis received every vote, including that of Georgia. Thus, despite the well-known fact that he did not desire the office, he was drafted into the Provisional Presidency. Alexander S. Stephens was, also by unanimous vote, elected Provisional Vice-President.

Mrs. M. E. Hamer, Davis' great-niece, has left this account of how the news reached him: "Mr. Davis was at 'Brierfield' . . . and when a committee arrived at 'Hurricane,' on their way to inform him of the fact, my grandfather and grandmother [Mr. and Mrs. Joseph Davis], accompanied them to 'Brierfield.' They found Mr. Davis ill, and Mrs. Joseph Davis went to his room to notify him of the arrival of the gentlemen and the purport of their visit. She said he rose up, and lifting his arms over his head, cried out, 'O God spare me this responsibility!' . . . He however saw the gentlemen, and reluctantly consented to assume the difficult and arduous task."

Accounts of the incident found elsewhere in the Davis papers show a wide variation from this simple narrative: and all that is certain is that he received the news with surprise, and reluctantly set about the task of preparing to start for his inauguration. He assembled his slaves and made them a farewell speech, the last which he ever addressed to them as slaves. He then distributed among them such supplies as he had on hand, and to old "Uncle

Bob," a rheumatic and therefore unproductive slave, he gave an enormous supply of blankets.

Having thus set his house in order, Davis started alone for Montgomery, with the understanding that his wife would complete necessary arrangements at the plantation, and join him later. Isaiah Montgomery, a slave, has left the following account of his departure: "The Davis plantation lay in a big bend of the Mississippi River, thirty miles below Vicksburg. We had a landing of our own which the smaller boats could make, but when passengers were to take one of the large river boats they had to be rowed to a landing three miles below our place. The morning Mr. Davis was to start for the inauguration we were late in getting away from the house. Before we got far out on the river we heard the steamer blow at the landing. We knew then that we could not get to the landing in time, so headed for an island which lay in the middle of the river, so as to meet the steamer when she came out from behind the island. She was Old Tom Leather's boat, the *Natchez*. The captain was expecting Mr. Davis, and when he found that we were not at the landing, he was looking out for our boat. When the steamer came along, Mr. Davis signalled to her, and the captain blew to show that he saw us and understood. He stopped the steamer, we rowed up, and Mr. Davis was taken on board. That was the last time I ever saw him."

February 12th found Davis at Jackson, Mississippi: and from the Governor's office he wrote:

Executive Office
Jackson, Miss., *Feb. 12, 1861.*

Govr. J. J. Pettus:

My dear Sir:

Circumstances of which you are aware render it necessary for me to tender you my resignation of the office of Major-General of the Army of Mississippi, conferred on me by the convention of the Republic of Mississippi. Proud of the station to which the too kind estimate of the people's representatives elevated me, I retire from it with sincere regret and will not attempt to express the additional sense of gratitude imposed on me by this further evidence of the favour by which all my efforts for the welfare of Mississippi have been cheered and sustained.

Very respectfully and
Sincerely yours,
JEFFERSON DAVIS

On that same day, and therefore before Davis' arrival at his Capital, the Congress of the Confederate States assumed charge of all questions pending between the several states of the Confederacy and the United States, regarding forts, arsenals, navy-yards, and other public establishments. Before his arrival, also, as Rhett's biographer declares, Rhett secured the post of Chairman of the Committee on Foreign Relations, with the object of setting the stage for foreign affairs before Davis, whom he suspected of reconstruction tendencies, could interfere. On February 13th he moved the appointment of a committee of three to proceed to Europe and open negotiations with foreign governments, expecting himself to choose these commissioners. The Congress, however, refused thus to take the control of foreign policy out of the hands of the President, and the appointments were suffered to await his inauguration.

Davis' trip from Jackson to Montgomery, says a contemporary dispatch, "was one continuous ovation. He made no less than twenty-five speeches. . . ." Propaganda, disguised as history, has altered the character of those speeches, depicting them as "invoking war, breathing defiance, and threatening extermination of the Union." They were, however, quite the opposite. "He approached the task of creating a nation," says Mrs. Davis, "with a longing beyond expression to have his extended hand of fellowship grasped by that of the North before blood had been spilt, and with many humble petitions to Almighty God for guidance and support." So little menacing was his tone that many Southerners lamented that "Jeff Davis has remained too long amongst the Yankees to make him exactly the kind of President the South needs." And Rhett confided to his Charleston *Mercury* that "Jefferson Davis will exert all his powers to reunite the Confederacy to the Empire."

In this Rhett misapprehended the situation. Davis believed that the sovereign states, in seceding from the Union, had acted within their constitutional rights, and, while desiring peace and friendship from the Federal Union which they had left, he accepted the separation as final. Coercion he was ready to resist by war if need be; but he hoped against hope, against almost certain knowledge, indeed, that coercion would not be attempted. "If we succeed," he said to his wife, upon many occasions, "we shall hear nothing of these malcontents; if we do not, then I shall be held accountable by the majority . . . friends as well as foes. I will do my best, and God will give me strength to bear whatever comes."

At the same time, in Springfield, Illinois, Abraham Lincoln was preparing, as he himself expressed it, "to assume a task more difficult than that which devolved upon Washington. Unless the great God who assisted him shall be with me and aid me, I must fail; but if [He] . . . shall guide . . . me, I shall not fail, I shall succeed." In comparing the two men, Edmund Ruffin confided to his diary the cynical and false opinion that Davis was hard-hearted and soft-headed, while Lincoln was soft-hearted and hard-headed.

Proceeding on his way, the President-elect was met eight miles from Montgomery and formally welcomed by a committee of the Confederate Congress, and one appointed by the authorities of the city. Two companies from Columbus, Georgia, joined him as an escort at Opelika, and the cortège reached Montgomery Friday night at ten o'clock. Salvos of artillery greeted his approach, and a large crowd, assembled at the station, hailed his appearance with tremendous cheering. Davis greeted and thanked them, and conscious, no doubt, of the criticisms of Rhett and others, declared: "Our separation from the old Union is complete. No compromise; no reconstruction can be now entertained." He then continued, through a dense and cheering crowd, to the Exchange Hotel, where he made his twenty-seventh speech since leaving Jackson, the keynote of which was the prayer that "Heaven will . . . prosper the Southern Confederacy and carry us safe from sea to the harbour of Constitutional liberty."

On February 18th in front of the Capitol at Montgomery, Davis was inaugurated President of the Provisional Government, of the Confederate States of America, and delivered his formal inaugural address, which, wrote the British consul at Charleston, in sending it to Lord John Russell, "has given great pleasure to the better classes . . . who had looked for more violent language and sentiments from a person of Mr. Davis' impulsive character." It had been hastily prepared in view of the unexpected election and lacked the literary qualities of the one which Lincoln, armed with the Constitution, Jackson's Nullification Proclamation of 1832, and Clay's speech on the Compromise of 1850, wrote in the big bare room over the store in Springfield.

A close comparison of the two addresses leaves one wondering that, while in education and culture, superiority was with the Southern Chief, eloquence and deep insight were with the unschooled leader of the Black-Republicans.

Davis argued the "inalienable" right of each state to secede, and based his contention on the philosophy of the Declaration of Independence. Lincoln, speaking a fortnight later, said: "I hold that in contemplation of universal law and of the Constitution, the Union of these states is perpetual. . . . No Government proper ever had a provision in its organic law for its own termination."

Davis declared: "If . . . passion or lust of dominion should cloud the judgment or inflame the ambition of those states, we must prepare to meet the emergency, and maintain, by the final arbitrament of the sword, the position which we have assumed among the nations of the earth." Lincoln answered with the challenge:

"In your hands, my disaffected fellow countrymen, and not in mine, is the momentous issue of civil war. The Government will not assail you. You can have no conflict without being yourselves the aggressors. You have no oath registered in heaven to destroy the Government, while I shall have the most solemn one 'to preserve, protect and defend it.'" And he closed with the eloquent words, said to have been written for him by Seward: "We are not enemies, but friends. We must not be enemies. Though passion may have strained, it must not break, our bonds of affection. The mystic chords of memory, stretching from every battlefield and patriot grave to every living heart and hearthstone all over this broad land, will yet swell the chorus of union, when again touched, as surely they will be, by the better angels of our nature."

Davis knew, however, and Lincoln must have known, that the oath which the latter was about to take bound him to no such obligation. What it declared plainly was: "I do solemnly swear that I will faithfully . . . defend the *Constitution*" [not the Government] of the United States.

In commenting upon Davis' inaugural address, Stephens, certainly no blind admirer of Davis, declared: "It clearly shows, as the acts of the convention show, that these states had quit the Union only to preserve for themselves, at least, the principles of the Constitution. It shows also that there was no purpose, wish, design, or intention, on the part of Mr. Davis, to make war, commit aggression, or do any wrong to those states, or the people of those states, which remained in the old Union, or to interfere improperly in any way, with the Government of their choice."

Thus these two leaders, born in the same state, reared under the same flag, had come, through deep and honest thought upon the baffling question of sovereignty, to positions diametrically opposed. Had Lincoln been asked, on March 4, 1861, what he considered the supreme motif of the Constitution of the United States, he would have replied, "the permanency of the Union"; to preserve which he later felt free to disregard provision after provision, of the Constitution itself, among others the habeas corpus clause. To the same question, on that day and ever afterward, Davis would have answered "the reserved rights which protect the sovereignty of the states"; for it is the state that fulfils the promise of the Declaration of Independence, of "life, liberty, and the pursuit of happiness" for the individual. And it was the consciousness of this irreconcilable difference, representative of the views of the North and South, which had caused Davis long ago to warn his fellow Southerners that secession would mean war.

"I was inaugurated on Monday, having reached here on Saturday night," he wrote to his wife on February 20th. "The audience was large and brilliant. Upon my weary heart were showered smiles, plaudits, and flowers; but beyond them I saw troubles and thorns innumerable. We are without machinery, without means, and threatened by a powerful opposition; but I do not despond, and will not shrink from the task imposed upon me. . . ."

That the task was heavy was already abundantly evident. His was the duty not only to execute the office of President, but to form, equip, and establish a government; and while organizing resistance to seek to preserve the peace. There was, moreover, a serious difference of opinion between him and many of the leading Confederates as to how peace could be best maintained. Most of Davis' colleagues still cherished the hope that secession would prove to be what it had been intended to be—a peace measure. The *Albany Argus*, toward the end of the year 1860, had announced—"If South Carolina or any other state, through a convention of her people, shall formally separate herself from the

Union, probably both the present and the next Executive will simply let her alone and quickly allow all the functions of the Federal Government within her limits to be suspended. Any other course would be madness." The *New York Herald*, a journal which answered to the reins of no party, had declared, toward the end of 1860: "Each state is organized as a complete government, holding the purse and wielding the sword, possessing the right to break the tie of the Confederation as a nation might break a treaty, and to repel coercion as a nation might repel invasion. . . . Coercion, if it were possible, is out of the question."

Davis, however, did not doubt that the North would appeal to force rather than see the country dismembered, and, though confident that law and tradition were on the side of the secessionists, he knew that the major force belonged to the other side. He therefore ardently pressed preparations for a war which, should it come, would be bitter and prolonged. He knew the North, and discounted the opinion that the commercially minded "Yankee" would not fight—replying to such assurances that only "fools doubted the courage of the Yankees."

CHAPTER XIV

"THE DRUMMING GUNS THAT HAVE NO DOUBTS"

WHEN considering the choice of a Cabinet, Davis remarked to his wife: "I can trust my own methods so
far, that they are humanitarian and, I feel sure, honest
—but I want the standpoint of other honest eyes, single to the
good of our people and of the country. I may look only at one
side." When choosing a Secretary of State, he anticipated Lincoln's plan of selecting his chief political rival. Toombs, like
Seward, had been a serious candidate for the Presidency; but,
unlike Seward, he proved to be an unwise selection. He was aggressive, uncompromising, disputatious and unstable, and it was
small grief to Davis when he retired to take a military command.
He next appointed Robert Taliaferro Hunter; and when after a
very brief service, the latter was elected to the Confederate Senate,
Judah P. Benjamin was made Secretary of State, and remained
the head of the Cabinet until the end of the Confederacy. Of all
his advisers, Davis relied most upon him, although when in the
Senate together, the two had on one occasion been very near
meeting on "the field of honour."

In making such appointments, Davis considered personality,
geographical location and political connexions; but never personal friendships. "No one of those who formed my first Cabinet," he later wrote, "had borne to me the relation of close
personal freindship, or had political claims upon me." When it
was complete, counting himself as representing Mississippi, he
had the satisfaction of knowing that each Confederate state had a
member.

While hunting for "honest eyes," Davis did not relax his search for working hands. Three days after his inauguration, he wrote to Raphael Semmes, who had resigned from the United States navy, to devote his brilliant talents to the Confederacy, authorizing the purchase of machinery and munitions, and the manufacture of arms. Having notified Governor Pickens of South Carolina that the Confederate Government would assume responsibility for military operations in Charleston harbour, he sent an experienced West Pointer, Major Whiting, to "inspect the various works in our possession and gain such knowledge of Fort Sumter as circumstances will permit."

But while acting upon the advice which Alexander Hamilton had given Washington as an item for his Farewell Address, "to place ourselves upon a respectable defensive," Davis believed, with Washington, that preparedness protects peace, and though pressing the former, organized what he hoped might prove a machine to bring about the latter. On February 25th, a week before Lincoln's inauguration, he appointed a commission to proceed to Washington and open with the latter, as soon as he should become President, a discussion of terms of peace between the "two Governments." He was conscious that fierce criticism would follow these activities, but consoled himself with the reflection that if a Government "can't stand the criticism of its friends, it will be in a bad way when it gets into the hands of its enemies."

It is strange, with war so evidently impending, that the Federal Government did not forbid the sale of arms to the potential enemy. But Buchanan was still President, and nothing was done to prevent it, or to stop the steady flow of military talent southward. In consequence, until the end of the term, Davis pressed his military preparations unimpeded.

When March 4th brought the retirement of Buchanan, Joseph H. Choate wrote that the loss was "like getting rid of an almost chronic disease"; but for a time many Republicans doubted whether Lincoln, the cure, would prove much better. On January 12, 1848, he had said: "Any people anywhere have the right to rise up and shake off the existing Government, and form a new one that suits them better. This is a most valuable, a sacred right—a right which we hope and believe is to liberate the world. Any portion of such people that can, may revolutionize and make their own so much of the territory as they inhabit. More than this, a majority of any portion of such people may revolutionize, putting down a minority . . . who may oppose their movements." Such a statement, and there had been many like it, seemed to indicate that there was no irreconcilable difference between the seceded states and the new Federal Executive, who had also announced that the Fugitive Slave law must be enforced, and that slavery within the slave states was legal and beyond the power of Federal interference.

Davis, however, was little disposed to accept such statements as proof that Lincoln would not attempt to reinforce Fort Sumter and compel the seceded states to return to their Federal connexion. And even Lincoln's inaugural address did not convince him, although the latter deliberately quoted the words of his platform denouncing, "the lawless invasion by armed force of the soil of any state or territory, no matter upon what pretext, as among the gravest of crimes." He saw clearly that Lincoln might invade the South, for either of the purposes just enumerated, without considering it "lawless invasion." Indeed, his words "perpetuity is implied, if not expressed, in the fundamental law of all national Governments," indicated the view that invasion of a state in order to preserve the Union would not be "lawless invasion," and that the right of secession so confidently asserted in the Confederate Constitution was not a right at all.

With this interpretation the *Edinburgh Review* was not in entire accord. The inaugural address of Mr. Lincoln, it declared, "augurs ill for the maintenance of the Union. The policy which it announces is neither that of conciliation nor that of defiance. He shuts his eyes to the fact of secession; and declares his intention of enforcing the Federal laws as if it did not exist. . . . The best defence which can be made of the inaugural address is, that it does not mean what it says, that its object is to gain time."

There is, however, ample reason to believe that Lincoln's aim was not only to gain time, but also to lead Davis into the first overt act of hostility, knowing that such an act would unite the North as arguments could never unite it. And unity was sorely needed. Neither House of Congress could be counted upon to accept the leadership of Lincoln, a minority President, and his very Cabinet was in part hostile, in part contemptuous. Moreover, it was far from certain to what extent he could count upon the support of the North. The abolitionists openly scorned both his ability, and his intuitions regarding slavery, to them the only issue.

Thus he wisely played for time, though with no such lack of purpose as Buchanan had shown, and while he waited, forming his plans with a patience akin to genius, the Northern papers and the European papers gratuitously warned him against trying to restore the shattered Union by force of arms. The *Detroit Free Press* declared that if "troops be raised in the North to march against the people of the South, a fire in the rear will be opened upon such troops, which will either stop their march . . . or wonderfully accelerate it." Horace Greeley, "a power behind the throne greater than the throne itself," as he has been described, continued to attack the idea of a Union pinned together with bayonets. Horatio Seymour demanded to know whether "successful coercion by the North [was] . . . less revolutionary than successful secession by the South. Shall we," he asked, "prevent revolution by being foremost in overthrowing the principles of our Government, and all that makes it valuable to our people and distinguishes it among the nations of the earth?"

Such a situation was calculated to induce caution, and, as Lowell later wrote, Lincoln was "at first . . . so slow that he tired out all those who see no evidence of progress but in blow-ing up the engine; then he was so fast that he took the breath away from those who think there is no getting on safely while there is a spark of fire under the boilers."

The Confederate commissioners saw only the slow Lincoln, and they respected his slowness. Not until March 11th did they definitely request an interview with the Secretary of State, which request was respectfully refused. The same day they addressed a communication to the Department of State, which declared: "The Confederate States constitute an independent nation, *de facto* and *de jure,* and possess a Government perfect in all its parts"; the Confederate Government desires "a peaceful solution" of all pending disputes, wishes to make no demand "not founded in strict justice," and requests an early opportunity for the presentation of the credentials of its commissioners.

Two days later, Mr. Justice Nelson, a friend of Seward's, assured Mr. Justice Campbell, a friend of the commissioners', that the Secretary of State was eager for peace, but desired to make no reply to the note for the present. Before reporting this interview, Judge Campbell sought out Seward, who apparently confirmed Judge Nelson's report of his attitude; for on the evening of the same day, Judge Campbell wrote to the commissioners: "I feel entire confidence that Fort Sumter will be evacuated in the next ten days . . . [and] that an immediate demand for an answer to the communication of the commissioners will be productive of evil, and not good. I do not believe that it ought at this time to be pressed."

Had the situation been as he supposed and as Seward apparently supposed, this would have been sound advice: but we now know that Lincoln had no intention of going peacefully. On December 12, 1860, he had written to the Hon. E. B. Washburne: "Please present my respects to the General [Scott], and tell him, confidentially, I shall be obliged to him to be as well prepared as he can be to either hold or retake the forts, as the case may require, at, or after, the inauguration."

On March 15th Secretary Seward filed in the State Department the Confederate commissioners' memorandum, with a note that after consulting the President he must decline "official intercourse with Messrs. Forsyth and Crawford." This decision was not, however, conveyed to the commissioners, and after waiting in vain for news of failure or success, Davis, on March 18th, wrote to Governor Pickens: "We have received nothing for several days from our commissioners, and I have not been of those who felt sanguine that the enemy would retire peaceably from your harbour. It is his choice as to how he will go; his stay must soon be measured by our forbearance. To have Fort Sumter uninjured is important to us, and for that reason, if there were no other, we should prefer that he should go peaceably."

On March 21st the Confederate Vice-President, Alexander H. Stephens, addressed a meeting at Savannah, in the course of which he said: "Many governments have been founded upon the principle of the subordination and serfdom of certain classes of the same race; such were, and are in violation of the laws of nature. Our system commits no such violation of nature's laws. With us, all of the white race, however high or low, rich or poor, are equal in the eye of the law. Not so with the negro. Subordination is his place. He, by nature, or by the curse against Cain, is fitted for that condition which he occupies in our system. . . . The substratum of our society is made of the material fitted by nature for it, and by experience we know that it is *best*, not only for the *superior*, but for the *inferior race*, that it should be so. It is, indeed, in conformity with the ordinance of the Creator. . . ."

Such opinions Davis had often expressed, but at this point Stephens announced a view entirely at variance with Davis' views. "This stone, which was rejected by the first builders, 'is become the Chief of the corner'—the real 'corner-stone' of our new edifice," he said.

This statement clearly meant that slavery was the foundation upon which the new Confederation stood and was determined to stand. It gave to the abolitionists the argument which they needed to convert a Constitutional controversy into a crusade, and they eagerly seized upon it, interpreting the speech as though it had been an article in the Confederate Constitution. "Nothing could be more absurd," commented the British *Quarterly Review*, "than to fix upon many millions of people, the great majority of whom had nothing to do with slavery, the sentence or epithet of a speaker expressing an individual view, on his own responsibility." It added the observation that there was in the Confederate Constitution "not a single provision for the protection of slavery which does not also exist in the Federal Constitution."

This was true enough, but propaganda takes little account of facts save only those which it can use for its purposes, and thereafter, protest though Stephens and Davis did, the North laboured, and in the end successfully, to make of Stephens' remark a battle-cry for the South: slave-holding minority, and non-slave-holding majority alike. Yet it is clear from the documents of the period that at the very time when Stephens was speaking, Davis was seeking to centre the controversy upon what to him, as to Lincoln, was the dominant issue—State Sovereignty vs. National Sovereignty, and to keep the slavery issue where Lincoln's inaugural address had placed it, in the area of things accepted by both sides as lawful.

Stephens' speech was followed by renewed pressure upon Lincoln to relieve the little garrison at Fort Sumter, and to hold what could be held against "rebels" bent upon making more secure the chains of their human chattels. "Seven Governors from . . . seven Northern states," says Stephens, ". . . hastened to Washington, and then and there organized their 'conspiracy,' and by appeals to Mr. Lincoln, and tendering him their organized military forces, caused him to change his policy and adopt theirs, which aimed at an entire overthrow of the Constitution of the United States, and the Federative principles of government on which it was based." It seems unlikely that Lincoln's course was the result of such direct pressure. But it is certain that some force or forces were pushing him ever nearer to the decision which Davis was prepared to accept as an act of war, namely, an attempt to reinforce Fort Sumter.

Meanwhile, as no news had come to confirm Seward's assurances that Sumter would be speedily evacuated, and as rumours of a contemplated relief expedition backed by force became more insistent, the Confederate commissioners, through Judge Campbell, sought new assurances. Having again interviewed Seward and received from him on April 7th, the assurance: "Faith as to Sumter fully kept—wait and see," Campbell reported to the commissioners that the failure to evacuate Sumter was "not the result of bad faith, but was attributable to causes consistent with the intention to fulfil the engagement."

Solomon said "in multitude of counsellors there is safety" and certainly Lincoln's counsellors in this hour of crisis were many, and their counsels were many. The Blairs, according to Gideon Wells, Lincoln's Secretary of the Navy, were now steering the ship, and following the direction indicated by Thaddeus Stevens, Sumner, and Wade, while Seward and General Scott planned an opposite course. Scott's advice was, "let the wayward sisters depart in peace," and Seward, says Wells, "was charged with giving a pledge to evacuate Fort Sumter. Mr. Thurlow Weed, the oracle and organ of Mr. Seward, in semi-official remarks on the rebel correspondence . . . says that 'Governor Seward conversed freely with Judge Campbell. We do not deny, nor do we doubt that in these conversations at one period he intimated that Fort Sumter would be vacated.' " But "if any such pledge as indicated in this correspondence was given, or any understanding was had, I was not aware of it, nor do I think it was known at the time to other members of the Administration." Wells also records a conversation with Lincoln in which the latter confessed that he had signed papers "some of them without reading them."

As to Lincoln's intentions, Stephens, after a careful study of

the records of the period, later wrote: "I have but little doubt
. . . that at that time, Mr. Lincoln had determined to withdraw
all United States forces from the limits of the Confederate States."
But Nicolay and Hay state that Lincoln's plan was "universal
statesmanship reduced to its simplest expression," namely to force
the enemy to strike the first blow. If when the Federal ships
should appear, carrying bread, but backed by others carrying guns,
the South "should set war in motion, they would lose their
Democratic allies in the Free States. If they hesitated to fight, the
revolution would collapse in the Slave States."

On March 29th, Lincoln wrote to Wells: "I desire that an expedition to move by sea be got ready to sail as early as the 6th of
April next, the whole according to memorandum enclosed; and
that you co-operate with the Secretary of War for that object."
The memorandum designated the *Pocahontas*, the *Pawnee* and
a revenue cutter, and specified that 300 seamen and 200 other men
should be ready at New York, with the necessary equipment.

The part of the plan to which Wells raised most objection was
that the Confederate authorities should be notified when the expedition was ready to start, as such notice would give Davis "time
to make preparations to defeat it." But, despite his protests, Lincoln "decided to send a message to Charleston when the expedition sailed, but not before, to notify Governor Pickens, of the
fact that the object was peaceful." If Seward knew of this decision, as confided to Wells on March 29th, he was certainly breaking a promise in the spirit, if not in the letter, when, on April 1,
1861, he gave Judge Campbell a written statement, that he was
satisfied that "the Government will not undertake to supply Fort
Sumter without giving notice to Governor Pickens": for notice
after the expedition was actually under way would be of little
practical value to the Governor of South Carolina, if he meant to
prepare for resistance. It seems fairer to Seward to assume that
he was ignorant of Lincoln's plans, rather than to accept Campbell's charge, that he was guilty of "systematic duplicity . . .

through me." But whether through ignorance or duplicity, he had kept the Confederate commissioners awaiting a reception which had never been contemplated by Lincoln.

More important still, Virginia had been kept waiting. On April 4th her convention rejected secession by a vote of 89 to 45, but caused Lincoln serious anxiety by remaining in session. On April 5th, fearing that his Fort Sumter expedition, now almost ready to put to sea, might cause a reversal of the vote of the convention, Lincoln held a conversation with one of its members, Colonel John B. Baldwin of Staunton, during which, according to an account which the Rev. R. L. Dabney claimed to have had from Baldwin's own lips, Lincoln said: "We have in Fort Sumter, with Major Robert Anderson, about 80 men. Their provisions are nearly exhausted. I have . . . written to Governor Pickens . . . that I will not permit these people to starve; but shall send them provisions. If he fires on that vessel he will fire upon an unarmed vessel loaded with bread." He explained, furthermore, that a fleet of armed vessels would accompany the relief ship to the entrance of Charleston harbour, with orders to go in only in case the provision ship should be attacked. "If you will go back to Richmond and get the Union majority to adjourn and go home without passing the ordinance of secession . . . I will take the responsibility of evacuating Fort Sumter. . . ." Baldwin in his account of the interview does not mention such a proposal, though he says that Lincoln lamented the fact that the interview had come too late.

In view of Davis' determination to avoid a conflict, and of his oft-repeated declaration that the helpless little garrison of Fort Sumter was a menace to peace, it seems certain that if so reasonable a proposal had come to his ears, he would have urged the Virginia convention to accept it. While distrusting Seward, as a man devoted to devious subtleties, he considered Lincoln honest and reliable, though misguided upon the issues of state sovereignty and the rights of slavery in the territories. But, whatever the reason, Baldwin reported no proposition from Lincoln, and the Virginia convention remained in session, and watched developments. It was apparent that any attempt to capture Fort Sumter would mean another state in the Confederacy, and that the Old Dominion.

Prior to these events, there had been no stated Cabinet meetings, but Lincoln now directed that such should be held twice weekly. This change Wells interpreted with satisfaction as the end of Seward's supremacy, as the other members of the Cabinet might now have more influence with the President.

The American Cabinet, so called, unlike that of Great Britain, contains many voices, but one vote. The voices offer suggestions, but the President alone makes decisions. Seward, Wells, and their fellow members continued to give opinions, but in the absence of Cabinet minutes, it is difficult to ascertain what these opinions were, or how they affected Lincoln. They certainly, however, did not cause him to abandon his expedition to Fort Sumter, which he insisted could not fairly be called either invasion or coercion. The preparations proceeded, and Major Anderson, "the first man holding a position of trust who did his duty to the nation," as James Russell Lowell declared, "grimly held his position, and as chance offered strengthened it."

Under such conditions, the Confederate commissioners, who had now waited twenty-three days, felt that further patience would be not virtue but folly, and this feeling became conviction when they read in the papers of April 8th a letter from Lincoln to Governor Pickens and General Beauregard, announcing that, "provisions will be sent to Fort Sumter—peacefully or otherwise by force." On that same day, Choate reported to his mother: "Ships of war, well freighted with soldiers and ammunition, are being fitted out with great expedition and leaving the harbour, but their destination is kept a profound secret." And he added with youth's tendency to generalization, "Nobody here would be much distressed to hear of a sharp skirmish southward."

JEFFERSON DAVIS

From a photograph by E. Anthony, of New York, which has been in the
family of the present author since it was taken about 1860 or 1861

These facts caused the Confederate commissioners to dispatch their Secretary, J. T. Picket, to the State Department with a demand for a definite answer to their earlier communications. Picket returned with a copy of the memorandum filed by Seward, with this note attached: "The foregoing memorandum was filed in this Department on the 15th of March last. A delivery of the same, however, to Messrs. Forsyth and Crawford was delayed, as was understood, with their consent. They have now, through their Secretary, communicated their desire for a definite disposition of the subject. The Secretary of State therefore directs that a duly verified copy of this paper be now delivered."

The commissioners not unnaturally concluded that they had been deliberately deceived regarding the intentions of the Federal Government, which had used the time thus gained to prepare its plan of the invasion, now under way. Therefore, on April 9th they wrote accusing the Federal Government of trickery and bad faith. "The memorandum, dated Department of State, Washington, March 15, 1861, with postscript under date of 8th instant, has been received. . . . Your refusal to entertain these overtures for a peaceful solution, the active naval and military preparations . . . and a formal notice to the commanding general of the Confederate forces in the harbour of Charleston that the President intends to provision Fort Sumter by forcible means, if necessary, are viewed by the undersigned, and can only be received by the world, as a declaration of war. . . . For the President of the United States knows that Fort Sumter cannot be provisioned without the effusion of blood. The undersigned . . . accept the gage of battle thus thrown down; and, appealing to God and the judgment of mankind for the righteousness of their cause, the people of the Confederate States will defend their liberties to the last, against this flagrant and open attempt at their subjugation to sectional power.

"The undersigned are not aware of any Constitutional power in the President of the United States to levy war, without the consent of Congress, upon a foreign People, much less upon any portion of the People of the United States." And, lest these words should be taken as a recognition of the fact that the seceded states still belonged to the Federal Union, now rapidly becoming a consolidated nation, they added: "You . . . refuse to recognize the fact . . . of a completed and successful Revolution. You close your eyes to the existence of the Government founded upon it. . . . Whatever may be the result, impartial history will record the innocence of the Government of the Confederate States, and place the responsibility of the blood and mourning that may ensue upon those who have denied the great fundamental doctrine of American liberty, that 'governments derive their just powers from the consent of the governed,' and who have set naval and land armaments in motion to subject the people of one portion of this land to the will of another portion."

This bland assumption that military preparation had been all on the side of the Federal Government disregarded the fact which T. C. De Leon had reported, that the South was ready to fight, though unprepared for war. Lincoln knew that on March 6th the Confederate Congress had authorized Davis to call out 100,000 volunteers, to serve for twelve months, and to employ also the militia, military, and naval forces of the Confederate States to "repel invasion, maintain the rightful possession of the Confederate States, and to secure public tranquillity and independence against the threatened assault." He knew, furthermore, that, as a result, General Beauregard now had thousands of men and many cannon ready to challenge an attempt to provision or reinforce Fort Sumter.

Such facts make it clear that in proposing to send force with his provisioning ships, Lincoln was only preparing to meet force with force; for clearly Beauregard's army was designed to prevent the operation of laws which had been duly passed and to impair rights long exercised and admitted. The South had thus furnished justification for the armed vessels which would attend Lincoln's

ABRAHAM LINCOLN

From a portrait taken in 1860, in the possession
of the Library of Congress

"vessels laden with bread," and on the day that the commissioners wrote to Secretary Seward, Governor Pickens reported to Davis that by tomorrow he would have 6,000 men on the harbour in positions of defence, ready to do their duty should force be required.

"Who is the aggressor?" is a question always difficult to answer when discussing war guilt, and we are still seeking a workable definition of the word. Hallam declared that, "The aggressor in a war is not the first who uses force, but the first who renders force necessary." But even by that apparently simple test it is difficult to determine the aggressor in this case, although Lincoln's biographers, Nicolay and Hay, have awarded the responsibility to him, by arguing that his aim in the Fort Sumter Expedition was to tempt the Confederates to fire upon the flag, and thus become the aggressors in a conflict which he felt to be inevitable.

Davis, agreeing with Hallam, wrote: "He who makes the first assault is not necessarily he that strikes the first blow or fires the first gun. To have awaited further strengthening of their position by land and naval forces, with hostile purpose now declared, for the sake of having them fire the first gun, would have been as unwise as it would be to hesitate to strike down the arm of an assailant, who levels a deadly weapon at one's breast, until he actually fired. The disingenuous rant of demagogues about 'firing on the flag' might serve to rouse the passions of insensate mobs in times of general excitement, but will be impotent in impartial history to relieve the Federal Government from the responsibility of the assault made by sending a hostile fleet against the harbour of Charleston, to co-operate with the menacing garrison of Fort Sumter."

Of the shrewdness of Lincoln's plan to play upon the psychology of the masses, there can be no question. Little intent upon his own place in history, he was concerned with what the wavering minds, North, South, Border state and European, would think when Confederate guns should open upon an unarmed vessel ladened with bread for a garrison starving under the floating flag of their country. As a wrestler, he knew how to find the weak spot of his antagonist, and shrewdly applied the tactics to statecraft.

To Davis, trusting the world to understand the complicated reasoning with which he ably sustained the South's position, it was not apparent that the public seldom concerns itself with subtleties. When one fires on the flag of one's Country, one is a traitor, and Lincoln had now placed Davis in a position where he must either capture Fort Sumter before the arrival of "unarmed vessels laden with bread" for "a few brave and hungry men," as Lincoln described it, and its armed convoy "eight vessels, carrying 26 guns and 1,400 men," as Davis described it, or risk a fatal loss of prestige at the very beginning of his Presidential term.

It is difficult, therefore, if not impossible, to answer the question, which was the aggressor. As Lincoln thought Davis' plan was to starve Sumter into surrender, he was perhaps justified in the conclusion that Davis had left him no alternative but to relieve the garrison, and was therefore the aggressor. On the other hand, as Davis thought of the supply ship, and its grim comrades steaming southward, he was perhaps justified in his argument that Lincoln had left him no alternative but attack. One thing, however, was clear: Lincoln had made his decision: and the hour for that of Davis had arrived.

Already the heavy labours and heavier responsibilities of office had left their effect upon Davis' never too robust constitution. T. C. De Leon, who visited Montgomery while Lincoln's provision ships and armed convoy were moving towards Fort Sumter, says, "Even in the few weeks since I had seen him [Davis] in Washington, a great change had come over him. He looked worn and thinner, and the set expression of his somewhat stern features gave a grim hardness not natural to their lines. With scarcely a glance around, he returned the general salutations, and sat down absently and was soon absorbed in conversation. . . . At this time the Southern chief was fifty-two years old—tall, erect, and spare by natural habit, but worn thin almost to emaciation by mental and physical toil. Almost constant sickness and the unremitting excitement of the last few months had left their imprint on face as well as figure. The features had sharpened and the lines had deepened and hardened. . . . Mr. Davis had lost the sight of one eye many months previous, though that member scarcely showed its imperfection; but in the other burned a deep, steady glow, showing the presence with him of thought that never slept."

The strain was heightened when, a few days later, General Beauregard requested instructions regarding the approaching Federal expedition. At once Davis summoned his Cabinet and passed on to them the question. Most of them felt that but one course remained: Fort Sumter must be challenged at once, and if Anderson would not surrender, force must be used to capture it before it should be too late. Toombs, on the other hand, vigorously dissented, declaring that "The firing upon that fort will inaugurate a civil war greater than any the world has yet seen. . . . At this time it is suicide, murder, and will lose us every friend at the North. You will wantonly strike a hornet's nest . . . and legions now quiet will swarm out and sting us to death. It is unnecessary; it puts us in the wrong; it is fatal."

Davis, however, agreed with the majority, and was prepared to act in accordance with Locke's theory that, "In all states and conditions the true remedy of force without authority is to oppose force to it. The use of force without authority puts him that uses it into a state of war as the aggressor." He felt that Lincoln's approaching warships, sent without consultation with Congress, was "force without authority," making Lincoln already the aggressor. Therefore, after hearing the opposing views he announced his decision: "The order for the sailing of the fleet was a declaration of war. The responsibility is on their shoulders, not ours. The juggle for position as to who shall fire the first gun in such an hour is unworthy of a great people and their cause.

A deadly weapon has been aimed at our heart. Only a fool would wait until the shot has been fired. The assault has been made. It is of no importance who shall strike the first blow or fire the first gun." With the quick decision of a man trained to command in a crisis, he directed that Beauregard be ordered to demand the surrender of Fort Sumter, and if that were refused, to reduce it.

Accordingly, on April 11th Colonel Chestnut and Captain S. D. Lee approached Fort Sumter and at 2:20 P.M. demanded its immediate surrender, as the Confederate States could "no longer delay taking possession of a fort which commanded one of their harbours." Anderson replied that a sense of responsibility prevented his immediate compliance, although "if you do not batter the fort to pieces about us, we will be starved out in a few days."

As this answer seemed to offer a chance of avoiding bloodshed, Beauregard reported it to President Davis, who replied, through his Secretary of War, Walker: "Do not desire needlessly to bombard Fort Sumter. . . . If Major Anderson will state the time at which . . . he will evacuate . . . you are authorized thus to avoid the effusion of blood. If this, or its equivalent, is refused, reduce the fort. . . ." Beauregard therefore dispatched a second message to the fort, that if Anderson would agree not to use his guns unless attacked, force might be avoided. This message was delivered at 12:25 A.M. of April 12th. At 3:15 A.M. Anderson returned the answer: "I will evacuate . . . Fort Sumter by noon on the 15th instant, and I will not in the meantime open my fires upon your forces unless compelled to do so by some hostile act against this fort or the flag of my Government . . . should I not receive controlling instructions . . . or additional supplies."

As it was known that the relief expedition would arrive before April 15th, such an answer appeared a pretext for awaiting its approach, at which time, the chance of taking Fort Sumter without a serious engagement would disappear. Furthermore, Roger A. Pryor, of Virginia, was convinced that an immediate attack would add his state to the Confederacy. Only the day before he had delivered a speech of congratulation to South Carolina upon the annihilation of this "cursed union," and had added, "I will tell your Governor what will put Virginia in the Southern Confederacy in less than an hour by the Shrewsbury clock—'strike a blow'!"

It is not possible to determine how much the other three messengers were influenced by this idea, but they would doubtlessly have agreed with William Tecumseh Sherman that: "if Major Anderson can hold out till relieved and supported by steam frigates, South Carolina will find herself unable to control her commerce." They therefore decided to act upon the discretion which their instructions had granted, and, without referring the matter again to Davis, or to Beauregard, sent Anderson this message: "By authority of Brigadier-General Beauregard, commanding the provisional forces of the Confederate States, we have the honour to notify you that he will open the fire of his batteries on Fort Sumter in one hour from this time."

The "honour" of firing the shot, which initiated the Civil War, was given to the veteran agitator, Edmund Ruffin, of Virginia, who had long and impatiently worked for secession and a new Confederacy. According to his *Journal*, on "April 12, 1861—Before 4 A.M. the drums beat for parade, and our company was speedily on the march to the batteries which they were to man. At 4:30 a signal shell was thrown from a mortar battery at Fort Johnston, which had been ordered to be taken as the command for immediate attack; and firing from all the batteries bearing on Fort Sumter next began in the order arranged, which was that the discharges should be two minutes apart, and the round of all the pieces and batteries to be completed in thirty-two minutes, and then to begin again.

"The night before, when expecting to engage, Captain Cuthbert had notified me that his company requested of me to discharge the first cannon to be fired, which was their 64-pound columbiad, loaded with shell. I was highly gratified by the compliment, and delighted to perform the service—which I did. The shell struck the fort at the northeast angle of the parapet. By order of General Beauregard, made known the afternoon of the 11th, the attack was to be commenced by the first shot . . . from the iron battery. In accepting and acting upon this highly appreciated compliment, the company had made me its instrument." We have this account from a Mobile paper of the period: "The venerable Edmund Ruffin, whose head is silvered over by more than eighty winters, and who, when the war cloud lowered over the gallant city of Charleston volunteered as a private, and with knapsack on his back and musket on his shoulder, tendered his services to South Carolina to fight against the aggression upon her rights, . . . pointed and fired the first gun at Fort Sumter."

The guns of Sumter remained silent till 7 A.M., and the duel which followed would have been fairly equal had Anderson had a full garrison, as the armaments were well matched. But with a defending force of only "about 80 men," and an attacking force of 7,000, the end was certain, save only for the chance that help might arrive before the power of resistance was exhausted.

As the firing continued, the people of Charleston thronged to the waterfront, to witness what was to prove not the consummation of their dream of separate sovereignty, but the beginning of the end of slavery. The *Charleston Courier* described the scene as a gala occasion. Throughout the day, the crowds watched, cheered, debated, and waited for the inevitable surrender. In the afternoon the guns of Sumter slackened, and, as night came on, ceased. They had seen the approaching end of their munitions. But the Confederate batteries thundered on through the night.

Early on the morning of the 13th the firing became fiercer: and at about nine o'clock a shot set fire to the officers' quarters of Fort Sumter, and the blaze spread rapidly. It was soon necessary to close the powder-magazine, the explosion of whose scant supply would have demolished the fortifications. Fifty barrels of powder were taken out; but the fire continued to spread so rapidly that forty-five of these had to be thrown into the sea. Then some of the magazines exploded, and the garrison, with wet cloths over their faces, crept to the embrasures to avoid suffocation.

At 1:30 in the afternoon Sumter's flagstaff was cut by a shell and her flag fell. Instantly Captain Hart climbed the stump and nailed the fallen colours back in the position of defiance. The disappearance of the flag for even so brief a space, however, had caused General Beauregard to suppose that the fort had fallen. He, therefore, dispatched three aids, with an offer of assistance. The result was surrender, the only possible course, and at 3 P.M. Anderson thus reported it:

"Having defended Fort Sumter for thirty-four hours, until the quarters were entirely burned, the main gates destroyed by fire, the gorge walls seriously injured, the magazine surrounded by flames, and its door closed from the effects of heat, four barrels and three cartridges of powder only being available, and no provisions remaining but pork, I accepted terms of evacuation offered by General Beauregard, being the same offered by him . . . prior to the commencement of hostilities, and marched out of the fort Sunday afternoon, the 14th instant, with colours flying and drums beating, bringing away company and private property, and saluting my flag with fifty guns."

Not a man on either side had been killed: but the gallantry of the defenders of Fort Sumter had wrung cheers from the enemy crowds on the battery during the fight.

After the fall of the fort, its garrison embarked on the *Baltic* and steamed away to New York. Governor Pickens with General Beauregard then crossed to the island and raised the Confederate flag over the smouldering ruins of regained Sumter: and President Davis expressed to Edmund Ruffin his "grateful acknowledgment of your heroic devotion to the South, to truth and to Constitutional Government."

Thus out of a tangle of facts imperfectly understood, of hesitations, uncertainties, and bold decisions, had come a war which

J. L. O'Sullivan later characterized as the "most dreadful and most absurd of wars yet witnessed by the world," and one which throughout the remainder of his life Davis never wearied of comparing with the American Revolution, which Pitt had declared: "most accursed, wicked, barbarous, cruel, unnatural, unjust and diabolical." In both cases, the individual, for whose welfare "governments are instituted among men," was sacrificed upon the altar of that mythical creature called sovereignty. For the South, Davis, Lee, Jackson, and the rest, the sovereign was the state: for Lincoln, Seward, Scott, Grant, and their Northern colleagues, it was the nation.

"The fall of Fort Sumter," wrote a British pamphleteer, "caused one of those sudden and shameless changes of feeling in the North to which democracies are most prone. Up to that time the secession had been more than excused." The *Times*, the most reliable exponent of British public opinion, manifested a strong sympathy for the South, and a tendency to censure the North. "What a spectacle is here!" it cried, "a Government going to war for no principle, for no object, save that of aggrandizement." Upon which Henry Ward Beecher indignantly declared: "When our rebellion broke out, if there was any nation under heaven that we looked to for sympathy and help, it was the mother country, England. But how did she treat us? She sympathized with our enemies."

As the President of the Confederacy was now in a position to claim for his government the qualifications which international law had specified for belligerents, and as he himself had openly advocated the right of revolution, Lincoln now sought a formula to prevent the seceders from enjoying belligerent rights. Unable to accept Seward's doctrine, that law and precedent had been superseded by "the higher law," he decided to rely upon the idea of the Federal Convention of 1787, and exercise the Federal power over the *individuals* involved, or to be involved, in the secession movement. He saw that if he could interpret this *rebellion*, seeking to become a *revolution*, in terms of a domestic uprising of individuals, he might deal with the secessionists as mere law-breakers, and on April 15th issued a proclamation declaring "the laws of the United States . . . opposed and the execution thereof obstructed . . . by combinations too powerful to be suppressed by the ordinary course of judicial proceedings," and commanding "the combinations aforesaid to disperse."

Davis later commented thus upon this ingenious interpretation of an appeal to the right of revolution by seven powerful states united into a definite Government: "It can but surprise any one in the least degree conversant with the history of the Union, to find states referred to as 'persons composing combinations,' and that the sovereign creators of the Federal Government, the States of the Union, should be commanded by their agent to disperse."

Lincoln's Proclamation furthermore called out "the militia of the several states of the Union, to the . . . number of 75,000, in order to suppress said combinations"; of which order William Tecumseh Sherman remarked, contemptuously, "You might as well attempt to put out the flames of a burning house with a squirt-gun." Davis, more concerned to discount Lincoln's legal position than his military judgment, declared that so large an army could only mean war, which the President could not lawfully enter upon without authorization by Congress, a view which had often been emphasized in that body by men of both political parties. As recently as March 15th Douglas had said, in the Senate: "Under the laws as they now exist, he [the President] cannot, consistently with his oath, do any act that will produce collision between the seceded states and the Federal Government."

Lincoln's Proclamation announced also, that: "the first service assigned . . . will probably be to repossess the forts, places, and property which have been seized from the Union," and summoned Congress in extraordinary session "at 12 o'clock noon, on Thursday, the fourth of July next," a generous allowance of time in view of the fact "that the present condition of public affairs presents an extraordinary occasion."

Pitt declared that no man can serve England in a great capacity without sacrificing the minor virtues, and it was easy for Davis and his associates to show in Lincoln's Proclamation proof positive that he was sacrificing the minor virtue of consistency. Inconsistency, however, disturbed him not at all. It was easy to assert that his proposed invasion of a sovereign state was lawless invasion, and as such according to his own platform "among the greatest of crimes." Lincoln clearly regarded invasion to preserve the Union not as lawless, but as lawful invasion. It was easy for Davis to argue that for Lincoln to keep Congress out of Washington until July 4th was a demonstration of his determination to rule alone: but even that did not disturb Lincoln. "My policy is to have no policy," he had often declared, and he might as truthfully have said, "My consistency is to be as inconsistent as the emergency." But, whatever the criticism, one thing was clear; the rapid Lincoln was in the ascendent. The eighty days had begun.

Thus Lincoln had been shrewd enough so to interpret the situation as to leave the South, and the people of the South, under American law, and without the protection which international law offers to belligerents. Should his interpretation be accepted, men captured in "rebellion" would be subject to trial as traitors, rather than as prisoners of war. This view offered manifest advantages, making recognition of the Confederacy difficult for foreign nations. He persistently adhered to the position that the States were still under the laws and the Constitution, because no state could get out of the Union, which was perpetual. The seceding states were only "out of their proper practical relation to the Union," and their citizens as individuals were still subject to the coercive power of the Executive, whose duty it was to "take care that the laws be faithfully executed." This interpretation made unnecessary a decision on the part of Congress to which the Constitution had assigned the right to declare war.

In his vain efforts to persuade the Virginia convention to adjourn, Lincoln had shown his distrust of popular action at such a crisis; and now, in his Proclamation he showed as clearly that he preferred not to risk the interference even of his own Congress. Thus eighty days, without the disturbing presence of Senate or House of Representatives, lay before him, and he proceeded to make full use of them, though conscious that he would face protest and indignant criticism when Congress should again convene.

On April 16th, Governor Pickens wrote to Davis that Mr. Dallas, the American minister at London, had appealed to Lord John Russell, Minister of Foreign Affairs, not to recognize the Confederacy, nor in any way to encourage its leader to hope for recognition. He declared that this action had been taken by Dallas, "by instructions from Washington," and that Lord John, while declining to give any pledge, and expressing the hope that reconciliation might be brought about, had warned Dallas that any attempt on the part of President Lincoln to blockade the Southern ports would "immediately lead to the recognition of the independence of the South by Great Britain." This information was given to the Governor of South Carolina by the British consul, in confidence, but with permission to convey it to President Davis.

To Davis, confident that Lincoln would attempt to blockade the Southern ports, this meant that English recognition might almost surely be counted upon, especially as Southern cotton was the basis of the industry of such cities as Manchester and Birmingham, and as the North was a formidable rival of England in the carrying trade.

In view of such facts, it was obviously to the interest of the Confederate States to repudiate Lincoln's interpretation of the war started at Sumter, and accept the character of a rebel government seeking recognition, and demanding belligerent rights. Robert E. Lee had expressed the view that "secession is nothing but revolution," and had added, "The framers of our Constitution never exhausted so much labour, wisdom, and forbearance in its formation, and surrounded it with so many guards and securities, if it was intended to be broken by every member of the Confederacy at will. It was intended for 'perpetual union,' so expressed in the preamble, and for the establishment of a government, not a compact, which can only be dissolved by revolution."

Thomas H. Hatts, later as Davis' Attorney-General, definitely urged him to accept the name "Rebel." "The war now waging," he wrote, ". . . is not a war between a part of one community with the other part of the same community; it is not a civil war, but a public war, between two nations. . . ."

Had Davis studied the authorities on international law as diligently as he studied the relationship between Lincoln's actions and the Federal Constitution, he would have found ample argument to induce foreign nations to reject Lincoln's position. The learned Swiss jurist Vattel had written: "When a nation becomes divided into two parties absolutely independent, and no longer acknowledging a common superior, the state is dissolved, and the war between the two stands on the same ground in every respect, as a public war between two different nations. They decide their quarrel by arms as two different nations would do. The obligation to observe the common laws of war toward each other is therefore absolute—indispensably binding on both parties, and the same which the law of nature imposes on all nations in transactions between state and state." The German jurist, Welckler, had announced the opinion that when: "a division of the nation has taken place into two hostile camps . . . every citizen is bound to declare himself for one or the other party, and then neither blame nor punishment can reach him, whatever the result of the battle may be. Then there are only victors and vanquished—not loyalists and criminals, and, although it is difficult to state the precise moment when rebellion ceases and civil war commences, there nevertheless exists an essential difference between them." And Francis Lieber, another eminent authority, was teaching Columbia students that: "No one incurs the guilt of treason by coherence to . . . a Government *de facto,* although that . . . Government has but the right of a successful rebel, and loses all by a subsequent defeat."

CHAPTER XV

"THE EIGHTY DAYS"

THE evacuation of Fort Sumter by the Federal garrison found both Lincoln and Davis intent upon the questions of how to secure the Border states; how to win the good will of England, which then, as now, set the compass of Europe; and how to create, rapidly, an effective army and navy. In facing these problems, Lincoln had two great advantages in addition to wealth and man-power—he was free from interference from Congress for eighty days; and he did not admit the existence of war, adhering steadily to the view that he was dealing with law-breakers "too powerful to be suppressed by the ordinary judicial proceedings."

Davis, on the other hand, had to contend with opponents in his Congress, and to convince Europe that war existed, though only for the defence of local self-government. He hoped that the commercial rivalry between the United States and the British Government would lead the latter to recognize the Confederacy, if not actually to intervene, and that the refusal of the United States to join the international agreement to abandon letters of marque and privateering, would counterbalance any complaints which England could make against Confederate use of the same weapons.

The most pressing of these problems was that of the Border states, all of which had been thrown into uncertainty by the attack upon Fort Sumter. Their closest connexions were with the South, and many of their citizens were slaveholders and sensitive to the criticisms which the abolitionists constantly published abroad, to convince the world that the war would be a life-and-death struggle for the preservation of slavery, and that Lincoln's attitude towards the institution had changed since writing his inaugural address, in which he had denied the purpose, "directly or indirectly, to interfere with . . . slavery in the states where it exists. I believe I have no lawful right to do so, and I have no inclination to do so. Those who nominated and elected me did so with full knowledge that I had made this and many similar declarations, and had never recanted." But, search as they might, no support of their claim could be found in Lincoln's utterances.

Immediately after the fall of Sumter, Lincoln was faced with the loss of the chief Border state. Two-thirds of Virginia's convention, which he had vainly urged to adjourn, were said to be Union men when Fort Sumter was attacked: but that attack had altered her point of view, and at once it was evident that the "Shrewsbury clock" had struck. At the news of the surrender, Richmond went frantic with delight. Thousands of people marched in procession to the Capitol, and the Fayette Artillery fired 100 guns in honour of the victory. They next proceeded to the Governor's house and Letcher made a few remarks, which, however, were interrupted by hisses, as lacking sufficient enthusiasm for secession. The crowd then returned to the Capitol, pulled down the Federal flag, and for three hours the Southern flag floated in the breeze. Governor Letcher, however, though ready to protect Virginia, if attacked, had no intention of allowing the excitement of the moment to carry her into the Confederacy. He therefore ordered the Confederate flag hauled down, and the Stars and Stripes were again raised over the Capitol.

Four days later, on April 17th, by a vote of 88 to 55, Virginia's convention adopted an Ordinance of Secession, to be binding if approved by the people. Accepting this act as final, without waiting for the result of the plebiscite, Davis now issued a proclamation, inviting applications for letters of marque, and Samuel Goddard in his report to the London *Daily Post*, a few days later, commented that Davis was "probably designing to replenish his treasury from some of the gold-ships." To Lincoln this meant that plans must be set on foot for the protection of Federal commerce; and, on April 19th, he declared what was in effect a "paper block-ade" of Confederate ports: "If any person, under the pretended authority of the said states . . . shall molest a vessel of the United States . . . such person will be held amenable to the laws of the United States for the . . . punishment of piracy."

The day on which this proclamation was issued, Davis sent Vice-President Stephens to Richmond, to seek an offensive and defensive alliance, and, the day after, Colonel Robert E. Lee, also confident that the people of Virginia would approve the Ordinance of Secession, wrote to General Winfield Scott the following letter:

Arlington, Va., *April 20th, 1861.*

General:

Since my interview with you on the 18th instant, I have felt that I ought not longer to retain my commission in the army. I therefore tender my resignation, which I request that you will recommend for acceptance. It would have been presented at once, but for the struggle it has caused me to separate myself from a service to which I have devoted the best years of my life, and all the ability I possessed.

During the whole of that time—more than a quarter of a century—I have experienced nothing but kindness from my superiors, and the most cordial friendship from my comrades. To no one, General, have I been as much indebted as to yourself, for uniform kindness and consideration, and it has always been my ardent desire to merit your approbation. I shall carry to my grave the most grateful recollections of your kind consideration, and your name and fame will always be dear to me.

Save in defence of my native state, I desire never again to draw my sword. Be pleased to accept my most earnest wishes for the continuance of your happiness and prosperity, and believe me,

Most truly yours,

R. E. LEE.

LIEUTENANT-GENERAL WINFIELD SCOTT.
Commanding United States Army.

He wrote also to his sister: "I know that you will blame me; but you must think of me as kindly as you can, and believe that I have endeavoured to do what I thought *right*"; and to his brother, "I wished to wait until the Ordinance of Secession should be acted on by the people of Virginia; but war seems to have commenced, and I am liable at any time to be ordered on duty, which I could not conscientiously perform. . . . I had to act at once."

By this devotion to duty, Lee, like Davis, sacrificed a certain present for an uncertain future. The Federal Government had, through Francis Preston Blair, offered to make him commander of the armies that were to be brought into the field: but he declined, "stating as candidly and courteously as I could that, though opposed to secession and deprecating war, I could take no part in the invasion of the Southern States." General Preston later said that upon Lee's refusal, General Scott declared: "If I were on my dying bed, and knew there was to be a battle fought for the liberties of my country, and the President were to say to me, 'Scott, who shall command?' with my dying breath, I should say, 'Robert Lee; nobody but Robert Lee, Robert Lee, and nobody but Lee.' "

These facts constitute a sufficient denial of the oft-repeated statement that Davis led his state into secession, and Lee followed his. On the contrary, Davis waited in the Senate until officially notified by the Governor that Mississippi was out of the Union; while Lee resigned his Federal commission and cast his lot with Virginia before the plebiscite had legalized the process of secession. "I could have taken no other course without dishonour," he later declared. Writing in old age, Davis thus summed up the reasons which led Lee, "the deathless martyr of our kingdom of the twilight," to reject the chief command in the gift of the Federal Government and to cast his lot with the Virginia militia: "General Lee did not leave the United States army to enter that of the Confederacy. He conscientiously believed that his allegiance was due primarily to Virginia, and that through her, so long as she remained in the Union, he owed allegiance to the United States; therefore, when Virginia withdrew from the Union and war was waged against her because of the exercise of that sovereign right, the alternative presented to him, was to fight against, or in defence of, his mother state—any one who knew him could have foretold what his choice would be." It is true, however, that Lee left the Union before the Virginia plebiscite had made legal the secession of his state. "It is hard to understand," writes Douglas Freeman, "why it has been so widely believed that he waited until the secession of Virginia."

Lee's decision, as unwelcome as it was unexpected at the North, raised the cry that he had acted from ambition, an absurd and unjust charge. "With a small part of his knowledge of the relative amount of material of war possessed by the North and South," Davis later wrote, "any one must have seen that the chances of war were against us; but if thrice-armed Justice should enable the South to maintain her independence, as our fathers had done, notwithstanding the unequal contest, what selfish advantage could it bring to Lee? If, as some among us yet expected, many hoped, and all wished, there should be a peaceful separation, he would have left behind him all he had gained by long and brilliant service, and could not have in our small army greater rank than was proffered to him in the larger one he had left. If active hostilities were prosecuted, his property would be so exposed as to incur serious injury, if not destruction. . . . Above the voice of his friends at Washington, advising and entreating him to stay with them, rose the cry of Virginia calling her sons to defend her against threatened invasion. Lee heeded this cry only. Alone he rode forth, . . . his guiding star being Duty, and offered his sword to Virginia."

Governor Letcher was authorized to appoint the now detached colonel to the command of Virginia's militia, and on April 21st summoned him to a conference in Richmond. Lee started at once by train, but before he arrived, war and secession threatened in a second border state. On April 19th, a mob had attacked the Sixth Massachusetts Regiment, which was attempting to pass through Baltimore on its way to invade the South, and despite the best efforts of the police, four men were killed, and thirty-nine wounded.

This indication that another star was soon to be added to the flag of the Confederacy was emphasized that evening when at a mass meeting in Monument Square, Governor Hicks declared that he "would sooner have his right arm cut off than raise it against a sister Southern state," and George W. Brown announced himself ready to "protect its soil with his life," against the invading foe. Brown was Mayor, and a member of the Board of Police Commissioners which, before midnight, ordered the destruction of the bridges which connected Baltimore with the North; and before dawn, all railway communication was at an end, and a call had been sent out for troops to protect the city from "further trespass" by the Federal Government. A notice, posted at Frederick, urged that defenders "report as soon as possible, providing themselves with such arms and accoutrements as they can. Double-barrelled shotguns and buckshot are efficient." The next morning Baltimore's City Council appropriated half a million dollars for defence against Federal troops moving towards the national capital at the call of the President.

To Davis this action of the people of Baltimore seemed entirely proper; and their right to secede, should they so decide, unquestionably legal, especially as he believed that the troops marching to Washington were "destined sooner or later to be the bearers of an emancipation proclamation or to stir up servile insurrection."

When, on April 23, 1861, Robert E. Lee appeared before the Virginia convention to receive from its president official notification of his appointment as major-general of militia, he was received by John Janney, its President, with the words: ". . . When the necessity became apparent of having a leader of our forces, all hearts and eyes, by the impulse of an instinct which is a surer guide than reason itself, turned to the old County of Westmoreland. . . . We knew that she had given birth to the Father of his Country, to Richard Henry Lee, to Monroe, and last though not least, to your gallant father; and we knew well by your deeds, that her productive power was not yet exhausted. . . .

"One of the proudest recollections of my life will be the honour that I yesterday had of submitting to this body, confirmation of the nomination made by the Governor of this State, of you as commander-in-chief of the military and naval forces of this commonwealth. When I asked if this body would advise and consent to that appointment, there rushed from the hearts to the tongues of all the members an affirmative response, told with an emphasis that could leave no doubt of the feeling whence it emanated. I put the negative of the question for form's sake, and there was an unbroken silence. . . .

"We have, by this unanimous vote, expressed our conviction that you are this day among the living citizens of Virginia, 'first in war.' . . . When the Father of his Country made his last will and testament, he gave swords to his favourite nephews, with an injunction that they should never be drawn from their scabbards, except in self-defence, or in defence of the rights and liberties of their country; and that if drawn for the latter purpose, they should fall with them in their hands, rather than relinquish them. . . ."

Lee's response was as brief and modest as Washington himself would have uttered upon such an occasion: ". . . Profoundly impressed with the solemnity of the occasion, for which I was not prepared, I accept the position assigned me by your partiality. I would have much preferred that your choice had fallen upon an abler man. Trusting in Almighty God, and in an approving conscience, and the aid of my fellow-citizens, I devote myself to the service of my native state, in whose behalf alone will I ever again draw my sword."

Although Virginia now seemed ready to form an alliance with the Southern Confederacy, Stephens, Davis' ambassador for Union, sought to make assurance doubly sure by gaining Lee's aid. "He met me at my quarters," he writes, "in a private conference that evening . . . I unfolded to him, with perfect candour, the object of my mission, the nature of the alliance I should propose, and particularly the effect it might have upon his official rank. . . . He expressed himself as perfectly satisfied, and as being very desirous to have the alliance formed. He stated . . . that he did not wish anything connected with himself, individually, or his official rank or personal position, to interfere in the slightest degree with the immediate consummation of that measure, which he regarded as one of the utmost importance." Thereafter, Lee gave his powerful influence to further Virginia's entrance into the Confederacy.

On April 24th Vice-President Stephens and a Virginia committee, headed by ex-President Tyler, agreed upon and signed a temporary Convention, placing Virginia's military force "under the chief control and direction of the President of the . . . Confederate States." This act was ratified by the Virginia convention on the following day, and two days later Davis received from Janney an invitation, sent by order of the convention, "to make this state the seat of government of the Confederacy."

On April 27th Lincoln issued his second proclamation of blockade, which declared that "persons claiming to act under authorities of the states of Virginia and North Carolina," had seized Federal property, obstructed the collection of Federal rev-

enue, and arrested Federal officials in the discharge of their duties. He knew that if the seceded states were still in the Union,
as he himself claimed, he had no legal authority to declare their
ports blockaded, and that if they were out of the Union, as he
denied, blockade was an act of war which Congress alone was
competent to make. He therefore declared his blockade only
"until Congress shall have assembled," on the 4th of the following July. Had he known, also, as Davis knew, of Lord John
Russell's threat to recognize the Confederacy as independent,
should an effort be made to blockade her ports, he might have
hesitated to issue such a proclamation. He, however, not only
issued it, but followed it up by an order to General Scott "to
suspend the writ of *habeas corpus*" if he should "find resistance
which renders it necessary."

Davis rightly declared this action a violation of the Federal
Constitution, and, with the hope that England would now recognize the independence of the Confederacy, issued a proclamation
offering the status of Confederate privateer to any vessel which
would arm herself and engage in attacks upon Northern shipping
under the Confederate flag. This fact was announced in the
Times [London] in the words, written by William Howard
Russell, its correspondent: "Today [May 9th] the papers contain a proclamation by the President of the Confederate States
of America, declaring a state of war between the Confederacy
and the United States, and notifying the issue of letters of marque
and reprisal. . . . Mr. Seward told me that but for Jefferson
Davis, the secession plot could never have been carried out. No
other man of the party had the brain or the courage and dexterity
to bring it to a successful issue. All the persons in the Southern
States speak of him with admiration."

Four days later, the Queen's proclamation of May 13th was
issued, but in terms disappointing to the South. Instead of independence, it recognized belligerency, and referred to the Confederacy as "certain States styling themselves the Confederate

States of America," a phrase which Davis never forgave. While pleased with the indignation which even the recognition of belligerency aroused in Washington, he realized that his picture of Europe's coming to his active assistance was still a far off dream, and on June 1st England added to his discouragement by closing her ports "to armed vessels and privateers, both of the United States and the so-called Confederate States." To the United States such prohibition mattered little; but Seward assured Lord Lyons that "this measure, and that of the same character which has been adopted by France, would probably prove a death blow to Southern privateering."

Lincoln had lost no time in pressing his preparations for turning a "paper blockade" into an effective one, and on May 21st Lord John Russell admitted to the American minister that the "blockade might . . . be made effective, considering the small number of harbours on the southern coast." Meanwhile Davis had discussed with his associates Virginia's suggestion in regard to the capital of the Confederacy. To his disappointment, he found that it met with general approval, and reluctantly notified Virginia that preparations would be made for moving to Richmond, where General Scott had boasted that he would take his 4th of July dinner. It was May 26th, however, before the preparations were complete, and on that day Davis started for his new capital. His aides, Wigfall and Toombs, accompanied him, and close guard was kept about his person, as letters warning him of pending assassination had been received. "The many scenes which transpired on this trip," reported the *Richmond Daily Enquirer*, show, "that the mantle of Washington falls gracefully upon his shoulders. Never were a people more enraptured with their Chief Magistrate than ours are with President Davis." He was "welcomed to Virginia by a deputation of the Governor of the state and the Mayor of Richmond," and conducted to his temporary quarters at the Spottswood House. Many signs of favour were shown him, including the offer of a handsome dwelling, purchased by certain prominent citizens for the purpose. "Following the rule that had governed my action in all such cases," he later wrote, "I declined to accept it." He, however, occupied it as an official residence, and it was thereafter known as "The White House of the Confederacy."

In general, the Richmond press was fair in its comments upon the new President: though De Leon facetiously declared in *Town Topics* that social Richmond "felt much as the Roman patricians might have felt at the advent of the leading families of the Goths." Davis, however, paid little attention to such comments, if, indeed, he was conscious of them, but continued to concentrate his energies upon preparations for defending the South against invasion. He knew that this would involve a degree of centralized control not likely to be welcomed by men who, as Russell assured the *Times*, "had but one battle cry—States Rights," and sought to secure it without offending the decentralizers.

It is interesting to compare at this point the conceptions of official duty held respectively by Davis and Lincoln. Davis believed that "no officer of the Government, whether civil or military, has any more right to create offences, or define them except only as the law prescribes, than he has to rob or murder on the highway, or proclaim himself king or sultan," to quote one of his ardent followers. "The Constitution and laws should be masters, and public officers, like private individuals, only their servants. Beyond the lines of their strict constitutional powers such officers are as literally without authority, before the law, as the humblest citizens; for they are, in fact, private wrong-doers, and not public officers, from the moment that they have transgressed those constitutional limits." To Lincoln, on the other hand, the limitations thus imposed upon the Executive by the Constitution, were subordinate to his major duty of preserving the Union. The aim of the Constitution is defined in its preamble: "to form a more perfect Union, establish justice, insure domestic tranquillity, provide for the common defence," and he felt no obligation to sacrifice these in order to observe its lesser requirements. He was ready to violate any specific clause of the Constitution if by so doing he could serve its main purpose; and he interpreted his powers as including anything to save the Union. Already he had so employed those powers as to suspend the writ of *habeas corpus* which "shall not be suspended, unless when, in cases of rebellion or invasion the public safety may require it."

Rawle had interpreted this clause to mean that "of this necessity, the Constitution probably intends that the legislature of the United States shall be the judges": and Chief Justice Taney had, on May 25, 1861, declared, in the case, ex-parte John Merryman: "I understand that the President not only claims the right to suspend the writ of *habeas corpus* himself, at his discretion, but to delegate that discretionary power to a military officer. . . . I had supposed it to be one of those points of constitutional law upon which there was no difference of opinion . . . that the privilege of the writ could not be suspended, except by act of Congress."

After attempting to assess the meaning of these opposing views, Colonel Henderson, with the detachment which only a foreigner could then bring to their contemplation, wrote: "Any fair-minded man may feel equal sympathy with both Federal and Confederate. Both were so absolutely convinced that their cause was just, that it is impossible to conceive either Northerner or Southerner acting otherwise than he did. If Stonewall Jackson had been a New Englander, educated in the belief that secession was rebellion, he would assuredly have shed the last drop of his blood in defence of the Union; if Grant had been a Virginian, and had imbibed the doctrine of states rights with his mother's milk, it is just as certain that he would have worn the Confederate grey."

Davis argued that the Union had been formed by the states for their protection, and the protection of their property, and that Lincoln's aim was the subjugation of the states and the destruction of their property. He saw himself, therefore, not as a rebel, but as a defender of the Constitution. Upon the basis of a similar argument, Nathaniel Bacon had defended the Virginia rebellion of 1676, against Governor Sir William Berkeley, and Jacob Leister had seized New York in 1689, to be held by him "until the king's pleasure be known." The Government owes protection to the people; it is therefore loyalty to the Government to resist oppression. Patrick Henry in his defence of the people in the Parson's Cause of 1763, argued that the Government was a compact between king and people, the king to protect, the people to obey, and that when the king fails to protect, the people are free to refuse obedience.

Thus Davis argued that the Confederate States were but following in the footsteps of the Fathers of the American Revolution, who defended the British Constitution against a Government which had perverted its meaning. His Attorney-General vainly sought to convince him of the unwisdom of pressing this analogy. "It is not a civil war," he wrote, in an opinion furnished to the President ". . . but a public war between two nations." The idea that "the relation which the citizens of the Colonies before the Revolution bore to the Government of Great Britain is the same as that which the citizens of the several states bore to the Government of the United States before the commencement of this war . . . is wholly unfounded. . . ." Each of the American Colonies "owed obedience and allegiance to a common sovereign, the King of Great Britain; and were all citizens of the British nation. . . . Here the citizens of the states never were, since the Declaration of Independence, citizens of the same political community." The people of each state constitute "a separate and distinct community."

It is doubtless true that it is more dangerous to a leader to be uncertain than to be wrong. The uncertain man confesses thereby the need to be led; and that other, when found, becomes the leader. Davis made many errors; but indecision was not among them, a fact which largely accounts for his continuing leadership, though it accounts also for many of his mistakes. As he was confident that his constitutional views were unassailable, so was he later confident with respect to his military views. Lincoln, on the other hand, saw more clearly the impossibility of interesting the public, either American or foreign, in constitutional arguments, and was content to trust his case to a few great principles which all could understand.

When we turn from domestic and international politics to a comparison of Lincoln's and Davis' military preparations during the "eighty days," it is clear that at first Davis enjoyed certain great advantages, despite the inferiority of the Confederacy in wealth and man power. The white men of the South, even the majority which owned no slaves, had been trained to consider themselves a master race, and so had acquired habits of command. Their agricultural life, often on a vast scale, had given them, moreover, familiarity with firearms, and experience in taking care of themselves in the open. Always, they had ridden, or tramped unsettled areas in search of game, camping at night, cooking their own food, improvising sleeping quarters for themselves. To them, therefore, army life was almost second nature, while the Northerner, whose days had been absorbed by commercial and industrial pursuits, found greater difficulty in adapting himself to it. In the long run, the North's capacity to manufacture more than counterbalanced these advantages, but not so in the earlier days.

When the crisis came, furthermore, Davis had the advantage of knowing, from long and intimate contact with Federal officers, which of the men available were likely to prove competent in high command. It has been estimated that, of the 1,200 West Point graduates then fit for service in the field, only one-fourth were Southern men; but if we take account of quality, the Southern strength was greater than the figures indicate, as army life had in general been more attractive to the able Southerner than to the able Northerner. Moreover, Davis had the regular officer's distrust of political candidates for army posts, while Lincoln was less conscious of the danger of such appointments. As a result, scarcely a volunteer statesman received from Davis a rank higher than that of provisional brigadier, and John C. Breckinridge was the only political major-general commissioner.

Thus Davis had officers in abundance, and of high ability. Lee, Johnston, Jackson, Stuart, Forrest, Longstreet, Ewell, Beauregard, Bragg, Early and A. P. Hill, in the early years of conflict were superior to the corresponding commanders whom Lincoln was able to secure. And later in the struggle the Grants, Shermans, Sheridans, and Thomases were less numerous than men of equal ability in the South. Henderson's expert opinion is that Davis' selections "were the best that could be made, and [that] he was ready to accept the advice . . . of his most experienced generals."

As was inevitable, however, his appointments were criticized by civilian candidates suspicious of the "military mind," and by "the professional clique," as well as by certain professional soldiers to whom he gave a lower rating than self-admiration demanded. General Joseph E. Johnston, to cite the most distinguished among the discontented, was deeply resentful. He had been quartermaster-general of the Federal armies before his resignation and felt that he should rank all who had taken a similar course, as to quote his own words: "No other officer of the United States of equal rank relinquished his position to join the Southern Confederacy." Recalling the ancient conflict between himself and his now commander-in-chief, in West Point days, he claimed that he was discriminated against for personal reasons. His early services during the war which followed lent weight to his theory that he should have been first in command at the beginning; but as we view Davis' appointments in the light of later achievements, it is fair to say that in general he chose wisely.

"The appointing power," he said when the controversies had forced him to consider the motives which had dominated him, "is a public trust, to be executed for the public welfare, not a private fund with which to discharge personal obligations." Moreover, he agreed with the theory later expressed by Colonal Henderson, that "If Napoleon, himself more highly endowed by nature with every military attribute than any other general of the Christian era, thought it essential to teach himself his business by incessant study, how much more is such study necessary for ordinary men." To Davis, as to Henderson, the only real military leader was the one trained to the task. As when defending General Taylor in Mexican War days he had won the everlasting enmity of Andrew Johnson by pointing out that a tailor could not have done what General Zachary Taylor had done in Mexico, he still believed that to find an effective military leader you must, ordinarily, search for him among men of military education.

Thanks also to Davis' training and experience, both of which Lincoln lacked, he understood, at the outset, far better than did the latter, the scale of preparation which the conditions demanded. During a visit which Sherman made to the latter at this time, Lincoln remarked, "We shall not need many men like you, the affair will soon blow over." Silent and enraged, Sherman retired, but outside the President's room said to his brother: "You," meaning the politicians, "have got things in a hell of a fix, and you may get them out as best you can." He knew the South too well to believe that the war would be a holiday parade, and at first would have nothing of it. Even the offer of the chief clerkship of the War Department failed to interest him: "If Congress meets," he later explained, "and if a national convention be called, and the regular army put on a footing with the wants of the country, if I am offered a place that suits me, I may accept."

The effect of Lincoln's proclamation in his "eighty days" was to drive the inner tier of four border states from the old into the new Confederacy, while his drastic actions prevented Maryland and Missouri, in the outer tier, from leaving the Union.

But in the struggle, both Lincoln and Davis, in their efforts to serve each his own side, had created a powerful opposition who cried "tyrant" whenever his name was mentioned. On June 3, 1861, Goddard assured his English readers that "nearly every merchant in the rebel states would be glad of the interference of England, or of any other power, if it would relieve them of the intolerable tyranny of Jefferson Davis," and Northern comments upon Lincoln's use of the power made possible by his postponement of the assembling of Congress leave no doubt that many Unionists wished that a less autocratic, less lawless leader, had been chosen.

The wise cannot be always wise, and both Lincoln and Davis often blundered: but the honest must be always honest, and by this test both take high rank; for each served what he conceived to be his duty, with a selflessness which is above praise.

Both would doubtless have enjoyed a "poem," signed A Young Rebel, which circulated in the South at about this time, one stanza of which is as follows:

> On night last week, I had a dream,
>   I may as well now give it,
> I dream'd I saw Old Abraham,
>   A-swinging on a gibbet;
> And who do you think, boys, held the rope,
>   'Twas Mr. Jefferson Davis,
> And as he pulled, Old Abram cried,
>   For a writ of Corpus Habeas.

CHAPTER XVI

MANASSAS AND ITS AFTERMATH

EARLY in July, 1861, came the first direct clash of wills between Lincoln and Davis. The Federal navy had captured the privateer *Savannah*, and, following Lincoln's interpretation of the war as a domestic insurrection, had placed its crew in irons, carried them to New York and charged them with "piracy and treason." As the Confederate Government had formally recognized the existence of war, though carefully excluding Missouri, Kentucky, Maryland, and Delaware from the category of enemy states, Davis determined to make a test case of the *Savannah's* crew and dispatched to Lincoln a demand that they be treated, not as pirates and traitors, but as prisoners of war.

"It is the desire of this Government," he wrote, "so to conduct the war now existing as to mitigate its horrors as far as may be possible, and, with this intent, its treatment of prisoners captured by its forces has been marked by the greatest humanity and leniency, consistent with public obligations. . . . It is only since the news has been received of the treatment of the prisoners taken on the *Savannah* that I have been compelled to withdraw these indulgences. . . . Painful as will be the necessity, this Government will deal out to the prisoners held by it the same treatment and the same fate as shall be experienced by those captured on the *Savannah*, and if driven to the terrible necessity of retaliation by your execution of any of its officers or crew . . . retaliation will be extended so far as shall be requisite to secure the abandonment of a practice unknown to the warfare of civilized men, and so barbarous as to disgrace the nation which shall be guilty of inaugurating it.

"With this view . . . I now renew the proposition made to the commander of the blockading squadron to exchange for the prisoners taken on the *Savannah* an equal number of those now held by us, according to rank."

Colonel Taylor, the bearer of this message, failed in his efforts to deliver it to Lincoln in person, and was obliged to accept from General Scott the assurance that it had been given to the President, and would be answered in writing at an early date. No answer, however, was received from Lincoln, save the answer which his later actions gave, and after waiting a reasonable time, Davis announced that a number of Northern prisoners would be selected by lot, and held ready for whatever treatment should be given the captured crew of the *Savannah*.

On July 20th the Confederate Congress assembled at the new capital of Richmond, to hear Davis' message on the state of the Union. He congratulated them upon the accession of "our loved and honoured brethren of North Carolina and Tennessee," and upon the fact that "the people of Virginia, by a majority previously unknown in her history, have ratified the action of her convention, uniting her fortunes with ours." In regard to the removal of the Confederate capital from Montgomery to Richmond, he stated that, in the face of the enemy's evident intention of invading Virginia, "I deemed it advisable to direct the removal . . . immediately after your adjournment. From no point could the necessary measures for her defence and protection be so effectively carried out as from her own capital." He declared that Lincoln's Government had now dropped its subterfuge, and had confessed "the intention of subjugating these states by war, whose folly is equalled by its wickedness," and ridiculed his "idle and absurd assumption of the existence of a riot which was to be dispersed by a posse Comitatus. The fact that the Federal Government has placed at the President's control 400,000 men and

$400,000,000," he correctly argued, is an "avowal, in the eyes of civilized man that the United States are engaged in a conflict with a great and powerful nation; they are at last compelled to abandon the pretence of being engaged in dispersing rioters." The Federal Government has recognized "the separate existence of these Confederate States, by the interdiction, embargo, and blockade of all commerce between them and the United States, not only by sea, but by land . . . not only with those who bear arms, but with the entire population of the Confederate States."

He denied the "false representation that these states intended offensive war, in spite of conclusive evidence to the contrary," and charged Lincoln with deliberately attempting to deceive the people "into the belief that the purpose of this Government was not peace at home, but conquest abroad; not the defence of its own liberties, but the subversion of those of the people of the United States. He declared that in the Federal conduct of the war, "rapine is the rule; private residences . . . are bombarded and burnt; grain crops in the field are consumed by the torch; and when the torch is not convenient, careful labour is bestowed to render complete the destruction of every article of use or orna-ment remaining in private dwellings, after their inhabitants have fled from the outrages of a brutal soldiery," adding a damaging comparison between the respect shown to private property, when the British troops invaded this same district near Fortress Monroe, in 1781, and the ruthless destruction of it by the present invaders, "who pretend that the victims are their fellow-citizens."

He denounced Lincoln's suspension of the writ of *habeas corpus*, and his attitude towards the prisoners taken from the *Savannah*, who were "treated like common felons. I informed President Lincoln," he said, "of my resolute purpose to check all barbarities on prisoners of war, by such severity of retaliation on the prisoners held by us as should secure the abandonment of the practice. As no suitable reply has yet been received, I still retain in close custody some officers captured from the enemy, whom it had been my pleasure previously to enlarge on parole, and whose fate must necessarily depend on that of the prisoners held by the enemy."

Fortunately, Davis was not obliged to put this threat of retaliation into effect as negotiations between the two Governments soon resulted in a cartel for the exchange of prisoners, and in the recognition of captured privateers' men as entitled to the treatment of prisoners of war. The agreement was not signed till February 14, 1862, however, and long before that day the number of prisoners was greatly increased by the first serious military engagement, which occurred at Manassas on July 21, 1861, as a result of the overweaning desire on the part of Lincoln's Government to capture Richmond. The movement was premature, rash, ill-advised, and calculated to emphasize the wisdom of the Davis-Lee policy of defensive warfare.

Davis was ill when the news that a Federal army was marching on Richmond reached him, but he insisted that it was his duty to take part in planning resistance to the coming attack, and in consequence, every detail passed under his experienced eye, and the council of war which immediately preceded the battle of Manassas was held beside his sick-bed.

On July 16th General McDowell had, against his judgment, been started southward with 60,000 men, with Richmond as his objective. At Manassas Junction, thirty miles southwest of Washington, General Beauregard with a scant 20,000 volunteers barred the road, and west of him were General Joseph E. Johnston's 11,000, cut off, as the Federals supposed, by General Patterson. "The advantages of the union of the armies on the Potomac had been more than once the subject of consideration by you," wrote Lee to Davis, in a later summary of the situation, "and . . . the difficulty of timing the march of the troops so as to benefit one army without jeopardizing the object of the other, was therefore mainly considered, and you decided that the movements of the enemy in and about Alexandria were not sufficiently demonstrated as to warrant the withdrawal of any of the forces from the Shenandoah Valley. A few days afterward, however, I think three or four, the reports from General Beauregard showed so clearly the enemy's purpose that you ordered General Johnston with his effective force to march at once to the support of General Beauregard."

Having helped to make this decision, Davis returned to his executive duties, though keeping closely in touch with the movement of the troops. Sherman later described the battle of Manassas as "one of the best planned . . . but one of the worst-fought" battles of history. "Both armies were fairly defeated," he added, with engaging frankness, "and whichever stood fast, the other would have run."

Before the day closed, Davis yielded to his habitual desire to follow the direction of the firing, and started for Manassas. He arrived at the end of the engagement: and the conditions that he found are thus described in a letter written to him later by J. R. Smoot, the first man whom he accosted.

"At . . . about 1 P.M. on July the 21st, 1861, when on my way from Manassas . . . to the battlefield, I was overtaken by two persons riding rapidly—one dressed in plain citizen's clothes riding a bay horse, the other a cavalryman, acting as courier and guide to the former. As the former passed me, he gracefully raised his hat and asked if I knew the headquarters of our General. . . . Recognizing you as our President, I replied in the affirmative and immediately volunteered to pilot you. On our way we met many wounded, but a larger number of straggling soldiers—to the former you gave . . . words of cheer and condolence; to the latter you appealed to their manhood & C., and urged them to return to the field: but the majority kept on to Manassas—all, however, declaring that our army was cut to pieces. You kept on and when within less than half a mile of the battlefield, I remember your meeting a very large Old Virginia four-horse wagon, containing some wounded." Learning that General Bee of South Carolina was in the wagon, Davis stopped, and Smoot used the delay to locate "General Johnston . . . in command and surrounded by a few of his staff. As you rode up . . . General Johnston said . . . 'Mr. President, I am happy to inform you that the enemy is at this moment in full retreat.' You immediately asked him what steps had been taken to follow the retreating enemy and continue the advantage gained by our army."

As the answer was not reassuring, upon reaching headquarters Davis pressed for an explanation, and finding that no plans had been made to follow the fleeing enemy stated that pursuit was advisable. Beauregard's Adjutant-General, Colonel Thomas Jordan, who sat opposite to Davis, asked if the latter would dictate the order. This Davis did, in terms directing immediate pursuit. Later he changed the order to pursuit at early dawn. Davis then sent to Lee the following dispatch:

"Manassas, July 21, 1861.
"We have won a glorious though dearly-bought-victory. Night closed on the enemy in full flight and closely pursued.
"JEFFERSON DAVIS."

This report proved in part untrue, as Davis' order was not carried out, and the panic-stricken Federals were allowed by the panic-stricken Confederates to escape unharassed; "the latter army," as Johnston later explained, being "more disorganized by victory than that of the United States by defeat." Johnston also admitted later, according to Gamiel Bradford, that "he believed it inexpedient to follow up the Confederate victory with a march on Washington." Beauregard's explanation was that "the fortifications on the south bank of the Potomac . . . were garrisoned by [Federal] troops who were not involved in the panic caused by the defeat at Manassas," and therefore too strong to be attacked. It has been generally held by military experts, however, that a prompt and vigorous pursuit, such as Davis had ordered, might have done much towards ending the war.

Beauregard, who had failed to carry out Davis' order, backed by the hostile editor of the *Richmond Examiner*, later laid the blame of the failure to pursue upon him: and the famous English military leader, and critic, Wolseley, doubtless following their lead, charged that "the Confederates did not follow up their victory" because, "political considerations at Richmond were allowed to outweigh the very evident military expediency of reaping a solid advantage from this, their first great success." Colonel Henderson stated that Davis, "expecting much from the intervention of the European powers, did nothing to press the advantages already gained."

Davis remained at Manassas in consultation with Beauregard and Johnston, until July 23rd, when he returned to Richmond, and to the cheers of enthusiastic crowds. A speech was of course demanded, and having compared the present elation with the anxiety of a few days earlier, he added: "Your little army . . . has met the grand army of the enemy, routed it at every point, and it now flees in inglorious retreat before our victorious columns. . . . The grand old mother of Washington still nourishes a band of heroes."

On August 1st Davis wrote to Johnston, still at Manassas, that it was important to take advantage of the weakness of the enemy "produced by their late defeat," but his letter shows that he was now disposed to think that the pursuit which he had ordered might have proved mistaken zeal. And three days later he wrote to Beauregard: "Under the circumstances . . . it would have been extremely hazardous to have done more than was performed. You will not fail to remember that, so far from knowing that the enemy was routed, a large part of our forces was moved by you in the night of the 21st to repel a supposed attack upon our right, and that the next day's operations did not fully reveal what has since been reported of the enemy's panic. Enough was done for glory, and the measure of duty was full; let us rather show the untaught that their desires are unreasonable than by dwelling on the possibilities recently developed, give form and substance to the criticisms always easy to those who judge after the event."

The battle of Manassas had two important results; it convinced the South that to establish independence would require years of ceaseless toil, with a final victory by no means assured, and caused the Federal Government to pass the Resolution, that: "This war is not waged upon our part with any purpose of overthrowing or interfering with the rights or established institutions of these states, but to defend and maintain the supremacy of the Constitution, and to preserve the Union, with all the dignity, equality, and rights of the several states unimpaired; that, as soon as these objects are accomplished, the war ought to cease." More important still, as Schouler reminds us, it converted a rebellion into a civil war.

The Union, however, was far from the certainty of preservation towards which the above-quoted resolution looked, and each side, by such light as was vouchsafed it, continued its preparation for the struggle.

The weeks which followed emphasized Napoleon's famous remark that "armies travel on their stomachs," and Davis now bent his energies upon the problems of subsistence for his rapidly increasing numbers. His experience as Secretary of War had given him excellent training for the work of organizing provisions and military stores; though the competing activities of the states increased his difficulties. "A whole line of states . . . organize their armies," complained the Commissary-General, "and . . . adopt the easiest mode of subsisting them with ample state funds. They consume the bacon of the country, leaving the gleaning to the Confederate commissariat, which had to come in almost without funds, and support an army of double the previous strength." The difficulty was rendered greater by the fact, also reported by the harassed Commissary-General, that "the supply of coffee depends on accident even if money were always in hand, and vinegar being a Northern production chiefly, the supply must often be precarious. Soap depends on soda ash; and the supply here is nearly exhausted, and the efforts to obtain it from Maryland and Kentucky have not yet proved successful. If salt could be spared, chemistry could extract the caustic soda. . . . These articles may fail. The real evil is ahead. There are not hogs in the Confederacy sufficient for the army and the larger force of plantation negroes. Hence, competition must be anticipated by arranging for the purchase of the animals and getting the salt to cure them. Furthermore, beeves must be provided for the coming spring; cattle must be collected from Texas before the rains set in, and be herded in ranging-grounds convenient to the Mississippi."

Such subjects occupied most of Davis' time; but at intervals he found a moment to indulge in a letter to a general in the field, discussing purely military movements. In these letters he faced the fact, which he stated to General Johnston, that "We cannot afford to fight without a reasonable assurance of victory, or a necessity so imperious as to overrule our general policy. We have no second line of defence, and cannot now provide one."

At times he employed the arts of diplomacy to prevent conflicts between rival commanders, as when he sought to appease the imperious and never friendly Joseph E. Johnston by assuring him that you are "not mistaken in your construction of my letter having been written to you as the commanding general. I have, however, sometimes had to repel the idea that there was a want of co-operation between yourself and the second in command, or a want of recognition of your position as the senior and commanding general of all the forces serving at or near the field of your late brilliant achievements." At times also he soothed the sensibilities of some state Governor, as when he patiently explained to Letcher, of Virginia, that, "with the very limited means possessed, it is not to be expected that the supplies of the Confederate Government can keep pace with the wants of every locality"; and at the same time courteously solicited from him "any information which will aid me in the effort to repel invasion of the State of Virginia." Diplomacy was for him a new weapon; but at times he used it with surprising skill.

Meanwhile the daring brain of Stonewall Jackson had conceived a plan to strike the North before it could recover from the effect of Manassas, which had been disastrous enough even without the pursuit which Davis had desired. With this in view, he sought out General G. W. Smith before leaving for his new command in the valley of Virginia, and solicited the latter's aid in securing permission for the attempt. He argued that, by "crossing the upper Potomac, occupying Baltimore, and taking possession of Maryland, we could cut off the communications of Washington, force the Federal Government to abandon the capital, beat McClellan's army if it came out against us in open country, destroy industrial establishments wherever we found them, break up the interior commercial intercourse, close the coal mines, seize and, if necessary, destroy the manufactories and commerce of Philadelphia and of other large cities within our reach; take the narrow neck of country between Pittsburgh and Lake Erie; subsisting mainly on the country we traverse, and making unrelenting war amidst their homes."

Smith heard the plan with sympathy, but remarked, when Jackson had finished, that "these views had been laid before the Government, in a conference which had taken place at Fairfax Court House, in the first days of October, between President Davis, Generals Johnston, Beauregard, and myself," and had been rejected. "When I had finished," Smith tells us, "he rose from the ground, on which he had been seated, shook my hand, warmly, and said, 'I am sorry, very sorry.' Without another word he went slowly out to his horse . . . mounted deliberately, and rode sadly away. A few days afterward he was ordered to the valley."

So sweeping a plan to capture the North, while convincing to Jackson's biographer, might well have sounded fantastic to Davis and his other generals, but in view of Jackson's later achievements, it is possible that he might have accomplished much of his proposed program had he been given the chance. It is also possible to believe, of even this great strategist, that the fate of his expedition might have been that of the Northern leaders who, a little later, contrary to McClellan's desire, pushed a reconnaissance in force across the Potomac southward, to meet disastrous defeat at Ball's Bluff.

Editorial writers, however, continued to censure Davis for his failure to do what Jackson had urged; and their insistence drew from Lee one of the few sarcastic remarks recorded from him, namely that "in the beginning we appointed all our worst generals to command the armies, and all our best generals to edit the newspapers." It is fair to remember also that Davis' decision upon this critical question was taken in accord with Johnston and Beauregard, and that it might have been more dangerous to disregard their views and accept Jackson's bolder but far more hazardous counsel. What might have resulted must, therefore, remain a matter of conjecture.

On November 6th Davis faced the great assize, a general election to test his leadership, and by unanimous vote was re-elected President to serve for six years. This, he properly interpreted as an approval of his career as provisional President, including his part in the battle of Manassas, and of his interpretation of his duty as Commander-in-chief of the Army and Navy. Under the permanent Constitution, the President continued to be Commander-in-chief, and Davis, as President, continued to exercise military control.

Two days after the election, occurred an event which might well have aroused Davis' flagging hope of British intervention in a conflict which Lord John Russell had recently characterized as the North "fighting for power" and the South "for self-government." On November 8, 1861, James Mason and John Slidell, newly appointed Confederate commissioners to England and France who were crossing on the British ship *Trent*, were captured by the Federal man-of-war *San Jacinto*, and lodged in Fort Warren.

The press of America broke into excited comment and Lincoln remarked "I would rather die than give them up." The North displayed a mad joy, mad indeed, in view of the probable effect of both the incident and the rejoicing upon the mind of England, always sensitive to the honour of her seamen and her neutral rights.

Davis saw at once that England would interpret the incident as an insult to the British flag, and ventured to hope that from it might result the long-desired recognition of the South. The reception of the news in England tended to strengthen this hope: for the British Government promptly denounced the action and demanded the release of the prisoners. In his message of November 18th, Davis reported the seizure in the words:

"The distinguished gentlemen whom, with your approval, at the last session, I commissioned to represent the Confederacy at certain foreign courts, have been recently seized by the Captain of a United States ship-of-war, on board a British steamer, on their voyage from the neutral Spanish port of Havana to England. The United States have thus claimed a general jurisdiction over the high seas, and entering a British ship, sailing under its country's flag, have violated the rights of embassy, for the most part held sacred even amongst barbarians, by seizing our ministers while under the protection and within the dominions of a neutral nation. These gentlemen were as much under the jurisdiction of the British Government upon that ship and beneath its flag as if they had been on its soil, and a claim on the part of the United States to seize them in the streets of London would have been as well founded as that to apprehend them where they were taken. Had they been malefactors and citizens of the United

States, they could not have been arrested on a British ship or on British soil, unless under the express provisions of a treaty and according to the forms therein provided for the extradition of criminals."

Seward, too, although at first merely indignant at the British demands, soon realized that the North's violation of the neutral rights of the world's greatest sea power might attach the latter to the Confederate cause, and began to pave the way to avoid such a result by a frank surrender to England's just demands.

CHAPTER XVII

DARK DAYS OF '62

THE need for diplomacy on the part of the President of so decentralized a Confederation as that over which Davis presided was not confined to dealing with generals and other military men local in their patriotism, and highly jealous of governmental encroachments. Nor was it confined to conciliating the Border states, or to international questions. He must also, in his every act and utterance consider the susceptibilities of a large body of men and women, upon questions far removed from public affairs. He received, for example, from Bishop Meade of Virginia a letter regretting that he had endorsed a book which the Bishop declared to be "an open assault on a fundamental fact and doctrine of our holy religion, and a disgusting vilification of the whole African race." It "absolutely denies the Scriptural account of the descent of the nations of the earth from our two first parents in Eden, ascribing the origin of different and varying tribes to different [causes], and placing the African race near to the ape, monkey, or gorilla. A more positive denial of the divine inspiration and truth of the Bible cannot well be, for the great fact of the connexion of all the families of man by descent from Adam is so interwoven with the Old and New Testaments that it is impossible to question that, without destroying the credibility of the whole. . . . The doctrine of this book strikes at the root of all effort to Christianize this race. Indeed, there is not a word in it which hints at such a thing. . . . It is most unfortunate that this infidel doctrine should be brought forward at this time, especially when the fond hope of Christian patriots and ministers

330

at the South is that our separation from the North would dispose
and enable us to be more zealous in our efforts for the religious
instruction of our slaves. We have charged, and most justly, on
the abolitionism of the North, that it leads to infidelity, for not a
few, unable to deny that the Scriptures sanction slavery, have
abjured the Bible rather than give up their anti-slavery system.
But what shall we now say of ourselves, if we also deny the Scriptures . . . and declare that four million of our fellow-beings, for
whose welfare we are contending, are beings of another order,
little above the ape and monkey, and only designed for the lowest
service to ourselves. I am confident that you were not aware of
the contents of this book . . . or you would not have permitted
its dedication to yourself."

But Lincoln's armies left Davis scant time to argue the bearing
of the Darwinian theory upon the Confederacy. In the first week
of February, 1862, Grant attacked Fort Henry, and having taken
it, turned his attention to Fort Donelson, which after bitter resistance, also yielded, and on February 16th Buckner was forced to
"accept the ungenerous, and unchivalrous terms offered." This
news found Davis preparing his inaugural address, as permanent
President of the Confederacy and, four days later, standing beneath the statue of Washington on Capitol Hill, he again asserted
the justice of the Confederacy's revolt against "the tyranny of an
unbridled majority," and the sacredness of a Constitution which
"admits of no coerced association," and continued, "My hope is
reverently fixed on Him whose favour is ever vouchsafed to the
cause which is just. With humble gratitude and adoration,
acknowledging the Providence which has so visibly protected the
Confederacy . . . to Thee, O God, I trustfully commit myself,
and prayerfully invoke thy blessing on my country and its cause."

This belief which embodies the mediaeval superstition which
caused the varied trials by ordeal, was shared by Davis' great
antagonist, who in his inaugural address declared: "If the Almighty Ruler of Nations, with his eternal truth and justice, be

on your side of the North, or on yours of the South, that truth and that justice will surely prevail by the judgment of this great tribunal of the American people." Three years earlier, John Stuart Mill, who had examined this doctrine in the light of history, wrote in his essay "On Liberty," that "The dictum that truth always triumphs over persecution is one of those pleasant falsehoods which men repeat after one another till they pass into commonplaces, but which all experience refutes. History teems with instances of truth put down by persecution. . . . The Reformation broke out at least twenty times before Luther, and was put down. Arnold of Brescia was put down. Fra Dolcino was put down. Savonarola was put down. The Albigeois were put down. The Vaudois were put down. The Lollards were put down. The Husites were put down. Even after the era of Luther, whenever persecution was persisted in, it was successful. In Spain, Italy, Flanders, and the Austrian Empire, Protestantism was rooted out; and, most likely, would have been so in England, had Queen Mary lived, or Queen Elizabeth died. Persecution has always succeeded, save where the heretics were too strong a party to be effectually persecuted. No reasonable person can doubt that Christianity might have been extirpated in the Roman Empire. It spread, and became predominant, because the persecutions were only occasional, lasting but a short time, and separated by long intervals of almost undisturbed propagation. It is a piece of idle sentimentality that truth, merely as truth, has any inherent power denied to error, of prevailing against the dungeon and the stake. Men are not more zealous for truth than they often are for error, and a sufficient application of legal or even of social penalties will generally succeed in stopping the propagation of either."

Davis' second inaugural address also attacked Lincoln for "bastilles filled with prisoners arrested without civil process or indictment duly found, and the writ of *habeas corpus* suspended by executive mandate"; and declared that "through all the necessities of an unequal struggle there has been no act on our part to impair personal liberty or the freedom of speech, of thought or of the press." It gloried in the belief that his Government had respected the "unalienable rights" of man; and there was no hint of a suspicion that slavery was a denial of the greatest of them all.

Davis' term as permanent President began under discouraging conditions. He knew that there was a large faction highly dissatisfied with his leadership: and, had he not known it, the press would have enlightened him. The Richmond correspondent of the *Charleston Mercury* voiced this dissatisfaction in the words: ". . . They have no one to look to, no leader. . . . Mr. Boyce proposes Toombs and Beauregard as generalissimos. But how to effect this? . . . Both of these gentlemen have already experienced the impracticable temper of the President. Were they to accept the post they would not be able to retain it. . . . The President has proposed to hand his name down to history as one who combined in his own person all the best qualities of Napoleon and Wellington."

The situation was far more difficult than Davis' critics understood. His Government comprehended only eleven states, all locally minded and jealous of any attempt at centralized control. These covered about 727,000 square miles and contained a little over 9,000,000 people, white and black, with taxable property aggregating about $3,500,000,000, not counting "slave property." Lincoln commanded some 941,000 square miles, not counting the territories, claimed equally by both sides, but largely controlled by Lincoln's forces. His twenty-two states had a population of more than 22,000,000, mostly white, and a taxable property estimated at more than $6,750,000,000.

It required much faith to believe Confederate victory possible in the face of such odds; but that faith Jefferson Davis possessed, and in it ventured even to announce that the states were free to leave the new Union should they so desire, although it was evident that Sovereign State and created Nation did not always walk together as two that are agreed.

The Confederate Congress had opened its new session at Richmond, on February 18th, and immediately after the inauguration it passed and sent up for the President's approval a resolution declaring that "the Congress of the Confederate States of America do enact that during the present invasion of the Confederate States, the President shall have power to suspend the writ of *habeas corpus* in such cities, towns, and military districts as shall, in his judgment, be in such danger of attack by the enemy as to require a declaration of martial law for their effective defence." Davis had many times denounced Lincoln for setting aside *habeas corpus* without Congressional action; but this bill, which he believed necessary to the success of the cause, had the sanction of Congressional action behind it, and he therefore quite properly signed it. He was, however, unfairly assailed as inconsistent, autocratic, and unjust to his opponent. It is the fate of every executive in time of war to suffer disparagement, if not actual libel, from allies, deeming themselves wiser than the man with the power, and Davis was no exception. He was censured for not having sufficient Cabinet meetings, though he held them practically every week, and at the same time was accused of clinging too closely to his Cabinet. He was criticized for his insistence upon his rights as commander-in-chief, and bitterly attacked when he entrusted any of those rights to others. Denounced for keeping his "generals in leading-strings," he replied: "My rule has been to seek for the ablest commanders . . . and to rely on them to execute the purposes of the Government by such plans as they should devise," a statement which must have been read with surprise, if it came under the eyes of Johnston, Beauregard, or even of his friend, Robert E. Lee, all of whom had seen him carrying the burden of military decisions, even when "the ablest commanders" were at hand. One critic announced that he had "scarcely a friend and not a defender in Congress or in the army," though, as Davis himself pointed out, if that were true, "our fate must be confided to a multitude of hypocrites."

Such criticisms Davis bore with a degree of patience, praise-worthy in one of his temperament, declaring only that these men "do us more harm than if twice their number should desert to Lincoln." But he confessed "if we can achieve our independence, the office-seekers are welcome to the . . . [post] I hold, the pos-session of which has brought no additional value to me than that set upon it when, before going to Montgomery, I announced my preference for the commission of a general in the army." Upon one occasion, when particularly tried by baseless attacks, he de-clared that he would gladly resign, but for the fact that the Vice-President would then become President, and he could not bear the thought of seeing Alexander H. Stephens in such an office. We now know, as Davis had not the consolation of knowing, that Lincoln was at the time suffering from a treatment not less un-reasonable; damned by his enemies, he was damned also by the faint praises of his friends.

In these dark days, Davis' mind reverted to the consolations of religion as he had known it in his father's house, and in the days of his dwelling with the monks of St. Thomas. But he had learned to love the beautiful ritual of the Episcopal Church and was confirmed in St. Paul's Church in Richmond, General Gorgas and his wife taking the vows of Confirmation with him.

On March 13, 1862, news reached Davis that Johnston had evacuated the Manassas line; and vigorous action was more than ever necessary if the Confederacy was to continue to hope for victory. Therefore, taking advantage of a power which Congress had recently conferred upon him by resolution, he directed Adju-tant and Inspector-General Cooper to dispatch the following tele-gram: "General Robert E. Lee is assigned to duty at the seat of Government, and, under the direction of the President, is charged with the conduct of military operations in the armies of the Con-federacy." This was a daring appointment, as Lee's recent opera-tions in West Virginia had been a great disappointment to his friends; but Davis trusted his own estimate of military talent in the face of adverse public opinion, and his choice of Lee over Toombs or Beauregard is among the proofs of his fitness for the high post which he held.

In view of the hostility felt toward Davis himself, this personal appointment did not seem likely to heighten Lee's reputation: but it gave him a chance, which is all that either genius or mediocrity has a right to ask, and set him on the road which led speedily to his place among the great commanders of history. For, as his biographer, Douglas Freeman, points out, his "first campaign might have been his last, but for the faith President Davis had in him," and this courageous decision was probably Davis' greatest military contribution to the cause of the Confederacy.

On April 6th was fought the fiercest of all the western battles, that of Shiloh, and with it came news which deeply distressed Davis, both personally and for the effect that it might have upon the cause. General Albert Sidney Johnston, commander of the Confederate forces at the beginning of the battle, was disabled by a wound on the first afternoon. He continued in the saddle, however, until exhausted, and upon being taken from his horse, died almost immediately. Grant considered him "a man of high character and ability," an opinion based in part on Mexican days, but in his later years Grant altered this opinion. "My judgment now is," he wrote in his *Memoirs*, "that he was vacillating and undecided in his actions," and "as a general he was over-estimated." To Davis, however, then and thereafter, the loss of Johnston seemed irreparable.

The effect of the engagement upon the mind of the successful commander, Grant, was much the same as that which the Confederate victory at Manassas had made upon Davis. It opened his eyes to the fact that the war was likely to be long and bitter. "Up to the battle of Shiloh," he states in his *Memoirs*, "I . . . believed that the Rebellion . . . would collapse suddenly and soon, if a decisive victory could be gained over any of its armies." After

Shiloh he believed that success would follow only "by complete conquest."

This engagement, partly, no doubt, as cause, marks also the time when Davis became convinced that if victory was to come, short-term enlistments must go, and that state sovereignty must yield something to centralization. He therefore urged upon Congress a policy of long terms for soldiers, and upon the states the necessity of more effective control by national authority. In the first matter, his will soon prevailed, and on April 16th Congress announced that all men between eighteen and thirty-five would be called to the colours. For the 148 regiments of twelve-months' men, now almost at the end of their enlistment, this meant three years more, unless the war should end sooner; and as an act of conciliation they were allowed to reorganize and to elect their own officers. For all other white men between the age limits designated in the conscription law it meant the immediate beginning of military training and at least three years of service, unless peace should bring relief. Under such conditions, there was danger that some of the less patriotic might escape service by seeking swivel chair employment, and Davis therefore directed the members of his Cabinet and other officials of the Government to select their employés from men not subject to military service. Fair as conscription was, and popular as it proved with the army already in service, it called forth bitter denunciations from such extreme states rights men as Vice-President Stephens, Governor Brown of Georgia, and Toombs, who denounced it as unconstitutional, and forced upon Davis a long and bitter contest for which he could ill spare either the time or the energy.

Meanwhile, other military and naval problems were also pressing, as the outlook had not brightened, especially in the southwest, where the Southern lines, commencing at Yorktown, were seriously threatened. As early as April 6th Lincoln had ordered McClellan to "break the enemy's lines from Yorktown to Warwick River at once." But, fortunately for the Confederate cause,

McClellan, whom Lee considered by far the ablest Federal general, had not carried out the order; indeed, it seems evident that he had determined not to try; for he had written to his wife: "The President very coolly telegraphed me yesterday that . . . I had better break the enemy's lines at once! I was much tempted to reply that he had better come and do it himself." Soon after that letter was written, Joseph E. Johnston took command of the Confederates at Yorktown, and with 53,000 men under his control appeared able to hold it against McClellan. Davis, however, still distrustful of Johnston's fighting qualities, felt no added security at the change. And when, on April 18th, Commodore Porter and Commodore Farragut, with a fleet of Federal war vessels, began closing in on New Orleans, he realized that the capture of that city was inevitable and would alter the whole southwestern and western problem.

Ten days later, New Orleans was taken and on May 3rd Johnston, regarding Yorktown as no longer tenable, withdrew his army toward Richmond. On May 5th Davis wrote to the Governor of Louisiana: "With regret I learned that the enemy had occupied New Orleans. Concur with you as to the changes necessary because of that event. I had previously concluded to form a Department west of the Mississippi. It is now a necessity."

Lincoln, though as eager as was Grant for rapid and complete conquest, had not yet recognized the instrument for it offered by Grant, the uninspiring soldier who had fought for him at Shiloh. McClellan had proved disappointing, at times insulting, and so unreasonable in his complaints that Lincoln said he seemed to think "that Heaven sent its rain only on the just, and not on the unjust." Sending him troops, Lincoln likened to "shovelling fleas across a barnyard: only half seem to arrive." Charles Eliot Norton named him "the hero of one hundred ungained victories"; and Emerson confided to his *Journal* that "the man McClellan ebbs like the sea." Lincoln, however, saw no course open but to support him; even as Davis, with equal reluctance, directed

Johnston to "exercise your judgment," though he gravely doubted whether there was much to be exercised.

In May Norfolk was evacuated by the Confederates who, before leaving, destroyed the *Merrimac*, thus from necessity robbing themselves of "that gift of God and Virginia." At once the Federal gunboats prepared to push up toward Richmond, as the inland waterway was now open.

On May 15th the *Monitor* and its accompanying Federal gunboats reached Drewry's Bluff, eight miles from Richmond; but they got little nearer, being repulsed by the determined defenders of the Confederate capital. Seward, then on a visit to the scene of battle, expressed the opinion that even yet a force of soldiers co-operating with the Federal navy on the James River, "would give us Richmond without delay." But McClellan, who might have made this conjunction, failed to do so and Richmond was saved, while the knowing ones did not seek to conceal their scorn of a general who had missed such an opportunity.

During all this trying period Davis was constantly harassed by enemies in his own household. Lacking the humour which enabled Lincoln to smile at McClellan's insults and Stanton's brutal thrusts, he suffered keenly under the ceaseless criticism, though outwardly bearing it with indifference. Few men would have fared so well in comparison with Lincoln, who at times, as Sir Frederick Maurice points out, "made him appear a dwarf, which he was not." He had proved, already, what Maurice pronounced him at the end of the conflict, "an administrator of more than average competence." The chief vulnerable point which he offered to his critics was that, preoccupied with military problems, he did not always gain the advantages which his administrative ability would have given him, and military experts have generally agreed that his control of matters purely military at times caused harm rather than good. These same critics have come to believe that Lincoln's frequent exercise of the military control given him by the Constitution worked, in general, for the advantage of the Federal cause.

On May 16, 1862, Davis returned from a journey down the James River, to investigate the protection provided against gunboats, and confidently declared that it ought to be possible to stop them. "Be of good cheer," he said to his wife, "and continue to hope that God will in due time deliver us from the hands of our enemies. . . . As the clouds grow darker and when, one after another, those who are trusted are detected in secret hostilities, I feel like mustering clans were in me, and that cramping fetters had fallen from my limbs. The great temporal object is to secure our independence, and they who engage in strife for personal or party aggrandizement deserve contemptuous forgetfulness. To me who have no political wish beyond the success of our cause, no personal desire but to be relieved from further connexion with office, opposition in any form can only disturb me in so much as it endangers the public welfare. . . ."

Meanwhile, Johnston, acting upon the President's permission to use his own judgment, decided to bring his army to the suburbs of Richmond: but left Davis ignorant of his plans. "We are uncertain," Davis wrote to his wife, on May 19th, "of everything except that a battle must be near at hand." Determined to know more than Johnston cared to confide, he sent for Lee, then at Richmond, and expressed the opinion "that McClellan should be attacked on the other side of the Chickahominy before he matured his preparations for the siege of Richmond." Lee consulted Johnston and reported that the latter proposed, on the next Thursday, to move against the enemy, giving the details of the movements which he contemplated. On the morning designated, Davis rode out toward Meadow Bridge to see the action: but there was no action; and "thus," he wrote, "ended the offensive-defensive program from which Lee expected much, and of which I was hopeful." This failure left him less disposed than ever to trust to either Johnston's ability or his zeal.

Despite his reiterated insistence, to Johnston and other generals, that his policy was to leave commanders the fullest powers of judgment and of action, Davis kept up his habit of visiting the front and taking an active, if not always a controlling, part in military councils; and the resulting criticisms, threats of impeachment, and calls for a dictator to displace him did not cause him to discontinue the practice. In a conference shortly before the battle of Seven Pines, he presented plans for the coming engagement, which were rejected. In consequence Johnston was left free to follow his own course, but, indignant at Davis' presence on the field when the battle began, according to Sir Frederick Maurice, actually rode into the front line to get rid of the sight of him. He did not, however, escape from Davis' view, but, in sight of both Davis and Lee, was brought back so severely wounded as to be beyond hope of resuming active service for some time to come.

After making certain that everything had been done for Johnston's safety and comfort, Davis turned to Lee with the words: "I shall assign you to the command of this army. Make your preparations as soon as you reach your quarters. I shall send you the order when we get to Richmond."

Before the close of the day a messenger brought Davis a letter from his wife, congratulating him upon the victory, and that evening he replied from camp: "Had the movement been made when I first proposed it, the effect would have been more important." He intimated also, and for her ear alone, that Lee was to take Johnston's place. "Lee rises with the occasion . . ." he said, "and seems to be equal" to the emergency.

The following day, June 1, 1862, saw Davis and Lee galloping together across the battlefield, and at 2 P.M. Major-General Gustavus W. Smith, who had been Johnston's second in command and who had automatically taken control when Johnston fell, was informed that Lee had succeeded to Johnston's command.

The next day, Davis wrote to his wife: "On Saturday we had a severe battle and suffered severely in attacking the enemy's entrenchments of which our generals were poorly informed. . . . Our troops behaved most gallantly, drove the enemy out of their encampments, captured their batteries, carried their advanced redoubts, and marched forward under fire more heavy than I had ever previously witnessed. . . . General J. E. Johnston is severely wounded. . . . I offered to share our house with him, but his staff obtained a whole house and seemed to desire such arrangement. . . . General Lee is in the field, commanding."

While showing every consideration and sympathy for Johnston, Davis condemned him for ignorance of the enemy's plans which had made the struggle, as he thought, needlessly severe. "The Yankees," he wrote, "had been eight or ten days fortifying the position in which we attacked them on Saturday, and the first intimation I had of their having slept on this side of the Chickahominy was after I had gone into an encampment from which they were driven. The ignorance of their works caused much of the loss we suffered. It is hard to see incompetence losing opportunity and wasting hard-gotten gains, but harder still to bear, is the knowledge that there is no available remedy."

Davis had, however, himself furnished the remedy in the person of Johnston's successor, though his choice of "Evacuating Lee, who has never risked a single battle with the invader," as the *Examiner* contemptuously called him, was bitterly criticized. Lee had not yet had the opportunity to display his gift for "finishing up," to quote the later characterization of Benjamin Hallowell, who had marked this as Lee's greatest "specialty" while preparing him for entrance to West Point. His critics condemned him upon his record. One "doubted his audacity"; but Davis' audacity in promoting him they flaunted in his face,—an audacity based upon knowledge of the man, and a firm belief in his qualities of leadership.

When the three days' engagement of Seven Pines was over, and even Lee's genius had been able to make of it only a drawn battle, there remained the task not of following up a victory, but of preparing to win one on another field. Lee's army was suffering from dire need of the food, clothing, and equipment which successful war demands; and worse still, from disheartenment, bred of repeated disappointment and defeat. In his effort to restore confidence, by organizing for victory, he had, however, one great advantage, perhaps the greatest; he enjoyed, as did no other man, the confidence of his constitutional commander. Freeman declares that at that moment no man of station save Davis and Johnston "realized what Lee might accomplish if given a fair chance." He himself apparently did not, for he wrote to his daughter-in-law, the night of his appointment: "I wish that [Johnston's] mantle had fallen upon an abler man."

A few days afterward, Davis writes: "I was riding to the front and saw a number of horses hitched in front of a house, and among them I recognized General Lee's. Upon dismounting and going in, I found some general officers engaged in consultation with him as to how McClellan's advance could be checked, and one of them commenced to explain the disparity of force, and with a pencil and paper to show how the enemy could . . . make his approach irresistible. 'Stop, stop,' said Lee. 'If you go on ciphering we are whipped beforehand.' " His problem was to win with a minor force, and he knew that success could not be gained by counting heads, but by putting confidence into a disheartened army and a disappointed people.

President Davis was conscious that his problem was the same, and he too faced it with gallant heart. He was leading a minority, brave beyond reproach, patriotic beyond question, but split by faction and disturbed by intrigue. Could he win the unity upon which hope of ultimate success depended? With courage, unselfish devotion to the cause, and a conscientious belief that he was serving the right, he faced his task, as Lee faced his, and as Abraham Lincoln, with no less reason for discouragement, was facing his.

It was soon apparent that the imminent "caving in" of the Confederacy which Edward Everett Hale had so lightly prophesied, more than nine months earlier, was not taking place, and he now recorded, the Federals "have just found out that it is not a picnic"; adding later, "Old Abe has called out 300,000 men by draft, and has informed us that if the 300,000 volunteers do not appear by the 15th he will draft for them. This is as it should be." And after ten days, "I have not seen a man who was not hoping to be drafted."

The Davis papers show, however, at least one example of a Southern boy who did not wish to stay drafted: "Dear Mr President—I want you to let Jeems, of Co. 1, Fifth South Carolina regiment, come home and git married. Jeems is willin, I is willin, his mammy says she is willin, but Jeems' Captain, he ain't willin. Now when we are all willin but Jeems' Captain I think you might let up and let Jeems come home. I'll make him go back when he's done got married and fight just as hard as ever." On the back of this letter we find in Davis' hand, "Let Jeems go."

In Robert E. Lee, the Confederacy had at last found, not a great, but a supreme leader, and one whose plans were quickly formed. "If it were possible to reinforce Jackson strongly," he wrote to Davis, on June 5, 1862, "it would change the character of the war. . . . Jackson could in that event cross Maryland into Pennsylvania. It would call off the enemy from our southern coast and liberate those states. McClellan will make this a battle of Posts." Lee had not seen the letter which McClellan had just sent to Stanton, outlining his plans for making Richmond accessible, but his military instinct had divined its contents. His own answer was characteristic: "I will endeavour to make a diversion to bring McClellan out." Able as he knew McClellan to be, he was confident of his own ability to meet him in battle.

Temptations come to statesmen in strange guises, and during the early summer of 1862, one of the strangest possible temptations came to Davis. Major Walker Taylor, a cousin of the first Mrs. Davis, appeared at Richmond, with a daring scheme to cap-

ture Lincoln and bring him South, and Colonel William Preston
Johnston, Davis' aide-de-camp, gives us an account of the interview between him and Davis:

"'Well, Walker,' said Mr. Davis, affably, 'what is it?' 'Mr.
Davis, I want to bring Lincoln a prisoner to you in this city.'
'Nonsense!' said Davis, 'How can such a thing be done?' 'Just as
easily,' said Taylor, 'as walking out of this town. I came across the
Potomac at no great distance from Washington, and while I
was there (in Washington) I watched Lincoln's habits closely
and know his outgoing and incoming. I tell you, sir, that I can
bring him across that river as easily as I can walk over your
doorstep.'

"'How could you do it?' said Mr. Davis. 'Lincoln,' replied
Taylor, 'does not leave the White House until evening, or near
twilight, and then with only a driver, he takes a lonely ride two
or three miles in the country to a place called the Soldiers' Home,
which is his summer residence. My point is to collect several of
these Kentuckians whom I see about here doing nothing and
who are brave enough for such a thing as that, and capture Lincoln, run him down the Potomac, and cross him over just where
I crossed, and the next day we will have him here.'

"Davis shook his head and said: 'I cannot give my authority,
Walker. In the first place, I suppose Lincoln is a man of courage.
He has been in Indian wars, and is a Western man. He would
undoubtedly resist capture. In that case you would kill him. I
could not stand the imputation of having consented to let Mr.
Lincoln be assassinated. Our cause could not stand it. Besides,
what value would he be to us as a prisoner? Lincoln is not the
government. He is merely its political instrument. If he were
brought to Richmond, what could I do with him? He would
have to be treated like a magistrate of the North, and we have
neither the time nor the provision. No, sir, I will not give my authority to abduct Lincoln.'"

On June 13th Davis wrote to his wife: "Beauregard claims by

telegram to have made a 'brilliant and successful' retreat. . . .
There are those who can only walk alone when it is near to the
ground and I fear he has been placed too high for his mental
strength," a criticism which recalls a couplet then going the
rounds:

> Here's to Toussaint Beauregard,
> Who for the truth has no regard,
> In Satan's clutches he will cry,
> I've got old Satan, Victori!

On June 14th Davis sent Colonel William P. Johnston to Beauregard's headquarters to ask explanations of his retreat from
the Charleston and Memphis Railway to the position now occupied, and information regarding his plans for future operations; why he had deemed it advisable not to occupy the hills
north and east of Corinth; what were the causes of the sickness
at Camp Corinth; whether it was not practicable to cut the
enemy's line of communication and thus compel him to abandon
the Tennessee River, or "permit us to occupy Nashville"; what
means had been employed, after the fall of Island 10, to prevent the descent of the Mississippi River by the enemy's gunboats,
etc., etc., throughout the list of Beauregard's recent actions. But
before Johnston had time to report, Beauregard turned over his
command to General Bragg and left on surgeon's certificate in
the hope of restoring his shattered health, and Davis telegraphed
to Bragg: "You are assigned permanently to the command of the
Department." Clearly, Beauregard's afflictions distressed Davis
little: but he had begun to miss Johnston, little as he had expected
it; for on June 23rd, he wrote to his wife: "I wish he were able
to take the field. Despite the critics . . . he is a good soldier,
never brags of what he did, and could at this time render most
valuable service."

Had Davis seen a letter which L. M. Child had recently sent
to Horace Greeley, it might have turned his thoughts into new
and promising channels. "Governments," it ran, "never mention

moral principles without expecting to serve some turn by it. . . .
I had previously seen letters from Europe, which stated that
Mason and Slidell were offering to abolish slavery as the price of
a league with France and England. I did not dare trust this report
until I read Lord Lyons' letter; but I at once concluded that that
letter was sent forth as a note of preparation. Bitter as the pill of
emancipation would be to the South, I have no doubt they would
swallow it, rather than acknowledge themselves conquered by
the U. S. And really there is no way in which they could so
effectively humiliate us, and revenge themselves upon us. We
should be the scorn and laughingstock of the world. . . . Perhaps Lincoln may have had trains of thought similar to those
that have occupied my mind of late; and his recent message may
be the result. . . . It says plainly enough, If the rebels continue
to resist, the U. S. government must and will resort to emancipation. . . . It seems to me that all will soon be resolved into one
question: 'Which party will emancipate first?' "

CHAPTER XVIII

EMANCIPATION PROCLAMATION

THERE is no evidence to show that Mason and Slidell had spoken with authority from Davis, or indeed with his knowledge, when holding out to England and France the idea that the Confederate Government was contemplating emancipation. Indeed, it is safe to say that Davis was considering no such flagrant denial of states rights. Always he had held that slavery in the states was a matter with which neither the Federal nor the Confederate Government had a right to interfere: and upon that subject he showed no shadow of turning.

Lincoln, on the other hand, had reached the conclusion that he must do something to attach the Border states to the Union cause, as their sympathies were divided, if not distinctly pro-Confederate. Therefore, unembarrassed by the fact that he too had always disclaimed the legal right to interfere with slavery in the states where it still existed, he summoned his Cabinet, on July 22nd, and read to them a proclamation announcing his purpose of again asking Congress for pecuniary aid for such Union states as would voluntarily abolish slavery; and his determination to declare, on the 1st of the coming January, "all persons held as slaves within any state or states wherein the Constitutional authority of the United States shall not then be practically recognized . . . for ever free." The proclamation declared such an act "a fit and necessary military measure," and showed that Lincoln was now ready to go within the seceded states and by virtue of military necessity, as far as the abolitionists had long been eager to go everywhere, upon the ground of ethical necessity. He, however, made it clear that his object was not the destruction of slavery but the restoration of "the Constitutional relation between the General Government and each and all the states wherein that relation is now suspended or disturbed; and that for this object the war, as it has been, will be prosecuted." In this pronouncement it would be difficult to find even the seeds of a crusade for the destruction of slavery. Indeed, Lincoln frankly recognized the fact that the proclamation, if issued, would free no slaves, as the Federal power did not extend within the Confederate lines, and the proclamation was not drawn to apply to regions outside Confederate lines.

Having announced his plan, with the statement that it was a plan, not merely a suggestion, he waited for the comments of his Cabinet, and was unmoved by the fact that only Stanton and Bates gave their unreserved approval, until Seward remarked that, following so close upon repeated military failures, such a proclamation might be regarded as the despairing measure of an exhausted nation—a cry for help—"our last shriek on the retreat." "The wisdom of the view of the Secretary of State," Lincoln later confessed, "struck me with very great force. It was an aspect of the case that . . . I had entirely overlooked. The result was that I put the draft of the proclamation aside . . . waiting for victory." He, however, made public the part which warned all men "to return to their proper allegiance to the United States on pain of forfeiture and seizure," and determined to issue the rest of the proclamation as soon as a Federal victory should be achieved.

Lord Harrington once expressed the view that "no Government can exist where the penny press lives," and the attacks which followed Lincoln's "hesitation" to go forward at once with emancipation, graphically illustrates his meaning. No abuse was too extreme for abolitionist editors who chafed at his delay without knowing its cause. In a thousand bitter articles they sought to stampede him into immediate action against slavery, regardless of Constitution, laws, or military problems. But Lincoln was not to be moved, and in a letter of August 22d, thus restated his position:

"My paramount object . . . is to save the Union, and is not either to save or to destroy slavery. If I could save the Union without freeing any slave, I would do it; and if I could save it by freeing all the slaves, I would do it; and if I could save it by freeing some and leaving others alone, I would also do that. What I do about slavery and the coloured race, I do because I believe it helps to save the Union; and what I forbear, I forbear because I do not believe it would help to save the Union." Patiently, with unfailing good humour, he continued to answer his critics, and he might have said with Lee, "I believe . . . looking into my own heart, and speaking in the presence of God, that I have never known one moment of bitterness or resentment."

On July 31, 1862, Davis reported to Lee that, on July 22, "the very day the cartel," for the exchange of prisoners had been signed, orders had been issued by the Secretary of War of the United States directing "the military commanders of the United States to take the private property of our people for the convenience and use of their armies without compensation," and that a general order had been issued on July 23rd by Major-General Pope, directing "the murder of our peaceful inhabitants as spies if found quietly tilling their farms in his rear, *even outside of his lines*." He added that Brigadier-General Steinwehr had seized "innocent and peaceful inhabitants, to be held as hostages, to the end that they may be murdered in cold blood, if any of his soldiers are killed by some unknown persons, whom he designates as 'bushwhackers.'" He declared, indignantly, that such actions had placed the Federal commanders responsible for them in the position of "robbers and murderers, and not that of public enemies, entitled, if captured, to be considered as prisoners of war." Thus, he added: "We find ourselves driven by our enemies . . . towards a practice which we abhor and which we are vainly struggling to avoid. . . . For the present we renounce our right of retaliation on the innocent, and shall continue to treat private, enlisted soldiers of General Pope's army as prisoners of war; but if, after notice to the Government at Washington of our intention to limit repressive measures to the punishment only of commissioned officers who are willing participants in these crimes, these savage practices are continued, we shall reluctantly be forced to the last resort of accepting the war on the terms chosen by our foes, until the outraged voice of common humanity forces a respect for the recognized rules of war.

"While these facts would justify our refusal to execute the generous cartel by which we have consented to liberate an excess of thousands of prisoners held by us beyond the number held by the enemy, a sacred regard to plighted faith, . . . prevents our resort to this extremity. Nor do we desire to extend to any other forces of the enemy the punishment merited alone by General Pope and such commissioned officers as choose to participate in the execution of his infamous orders.

"You are therefore instructed to communicate to the Commander-in-chief of the armies of the United States the contents of this letter . . . to the end that he may be notified of our intention not to consider any officers hereafter captured from General Pope's army as prisoners of war."

These orders dispatched, Davis turned to the study of other reports concerning "alleged murders committed on our citizens by officers of the United States army," and, the next day, instructed General Lee to inquire whether the charges cited are "admitted to be true, and whether the conduct of those generals is sanctioned by their Government," and to warn the officers of the Federal Government that, "in the event of our failure to receive a reply . . . within fifteen days . . . we shall assume the alleged facts are true and are sanctioned by the Government of the United States," and "on that Government will rest the responsibility of the retributive or retaliatory measures which we shall adopt."

Davis had no intention of allowing in his own armies actions even vaguely analogous to those complained of in the enemy's armies, unless it should become evident that protests had failed. He was doing his utmost to keep the war upon a civilized basis, but, was discovering, as he wrote next day, that though "revolutions develop the highest qualities of the good and the great . . . they cannot change the nature of the vicious and selfish."

The deep furroughs in Lincoln's face grew deeper, as one disappointment followed another; each calling forth fresh insults from his own side of the border. One critic declared that "the coat-tail of Andrew Jackson . . . would make a better President than Lincoln." Another complained that New York was held by a provost marshal empowered to "capture anybody and clap him into any prison that may suit his fancy." A volume of such senseless abuse might be compiled from the press and private papers of the time; but still Lincoln waited for the victory, which Lee's genius as steadily denied. With his scant forces Lee was performing astonishing feats. On August 15th, Davis described to Governor Lubbock, of Texas, "a series of victories in Virginia," and added, "the determination displayed by the Southern troops everywhere gives us assurance of the final expulsion of the enemy from the gulf states." Three days later, in a message to the Confederate Congress, he announced that, "the vast army which threatened the Capital of the Confederacy has been defeated and driven from the lines of investment, and the enemy, repeatedly foiled . . . is now seeking to raise new armies on a scale such as modern history does not record, to effect the subjugation of the South. . . . The perfidy which disregarded rights sacred by compact, the madness which trampled on obligations made sacred by every consideration of honour, have been intensified by the malignity engendered by defeat."

Lincoln had evidently not seen fit to denounce the actions of the generals complained of through General Lee in early August, for, after reciting a long list of instances of "malignity engendered by defeat," Davis added, "two at least of the generals of the United

States are engaged, unchecked by their Government, in exciting servile insurrections, and in arming and training slaves for warfare against their masters. . . . The rebuke of civilized man has failed to evoke from the authorities of the United States one mark of disapprobation. . . . To inquiries made of the Commander-in-chief of the armies of the United States whether the atrocious conduct of some of their military commanders met the sanction of that Government, answer has been evaded on the pretext that the inquiry was insulting."

Meanwhile Lincoln had still not played his trump card, emancipation, explaining that he "did not wish to imitate the Pope who issued a Bull against a comet." And while he waited, the abolitionists continued their effort to convince the public, at home and abroad, that the war was no mere contest of Union against disunion, but a fight for the liberation of an enslaved race. Early in the year, Mrs. Julia Ward Howe had marched in a military parade in Washington, and had joined in the singing of patriotic songs. At the end, one of her companions suggested the need of a hymn to arouse America to the meaning of the war, the verses just sung being trivial. Before dawn of the next morning the words of the "Battle Hymn of the Republic" suddenly came to her. She rose quietly, that she might not waken her baby, and without making a light wrote them down. The facsimile of their first draft, given in her *Reminiscences*, bears convincing testimony to that fact, some lines being almost illegible; but their inspiration is unmistakable. They were copied and sent to the *Atlantic Monthly*, which published them in its February number of that year.

Mine eyes have seen the glory of the coming of the Lord.
He is trampling out the vintage where the grapes of wrath are stored,
He hath loosed the fateful lightning of his terrible swift sword,
His truth is marching on.

Since then the song has been widely circulated, in many lands, leaving, wherever it went, the ineffaceable impression that the world was once more organizing for a crusade. As London read, she began to doubt the truth of the *Times'* assurance that "slavery counts for little" in the American war, and that of similar declarations in the *Quarterly Review* and other leading publications. The effect was heightened by the subsidized circulation of more substantial abolitionist literature, notably *Uncle Tom's Cabin*, Helper's *Impending Crisis*, and Olmsted's *A Journey Through the Slave States*, and as a result the public mind was prepared to accept a Federal proclamation of emancipation as a second call of Peter the Hermit to a new crusade.

In the meantime, events pointed to a possible curtailment of Lincoln's need of patience. Lee had formulated a plan to invade Maryland and Pennsylvania, in order to demonstrate the aggressive power of the Confederacy. It was distinctly his plan and, after explaining it to Davis, he warned the latter not to expect too much from it, as it was to be no more than "an impressive demonstration." Accordingly, on the morning of September 17th, General Lee, with 40,000 men, confronted some 60,000 under General McClellan, in the battle of Antietam. McClellan, counting upon his vast numbers, attacked Lee's left flank with vigour and confidence, forcing it back, after fierce resistance. But reinforcements, arriving at the moment of crisis, enabled Lee to recover his lost ground, and the result was indecisive. The Federals lost 12,410 to 11,172 on the Confederate side.

While this battle could hardly be elevated into the longed-for Federal victory, it checked the advance of Lee and Jackson, who had contemplated the establishment of a foothold on Federal soil. Had McClellan followed it up with promptness and determination, he might have made it into a real victory, as Lee's ammunition was almost spent and his army shattered. But McClellan failed to do so, and thereby drew from Lowell the remark that, "our chicken was no eagle, after all." The failure, however, did not prevent Lincoln from accepting Antietam as the victory for which he had waited, and, on September 22nd he called together his Cabinet and announced that the time had arrived for his proclamation. Chase in his *Diary* tells us that:

"All the members of the Cabinet were in attendance. There was some general talk, and the President mentioned that Artemus Ward had sent him his book. Proposed to read a chapter he thought very funny. Read it and seemed to enjoy it very much; the heads also (except Stanton, of course). The chapter was 'Highhanded outrage at Utica.'" Then a graver expression came into Lincoln's face. He reminded his advisers that he had read them a proclamation several weeks before, the publication of which he had postponed after discussion. "I think the time has come now . . ." he added. "When the rebel army was at Frederick I determined, as soon as it should be driven out of Maryland, to issue a proclamation of emancipation. . . . I said nothing to anyone, but I made a promise to myself, and (hesitating a little) to my Maker. The rebel army is now driven out, and I am going to fulfil that promise. . . . I do not wish your advice about the main matter, for that I have determined for myself."

Seward suggested a few verbal changes which were adopted, and, after a good deal of discussion, carried the amended Proclamation to the State Department where the Great Seal was affixed. Lincoln signed it and it was countersigned, not by the Secretary of War as a military measure should have been signed, but by Seward himself. It was immediately released to the press, and warned the officers and citizens of the Confederate States that, on January 1, 1863, the President of the United States would declare free all slaves belonging to the citizens of the Confederate States unless before that date they should have returned to their allegiance to the United States.

With the issuance of this document, Davis faced the great divide. Time and time again he had declared that the South was not fighting to defend slavery, but to save her liberty, threatened by the determination of the North to seize powers unwarranted by the Constitution. Lincoln had now, in effect, challenged this statement, and the Confederacy would henceforth stand before the world as the champion of slavery, risking life itself in its defence, unless some answer more effective than a mere denial could be given.

The only adequate answer was a counter-proclamation of emancipation. Lincoln had left over three months during which Davis might reply that by January 1, 1863, there would be no slaves in the seceded states to be emancipated. Clearly, such an action upon his part would convince a now uncertain Europe that the subject of the conflict was Constitutional liberty. With views similar to those of Lincoln upon the legal rights of slaveholders, Davis could have made this answer, but for one fact: in so declaring, he must assume for the Confederate Government the right to control property reserved to the states by the theory of state sovereignty, which would be to destroy the very principle which had led him to join the secession movement and accept the leadership of the Confederate cause, and there would thereafter remain no reason for resisting reconstruction. Therefore, Davis could not make the only reply which would convince the world that the South was not fighting for slavery.

Lincoln's proclamation was interpreted by the abolitionists as the mark of his conversion to their long-proclaimed views, which it was not. They hailed it with rapture, confident that emancipation would now go on, from glory to greater glory, until the whole task should be accomplished. "Great is the Proclamation," wrote Emerson in his *Journal*. "It works when men are sleeping, when the army goes into winter quarters, when generals are treacherous or imbecile." "God be praised," wrote Charles Eliot Norton. "I can hardly see to write—for when I think of this great act of freedom, and all it implies, my heart and my eyes overflow with the deepest, most serious gladness." Horace Greeley, whose caustic criticisms had so often embarrassed him, exclaimed, "God bless Abraham Lincoln!" Wendell Phillips who had indignantly described him as "a man without a backbone," and had denounced his policy of coercion so fiercely that his Northern audience had hissed, and William Lloyd Garrison, who had declared Lincoln's idea of "whipping the South into subjugation and extorting allegiance from millions of people at the cannon's mouth . . . utterly chimerical," now thanked God for such leadership. Grant, however, as yet remained with the hosts of the unconvinced. "If I thought this war was to abolish slavery," he said, "I would resign my commission, and offer my sword to the other side." The overwhelming response from the North, however, was as Lincoln said, "All that a vain man could wish"; but, with a keen eye upon the work still to be done, he added, "the North responded . . . sufficiently, in breath; but breath alone kills no rebels."

In the meantime the Southern press abounded with articles to prove that the South was not fighting for slavery. One declared that there were "318,000 slaveholders or sons of slaveholders in the Northern army, men who enlisted from the border states, Illinois, Pennsylvania, New Jersey and Delaware," while "there were only 200,000 slaveholders in the Southern army." Another, that General Scott, Admiral Farragut, General George H. Thomas, and Mrs. Lincoln had either owned slaves or married slaveowners, while General Lee had freed his slaves before taking his place at the head of the Confederate armies, General Albert Sidney Johnston had never owned a slave, and General Stonewall Jackson had owned only two, whom he had purchased to prevent their separation. General French exclaimed: "Palsied be the hand . . . that writes that 576,000 fight to maintain slavery," and Davis' papers contain many similar arguments, and denials of the charge. But the perusal of such arguments required time and a degree of interest which did not exist in the regions to which they were directed. The South needed no such proofs; the North regarded them as examples of special pleading, and England, so long the centre of Davis' hopes, was too busy with her own affairs to consider whether or not they proved their contention. Indeed so indifferent was the English public that James Russell Lowell remarked that there would be less danger of British intervention in the contest "if her governing classes knew something less about ancient Greece and a little more of modern America." And Cobden, after travelling in America, assured Americans that it was absurd to expect any great interest in her public men, or her internal affairs.

For reaching distant and indifferent minds Lincoln's proclamation was admirable: and he perfectly understood the necessity of reaching them. From the reports of Charles Francis Adams, minister at the Court of St. James, and letters which John Bright regularly sent Seward, he knew that the majority of England's governing class accepted Davis' assurance that the war was a fight for local autonomy and Constitutional liberty, and was convinced, as was Adams, that under the guidance of Lord Palmerston, the Premier, and Lord John Russell, the Foreign Secretary, England's leaders were in full sympathy with the South. The Earl of Shaftesbury, the Duke of Sutherland, the Earl of Donoughmore, Sir Henry Holland, Lord Harrington, had one and all been open in their expressions of Confederate sympathy: while Beresford Hope had defended the Southern cause in three lectures in 1861. "The Results of the American Disruption," which he published, prematurely in 1862, reached six editions. Sir William Gregory had recently been cheered in Parliament when he declared, "the adherents of the North in the House of Commons might all be driven home in one omnibus."

From these facts it is evident that Lincoln's Emancipation Proclamation had come none too soon, and although Sir Robert Peel declared it is odious and abominable, without it England and, following her, the most important continental nations, would probably have recognized the independence of the Confederacy. Already, the *Gentleman's Magazine* had argued that in so doing, England would do nothing which the Federal Government had not itself done. They have, it declared in its issue of September, 1862, "recognized the Southern Confederacy as an established Government, by entering into an arrangement with it for the exchange of prisoners." To the British mind that recognition had appeared unavoidable; for as the British *Quarterly Review* later commented, "undoubtedly at that time the South possessed all the attributes of an independent state." Upon the arrival of the news of the battle of Antietam, Lord John Russell had written to Palmerston: "Whether the Federal army is destroyed or not, it is clear that it is driven back to Washington and has made no progress in subduing the insurgent states," and had suggested a speedy recognition of the Confederacy, by proposing it first to France, and then on the part of England and France, to Russia and other powers.

This suggestion had grown out of no love of slavery, but was made in the belief that the issue was between a people fighting for domination and a people fighting for liberty and the right of self-government. Indeed, a few days later Russell had frankly avowed that he regarded the American war as simply another instance of the long Anglo-Saxon struggle against the spirit of dominant control of minorities by superior physical force, and Palmerston had answered with manifest sympathy.

Two weeks after the appearance of the Emancipation Proclamation, Gladstone made a speech at Newcastle, in which he declared: "There is no doubt that Jefferson Davis and the other leaders of the South have made an army; they are making, it appears, a navy; and they have made what is more than either— they have made a nation," which speech, although later denounced by himself as "most unwarrantable . . . with no authority other than his own . . . a mistake, but one of incredible grossness," has caused much discussion as to Gladstone's sympathies. Henry Adams regarded him in this whole affair at Newcastle as a "resolute, vehement, conscientious champion of Russell, Napoleon, and Jefferson Davis. Every act of Russell, from

April, 1861, to November, 1862," he adds, "showed the clearest determination to break up the Union." Justin McCarthy, in his *Reminiscences*, presents a different view:

"I have a distinct recollection," he wrote, "of a conversation with Mr. Gladstone and the emphasis with which he declared to me that he had never asserted, and had never intended to assert, that he believed in the failure of American institutions. He reminded me that a member of Parliament, the late Sir John Ramsden, had said during a debate in the House of Commons that the Republican bubble had burst in the United States, and that he himself, following Sir John Ramsden, in the same debate, had strongly dissented from and emphatically condemned any such expression of opinion. He went on to say that, even if the war of secession had ended in permanent separation, or if any such separation were at any future time to occur, such a fact would not of itself tend in the slightest degree to prove the failure of the institutions of the United States." McCarthy adds: "Those who believed Mr. Gladstone hostile to the United States merely because he thought it possible, if he did think it possible, that the Southern states might succeed in setting up for themselves, might well have remembered how many of the most devoted, loyal, and distinguished citizens of the Northern states were forced at one time to declare that the free republic would fare all the better if the seceding states were allowed to go, and set up their slavery system for themselves, and thus clear the air of the free republic from its tainting and enfeebling influence."

The protests which followed Gladstone's Newcastle speech, however, emphasized the fact that Lincoln's Proclamation had checked the movement towards England's recognition of the Confederacy, giving a new and powerful argument to the "workers and the thinkers," who, as John Morley later declared, were impotent sympathizers with the North. Politically, the labourers of England were, as yet, unenfranchised, and therefore unprepared to resist the nation's political leaders, drawn largely from the ruling class, who believed what Gladstone had said, and who, even after the outcry which greeted his speech, were ready to accept Davis' contention, advanced seven days after the Newcastle meeting, that the Confederacy had been "forced to take up arms to vindicate the political rights, the freedom, equality, and state sovereignty which were the heritage purchased by the blood of your revolutionary sires; you have but the alternative of slavish submission to despotic usurpation, or the independence which vigorous, united, persistent effort will secure."

That the desire for recognition of the Confederacy persisted in certain quarters is shown by the continued demand in leading British journals. The *Gentleman's Magazine* of November, 1862, expressed the hope that European powers will shortly intervene, "otherwise the Proclamation of President Lincoln for freeing the slaves, with its too evident tendency to cause a servile war in the South, and the fierce retaliation threatened by the Confederates, make it plain that a scene of horror is impending which Christian statesmen assuredly would risk much to prevent." And *Blackwood's* declared, in its issue of the same month: "Not only does international law justify our recognition of the Southern Confederacy, but humanity demands that we should take measures to put an end to such horrible war. . . . And if the great powers of Europe—or at least England, Russia, and France—would solve the difficulty which each power separately feels, by agreeing to undertake a joint mediation, and if necessary, intervention, they would render an important service to civilization, humanity, and mankind at large, and would show a better example of a 'Holy Alliance' than any which yet stands recorded in the pages of history."

Slowly, but very surely, however, Lincoln's Emancipation Proclamation forced both the European powers, and the English leaders, to face the fact that recognition of the Confederacy would mean assistance on the side of slavery. General French truly interpreted the situation when he later wrote: "The cry that the South was fighting to maintain slavery was proclaimed to prejudice the Emperor Napoleon III, and the English Cabinet from forming an alliance with the Confederate States. Had the South freed the slaves . . . after Lincoln's Proclamation, our independence would have been acknowledged." And the British *Quarterly Review* declared that such a move upon Davis' part, at this psychological moment, "would have turned the scale in favour of the South."

On November 26th Davis addressed a circular letter to the Governors of the Confederate States, warning them of a plan on the part of the Federal Government to enlist such "slaves of the South as they may be able to wrest from their owners, and thus to inflict on the non-combatant population of the Confederate States all the horrors of a servile war," and urging the necessity of prompt counter-preparations. Among these, he suggested recommending to the various state legislatures "such legislation as will enable the Governors to command slave labour to the extent which may be required in the prosecution of works conducive to the public defence." While under the doctrine of state sovereignty he could not use the slaves as soldiers, as Lincoln was now doing, he felt the necessity of using them as army labourers in so far as the states could be induced to co-operate with the Confederate Government.

In the meantime Northern leaders, from Lincoln and Seward down, continued to employ every opportunity to convince the world that the South was merely the champion of slavery. Sumner caustically capitalized the fact that "Mason is the author of the Fugitive Slave law, and Slidell the chief leader of the filibustering system," but he was too shrewd to mention that the law had been sustained by Northern as well as by Southern votes, and that New England's most commanding voice, that of Daniel Webster, had joined with Abraham Lincoln to urge its rigid enforcement.

On the other hand, every available means was used by the

South to fix in the minds of its people the idea that the war was the result of Northern ambition and greed. In some of the school books of the period, printed often upon the reverse side of wall paper for lack of better material, we find ingenious propaganda designed to fix that idea firmly in the minds of the coming generation. It could not, however, stop the course of the "Crusaders of Liberty," for there was Lincoln's Proclamation offering to make the slaves "for ever free," and no answering voice from the South to prove a similar intention. It created a situation which Lowell later described in the words: "For the first time in history it [Democracy] has mustered an army that knows what it is fighting for." But if we may accept the opinion of James Redpath, certainly a writer not pre-disposed to sympathy with any movement to perpetuate slavery, the South knew quite as well what it was fighting for. "What we of the North do not understand," he wrote, in summing up the results of his personal observations, "is that the South—meaning thereby the brains of the South—instead of regarding the states rights doctrine as a mere theory, to be debated like any other theory, held it as a sacred inheritance for which they were ready to die and to which they owed unfailing allegiance. This was the case almost universally."

On January 1, 1863, Lincoln issued his final Emancipation Proclamation, which declared: "By virtue of the power in me vested as Commander-in-chief, of the army and navy of the United States, in time of actual armed rebellion . . . and as a fit and necessary war measure for suppressing said rebellion . . . I do order and declare that all persons held as slaves within the said designated states and parts of states (previously mentioned by name), are, and henceforth shall be, free . . . And upon this act, sincerely believed to be an act of justice, warranted by the Constitution upon military necessity, I invoke the considerate judgment of mankind and the gracious favour of Almighty God."

At a critical period during the American Revolution an anti-American propagandist wrote and circulated over Washington's signature a statement indicating his desire to have America reconciled with England and returned to her old place in the British Empire. It was pure fiction, but was accepted as fact, until the forgery was made clear by Worthington C. Ford.

On January 5, 1863, an equally daring forgery was launched over the name of Jefferson Davis, a document purporting to be his reply to Lincoln's Proclamation of four days earlier. It is still preserved in the Boston Public Library, and reads as follows:

An Address to the People of the Free States
By the
President of the Southern Confederacy.

Richmond, January 5, 1863.

Citizens of the non-slaveholding states of America, swayed by peaceable motives, I have used all my influence, often thereby endangering my position as President of the Southern Confederacy, to have the unhappy conflict now existing between my people and yourselves, governed by those well-established international rules, which heretofore have softened the asperities which necessarily are the concomitants of a state of belligerency, but all my efforts in the premises have heretofore been unavailing. Now, therefore, I am compelled *e necessitate rei* to employ a measure, which most willingly I would have omitted to do, regarding, as I always must, States Rights, as the very organism of politically associated society.

For nearly two years my people have been defending their inherent rights—their political, social, and religious rights—against the speculators of New England and their allies in the states heretofore regarded as conservative. The people of the Southern Confederacy have—making sacrifices such as the modern world has never witnessed—patiently, but determinedly, stood between their home interests and the well paid, well fed, and well clad mercenaries of the Abolitionists, and I need not say that they have nobly vindicated the good name of American citizens. Heretofore, the warfare has been conducted by white men—peers, scions of the same stock; but the programme has been changed, and your rulers, despairing of a triumph by the employment of white men, have degraded you and themselves, by inviting the co-operation of the black race. Thus, while they deprecate the intervention of white men—the French and the English—in behalf of the Southern Confederacy, they, these Abolitionists, do not hesitate to invoke the intervention of the African race in favour of the North.

The time has, therefore, come when a becoming respect for the good opinion of the civilized world impels me to set forth the following facts:——

First. Abraham Lincoln, the President of the Non-Slaveholding States, has issued his proclamation, declaring the slaves within the limits of the Southern Confederacy to be free.

Second. Abraham Lincoln has declared that the slaves so emancipated may be used in the Army and Navy, now under his control, by which he means to employ, against the Free People of the South, insurrectionary measures, the inevitable tendency of which will be to inaugurate a servile war, and thereby prove destructive, in a great measure, to slave property.

Now, therefore, as a compensatory measure, I do hereby issue the following Address to the People of the Non-Slaveholding States:——

On and after February 22, 1863, all free negroes within the limits of the Southern Confederacy shall be placed on the slave status, and be deemed to be chattels, they and their issue for ever.

All negroes who shall be taken in any of the states in which slavery does not now exist, in the progress of our arms, shall be adjudged, immediately after such capture, to occupy the slave status, and in all states which shall be vanquished by our arms, all free negroes shall, *ipso facto,* be reduced to the condition of helotism, so that the respective normal conditions of the white and black races may be ultimately placed on a permanent basis, so as to prevent the public peace from being thereafter endangered.

Therefore, while I would not ignore the conservative policy of the slave states, namely, that a Federal Government cannot, without violating the fundamental principles of a Constitution, interfere with the internal policy of several states; since, however, Abraham Lincoln has seen fit to ignore the Constitution he has solemnly sworn to support, it ought not to be considered polemically or politically improper for me to vindicate the position which has been, at an early day of this Southern republic, assumed by the Confederacy, namely, that slavery is the cornerstone of the Western Republic.

It is not necessary for me to elaborate this position. I may merely refer, in passing, to the prominent fact, that the South is emphatically a producing section of North America; this is equally true of the West and Northwest, the people of which have been mainly dependent on the South for the consumption of their products. The other states, in which slavery does not exist, have occupied a middle position, as to the South, West, and Northwest. The states of New England, from which all complicated difficulties have arisen, owe their greatness and power to the free suffrages of all other sections of North America; and yet, as is now evident, they have, from the adoption of the Federal Constitution, waged a persistent warfare against the interests of all the other states of the old Union. The great centre of their opposition has been slavery, while the annual statistics of their respective state governments abundantly prove that they entertain within all their boundaries fewer [free] negroes than any single state which does tolerate slavery.

In view of these facts, and conscientiously believing that the proper condition of the negro is slavery, or a complete subjugation to the white man—and entertaining the belief that the day is not distant when the old Union will be restored with slavery nationally declared to be the proper condition of all of African descent—and in view of the future harmony and progress of all the states of America, I have been induced to issue this address, so that there may be no misunderstanding in the future.

JEFFERSON DAVIS.

At this point Horace Greeley, one of the most powerful of the Abolitionists, and one credited, as we have seen, with a major part in precipitating the war, intimated that the Federal Government should come to terms with the Confederacy by offering to restore slavery to the status of the early fifties. At once Vallandingham, most notorious of copperheads—Northern men with Southern principles—hailed him as a convert. On January 10th he wrote to Greeley: "If all you ask is the Union, with slavery on the old basis of fifty years ago, with no new concessions, but *new guarantees* for *old rights and privileges* in states and territories, we shall not differ greatly at last. The idea of getting rid of slavery . . . must be abandoned—unless the South does it herself—which she will not. To give up a cherished notion—one so long held and repeatedly proclaimed by you is a severe trial—but worthy of a patriot and statesman."

Confirmation of Vallandingham's opinion, that the South would not abandon slavery, came two days later, when Davis sent to Congress an authentic reply to Lincoln's Emancipation Proclamation. "The public journals of the North," he said, "have been received, containing a proclamation, dated on the first day of the present month, signed by the President of the United States, in which he orders and declares all slaves within ten of the states of the Confederacy to be free, except such as are found within certain districts now occupied in part by the armed forces of the enemy. We may well leave it to the instincts of that common humanity which a beneficent Creator has implanted in the breasts of our fellow-men of all countries to pass judgment on a measure by which several millions of human beings of an inferior race, peaceful and contented labourers in their sphere, are doomed to extermination, while at the same time they are encouraged to a general assassination of their masters by the insidious recommendation, 'to abstain from violence unless in necessary self-defence.' Our own detestation of those who have attempted the most execrable measure recorded in the history of guilty man is tempered by profound contempt for the impotent rage which it discloses."

He informed Congress of his intention, "unless in your wisdom you deem some other course more expedient," to deliver up to state authorities, for such punishment as they have decreed against criminals exciting servile insurrections, "all commissioned officers of the United States that may hereafter be captured . . . in any of the states embraced in the proclamation." The enlisted men, "unwilling instruments in the commission of these crimes," he would return on parole as usual. These words indicate a spirit very different from that suggested in the forged address, which proposed to make free negroes in the Confederate States for ever slaves.

Davis furthermore declared that the Emancipation Proclamation was "the complete and crowning proof" that Lincoln and his party had intended from the first just such action, despite their assurances to the contrary, and despite Lincoln's declaration "repeated in formal official communication to the cabinets of Great Britain and France," that he had no power and no desire to make any change in the domestic institution of the states.

Whatever may have been the original intentions of his party, this charge was unjust, so far as Lincoln was concerned. All available evidence confirms the statement later made by him at the Hampton Roads conference: that "it was not his intention in the beginning to interfere with slavery in the states; that he never would have done it, if he had not been compelled by necessity to do it, to maintain the Union."

DATE DUE

DEC 17 1997			
GAYLORD			PRINTED IN U.S.A.

Emory & Henry College · Kelly Library

3 1836 0013 4101 5